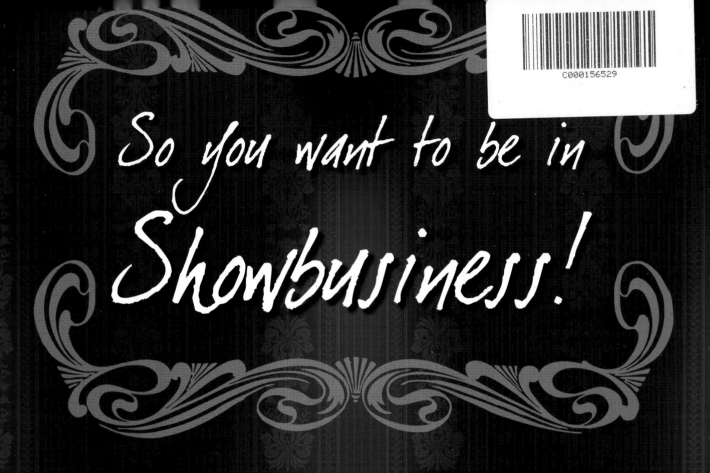

So you want to be in Showbusiness!

Val Jellay

JoJo

PUBLISHING

Published by JoJo Publishing

'Yarra's Edge'
2203/80 Lorimer Street
Docklands VIC 3008
Australia

Email: jo-media@bigpond.net.au or visit www.jojopublishing.com

JoJo Publishing "Making a difference"

Jellay, Val, 1927- .
        So you want to be in Showbusiness!

        1st ed.
        ISBN 9780980283631 (pbk.).

        1. Jellay, Val, 1927- . 2. Actors - Australia - Biography.
        3. Women entertainers - Australia - Biography. 4.
        Entertainers - Australia - Biography. 5. Performing arts -
        Australia. 6. Performing arts - Europe, Western. I. Title.

        792.028092

Designer/typesetter: Rob Ryan (Z.designmedia)
Project and text editor: Charlotte Strong
Editorial and publishing consultant: Liz Copping
Printed in China by Everbest Printing

ISBN: 978 0 9803 5478 2

Acknowledgments
Getty Images/Joe Sohm, pp.ii–iii; Newspix/David Caird, pp. vi–vii; The Production Company, 2000, p.140; Channel Nine, p.173; Sunday Herald Sun, p.254; Rodney Dobson, p.303. All other images are from the author's private collection.

The publisher wishes to thank the various individuals and organisations for permission to reprint the photographs, quotes and extracts from their publications. We have made every effort to contact those concerned and, where this has not been possible, we welcome the opportunity to include acknowledgments in future printing of this publication, should any individual or organisation bring an omission to our attention.

Accolades

There's no one I know who loves showbusiness more than Val Jellay. She lives and breathes it; she'd spread it on her toast in the mornings if possible. It's this passion mixed with a god-given talent, self-belief, drive and boundless energy that's enabled her to experience and excel in all aspects of the trade over a lifetime in the industry.

To successfully survive the heady days of vaudeville, live theatre and the advent of television, with its voracious appetite for artists and material, versatility was essential: to dance and tap, to sing, to act, play an instrument, do comedy, produce, direct, write sketches or even drama, do your own make up, make costumes and props or even negotiate your own contract, Val has not just been there and done it all, she has an innate sense of what it's all about. More than a slice of history on Australian showbiz, this is a valuable insight for those considering it as a career. May I suggest before you decide to take the plunge—read this book.

Daryl Somers

How to encapsulate the joy Val Jellay has brought so many with the gifts she has been graced with?

A gorgeous show girl, a great dramatic actress, a queen of the vaudeville stage, a theatre and television star ... she sits at the top of our industry, and serves as an inspiration to people like me for her amazing versatility, her longevity of career, and her sheer ladylike glamour.

She is divine, and I love her!

Marina Prior

As its title suggests this book is about the exciting, worrying, difficult world of showbusiness. Val Jellay probably has more experience in all aspects of the performer's world than anyone in Australia—or perhaps the world! I have been privileged to work with Val (and her late husband Maurie Fields) over a very long period and in many productions. I have always been astonished at the range of Val's experience in every branch of the performing arts.

For those who are contemplating a career, or even casual work in showbusiness, Val Jellay's experience will be enormously helpful and an inspiration.

Bud Tingwell

Val Jellay is an extraordinary woman and an incredible inspiration. She walks onto stage and her mega-watt energy and passion for her craft is obvious.

As a performer myself, I have admired and respected Val ever since I can remember—watching her charismatic and stunning performances, both live and on television, she is a true 'woman of quality' and a brilliant performer.

Rhonda Burchmore

I know it's a big statement but I believe there is no-one in Australia more qualified to talk about all aspects of showbusiness than Val Jellay.

Come to think of it, how sad would Australian showbusiness have been without this wonderful lady whom I call personally a friend and professionally a shining star.

Bert Newton

Val Jellay has been in showbusiness for a long, long time. She's learned from the legends, and she's worked with most of them. She's done it all—from old fashioned pantomime to modern major musicals, via the Tivoli, television and travelling shows. She probably knows more about the Business of Show than anyone else. And, of course, she knows how to tell a good story—especially her own. If you don't believe me, just read this wonderful book!

Frank Van Straten OAM

Val Jellay is one of a handful of people whose theatrical career and skills helped her to ride the wave of success that occurred at the dawn of Australian TV. She is also one of the few to ride out that storm and is still able to strut her stuff with the best of them.

A few years ago I had the pleasure of producing the Australian production of what was then a Broadway hit musical called *The Full Monty* (based on the film of the same name). In the show there was a character that required a veteran performer who could sing, dance and act up a storm and deliver comedy with drop dead timing. I said it was written for Val. I asked her to audition for the American Director and of course she was offered the part. I would do it all again tomorrow just to see Val steal the show, as she did at every performance of that show.

Anyone with even a passing interest in the business should read this book as Val has a legacy to impart and it's one of great value and humour.

David Atkins OAM

The Tivoli circuit was fondly known as 'The Tiv' by the regular patrons who lined up for the change of programme every five weeks. I was one of those audience merges, a 13 year-old.

There was one girl I watched like a hawk. Her name was Val Jellay, and to me she was the epitome of what I wanted to become. There was just one drawback—she was tall, brunette, slim and shapely; and I was short, blonde and chubby. Oh well, I could dream couldn't I?

A couple of years later I got my chance. A new variety theatre was opening in the suburbs of Melbourne. A choreographer was brought in. Guess who? My idol Val Jellay, and then my real training began. She taught me so much, not the least, how to walk on and off the stage.

Val went on to perform in television variety and later became a beloved character actress in television drama.

I am certain that this book, apart from being a 'great read' with the many 'backstage' stories she has to tell, will have lots of valuable tips for the aspiring performer.

Tricks of the trade—just like she showed me.

Toni Lamond

Contents

Tips and advice
from Val Jellay

Dedication
For my wonderful Grandaughter
Hayley

Thanks

My enthusiasm for this project was never in doubt, thanks to the
dependable encouragement of a very special friend. This book is a salute of
gratitude, to the remarkable Liz Copping.
Val Jellay

My involvement with this unique project has been a personal vision realised.
The detailed honesty in presentation will inspire all who are artistic.
Liz Copping

Introduction: An entertaining life

Val Jellay has written several books that have gained a wide readership throughout Australia and Europe. In this book, a splendidly visual, humorous and candidly written narrative, she shares her life's experiences from the very beginning to the present day.

Val Jellay's story is not only a personal history but also a unique record of entertainment in Australia, covering vaudeville, showbusiness, comedy and drama on stage, radio, film and television. The professional dramas also reflect her own personal 'highs and lows'. Val Jellay has been a part of it all.

It's also a great Australian love story—a document of then and now.

The career that began with dance lessons in 1931 when she was four years old continues to this day. Her popularity overseas is further propelled by her long running television appearances still filling the screens in the northern hemisphere. The respect she receives from fellow high-profile industry professionals is perhaps the greatest testament to her reputation as one of Australia's most versatile and loved performers.

So you want to be in Showbusiness! is also a handbook for hopeful showbiz students and their parents. Today performing arts are a part of every school's curriculum as children are encouraged to speak up, perform and grow with confidence.

Val Jellay shows the way—a way that is open to all who choose to follow.

So you want to be in Showbusiness!

It was time for school. Did I *have* to go to school with my hair in curlers? It made me feel so different! Admittedly, my mother did a fine job—she knew how to curl the hair around her middle finger and expertly slide a bobby pin up into each perfect curl. Some mothers set their little girl's hair in 'rags'—thin strips of torn up cotton material, wound around and around and then tied up in a knot—a very unpleasant sight. But then, by wearing a homemade cap of cotton, rather like a bathing cap, over my professional 'set' curls, who was to know what was underneath? Perhaps Valerie Jelley had a skin disease, or head lice, or even worse—no hair at all!

Whenever this ritual had to be endured, it always seemed to coincide with the class photograph being taken for posterity, or sides being chosen, or often, a new teacher arriving and, to my mind, deciding immediately that this five-, six-, seven-year-old definitely had her priorities wrong.

I learned that dress can impress. At school, still feeling apart from the rest of the world, we were asked to vote for a reading leader. When the votes were read out by the teacher, one vote went like this: 'The girl with the butterflies on her dress'. It was me. I actually got a vote, or at least my butterflies did. I never forgot it. But then, with whom could I share this? Who could possibly understand? Surely appearances must be the answer—put on a happy face. Is that what it was all about?

Church was the only place I was allowed to go to unattended. I was permitted to go there each Sunday because it was good, it was teaching, and it was free. Matter not that it was damp, cold, and dark, and that the mournful Sunday sermons were totally lost on me. I couldn't understand why I didn't come away feeling good, or at least feeling like I'd learned something. Everyone understood, why didn't I! My mother had taught me the Lord's Prayer and I always said my prayers every night, including God Bless everyone I could think of. But who was listening? Jesus? the Lord? God? Which was which? Were they the same person? It was no good asking anyone. *(Valerie! You should know that!)* I still have the little Bible my mother gave me, and during my lonely childhood I turned to it many times, determined to read it, to find comfort. But I could never understand a word of it. What did New Testament and Old Testament mean? It *all* seemed old to me. I was ashamed at not knowing—was I the only one in the whole world who was stupid? My parents brushed aside my queries.

Why did other children have a brother or a sister? Perhaps it was the Depression years and poverty prevented us expanding our family to more than three—my mother, my father and me. Wouldn't it have been wonderful to quarrel with the vocabulary of a child? My loneliness belied the

❦ The importance of props – always hold something.

⚘ *Second row from the back, fifth from the right – caught with my hair in a cotton cap, set for an evening's work at six and a half years old amid faces of the Depression at George Street Primary School. Did I have any hair at all?*

adage: what you never know you never miss.

I managed to get permission to keep silkworms. This was wonderful, and I spent hours watching them feed on mulberry leaves picked from the trees along the street. They would spin their golden cocoons around themselves and eventually emerge as butterflies, so beautiful. The whole evolution was fascinating, and I didn't need a companion to be able to occupy myself.

The house for my silkworm butterflies was an old blue shoebox, and into the lid I had punched little air holes. It was my box, and it was an interesting pastime. I kept the box

in the backyard, in the laundry where my mother boiled the washing in the 'copper' with its fire burning underneath. The old frayed copper stick for prodding and lifting had seen better days. One day I came home from school and my shoebox was missing. I asked my mother what had become of my silkworms. She said: 'they had become too many, so I burned the box under the copper'. What a death! They were harmless. It was so final. Stifling emotions can be learned at a very early age and the false coat of armour can be put in place at a moment's notice, with practice. But underneath, the

🌿 *Parents Jack and Alma Jelley.*

vulnerability just grows.

It has been said more alcohol is consumed in times of trouble, that the poor breed drunks, particularly drunken fathers. My father Jack was a man among men, always with mates, always at the pub. He made people laugh. He was funny, jolly and never seemed to be without a beer.

My mother Alma was the younger of two sisters. She was a dancer, and performed evenings on Clay's Circuit and various Sydney venues while cleaning the boarding house her mother ran in the daytime. She often spoke of artists she shared her teen years with—Lily Coburn, Heather Angel, The Harmony Four, Dinks and Onkus, Evey Allbright and George Sorlie, whose revue included her—Alma Humphries—in the well-known touring company.

It was easy for the pretty 19-year-old Alma to be smitten by the happy-go-lucky 20-year-old Jack Jelley; life was fun with no tomorrows. They married at 21 and 22 respectively. The very next year in September 1927, Valerie was born and the young mother never danced again.

My September birthday present was always a day at the Melbourne Agricultural Show. The showbags then were mostly referred to as sample bags because they contained lots of miniature samples and were free. McAlpins flour was my favourite, with its dear little replica boxes of plain, corn and self-raising flour about $1^{1/2}$ by 2 inches. A tiny set of scales was sometimes included, and the hours I would spend weighing pumpkin seeds and watermelon seeds were amazing. Backyard dirt was good too. It could be pretend anything, like sugar or butter. Local grocer shops personally weighed everything then so it was quite a serious game.

Hot, steamy, freshly dropped horse manure brought out the worst in neighbours. Most householders kept a bucket and shovel close to the front gate, and with most traders passing in horse and cart, it was a sprint of the fittest to the centre of the street, after any unsuspecting horse emptied its bowels. It apparently did wonders for the garden, although I don't remember us ever having one. *'Don't say manure, say fertiliser.' 'Turn it up—it's taken me six months to get him to say manure.'*

With so few belongings, families treasured every small possession. Clothes were made, mended and altered and were always kept crisp, fresh and spotlessly clean. There was pride in tidiness and cleanliness and woe betide the housewife with yellow or greyish washing on her line. Being house-proud was considered compulsory behaviour. With this spotless, though poor existence, it's a wonder that the mid-1930s presented an outbreak of diphtheria and scarlet fever. Could the constant attacks of infectious diseases in all children be caused by food handling? Bulk butter was always on display, as were sweets; and biscuits were served by hand from large tins—the kind that millionaires were said to keep their money in. Billy cans of milk, swung in a circle over the head and down without spilling a drop, must have gathered the odd bit of contaminated dust. Lids were a nuisance—no fun in them! Washing fruit before eating would have seemed eccentric behaviour. Flies were lured into kitchens by two-foot-long amber-coloured sticky curly paper, known as fly paper, which usually hung from the centre of ceilings—over the kitchen table was a popular spot. Fly paper was never replaced until the yellowish sticky paper was completely concealed by dead flies, massed on top of each other in an orgy of self-destruction. And of course, the hot steamy horse dung wouldn't have helped in the hygiene stakes. So most depression-raised children were exposed to infections such as whooping cough, chicken pox, measles, scarlet fever and, of course, diphtheria and suffered the accompanying vomiting, rashes, delirium, sore throats and so on.

If I wanted to be included in the majority, this time I got my wish. Fairfield Infectious Diseases Hospital was bulging with patients, including Valerie Jelley, and my diphtheria days were a constant montage of throat and nose swabs, phenol baths, starvation diets … and enemas. On one of the stays at Fairfield Hospital, feeling sick and lonely, I noticed the children who received attention were the ones who answered 'no' to the question 'Have you had a bowel movement?' They even got to have a screen put around them. So secretive, just like a cubby house. So one day I said 'no' to the question. I soon learned that an enema does not hold the same excitement or pleasure as a cubby house. Better not to receive attention, and better not to lie.

When I was discharged from Fairfield Hospital it was my mother's turn to be admitted with a severe case of scarlet fever. My paternal grandmother from Geelong was sent for to do the necessary maternal chores. This very elderly lady was a stranger who, to my mind, knew nothing about little girls,

especially little girls who spent most of their days attending dancing classes or practising. Mysterious things like bows and sashes and ankle socks were dispensed with and, as for tending hair, I was promptly taken to a hairdresser and given a permanent wave. I can still see myself in the mirror—a Medusa-like apparition with two-foot lengths of electrical wiring reaching vertically to some monster of a machine. Apart from the whole ordeal scaring the living daylights out of me, it didn't do a great deal for my naturally curly hair.

As soon as my mother was discharged from hospital, I was once again admitted with a second attack of diphtheria, this time more severe. Of course visitors were not allowed except for a little girl in the bed next to mine who had been moaning throughout night and day. One morning her parents arrived like two white ghosts in long gowns, caps and masks. The entire crowded ward was a little jealous; after all, we were all lonely, we were all experiencing the same illness. It was on my return early one morning from yet another bath in disinfectant that I found the bed next to mine empty. The little girl I envied had died during the night. Like most small children, I would have thought that thirty was real old and that I'd never reach that age. Ironically, over half a century later I would spend many hours filming in that very same hospital.

Acrobats and Tip Top Taps

With Alma's dancing days having come to an abrupt end, is it any wonder little Valerie was taken to dancing school, even before State School. I was four years old. The teacher was Alice Uren, and her dancing school had been recommended by Alma's old theatre friends in Sydney.

I was taken there on a Saturday afternoon, to Flinders Street, on the first floor of the Mutual Arcade (since gone), opposite the railway station. We climbed the stairs, then through a door with the top half glass expounding 'Alice Uren's School of Stage Dancing'. That glass panel was to remain a fixture in my memory forever. But that first day we gazed at that huge room, it was a sight to behold. It seemed to be swarming with little girls in various styled black tunics, all with matching black knickers. How did I know so much about their undergarments? Because every single one of them was standing on her head! For a four-year-old, this was truly a lasting first impression.

I was enrolled and became a Saturday class student and also had private lessons twice a week. This suited my father down to the ground as he spent each Saturday at the pub anyway. While my school days at George Street State were making me feel less acceptable to the human race, the other 'race' I seemed to be winning. On reflection, it's a wonder there was time for education at all.

Alice Uren was a wonderful teacher for the stage, having been part of the great stage act *Hank, Frank and Alice*. She taught tapping as combination rhythms and made me understand 'rounded' beats that flow. She taught style, and did all her own 'bearing' when teaching acrobats. I became one of the miniature Fred Astaire and Ginger Rogers dancing act—Valerie and Kevin. Miss Uren had cards imprinted *Tip Top Tappers—open for engagements, phone f6761*. She even had a phone!

About this time the many dancing schools, including May Downs and Ivy Emms, decided that Toe Dancing was to become *ballet*. Espinosa, the great ballet exponent, came to Australia with performers of his great work, one of whom was Eunice Weston, and from then on Alice Uren's school went up a notch in prestige. I remember the pain of bleeding toes being dipped into methylated spirits for toughening purposes. As French is the language of ballet, it was necessary to suddenly become a linguist, a bigger challenge than achieving 1st position!

I know now the value of having a basic knowledge of dance, even if one does not proceed in the performing arts. The carriage remains, the posture, the art of sitting, and walking—they are never wasted. But at the time I didn't find all that nearly as much fun as tapping and in particular, acrobating.

Alice Uren's best acrobats were a troupe called The Melbourne Marvels and when I became its youngest member I was as proud as punch. One of the troupe's acrobatic tricks was a pyramid

◄ Valerie and Kevin, Tip-Top Tappers.

Mother doing the splits.

wherein the larger girls formed a small circle by clasping shoulders and leaning their heads towards the centre of the circle. The next tier of smaller girls formed a smaller circle by climbing up on their shoulders and standing arms stretched shoulder to shoulder, heads meeting in the centre; then the next tier of three girls followed the same procedure. So much climbing and obvious strain on all concerned was a certain hand getter. But the big finish was when the tiniest acrobat—me—proceeded to climb the three-storey human pyramid, reached the top, and slowly achieved a head stand at the top of it. The audience always found humour in the scrambling antics of the little one trying to manoeuvre up the precarious ascent, and would go wild at the head stand. Unless you have balanced in the centre of three little heads all pushing in to sustain contact, with your own head trying to find a semblance of balance, you will never experience a true 'bump on the head'! The climbing up and down was fun, but those heads were torture. It's amazing how often it seemed audiences applauded for the wrong reasons.

In classes, being half unconscious from a heavy fall mattered not. Fear of difficult acrobatic tricks was meant to be dispelled by being ordered to do it again—immediately.

An unlikely spider-like lady played piano for Saturday's dancing classes. The piano was at one end of the huge hall, where there was an enormous wall mirror which is, of course, essential when students are endeavouring to emulate the teacher. The other end of the hall, with its centre doorway (with no door), was the change room for the students. The walls in between were a mish-mash of photographs of the school's stars. The oversized colour photo of Valerie and Kevin was above a large clock. I was aware, at that age, that looking at the time was something everybody does a lot, so looking at my picture was unavoidable.

Alice Uren played piano herself for all the private lessons and although not a great pianist, she was a great sight-reader and would watch in the mirror, talk, sing, bang her feet, wave her arms, yell and play all at the same time. The music publishers Albert and Chappell would send to her copies of their newest publications. I suppose I was but one of many during a private lesson who stood beside her and would go through

Opposite page: Espinosa was about to fix those hands and feet.

With love
Valerie

With Kevin Swain (Tin Top Tappers), 50 years on at the ABC – a chance meeting.

Down Bourke St with mother Alma after a Princess Theatre matinee. Never leave taps in the theatre.

"She can't change in that time." In the cellophane dress out of which I had to change.

the new songs, deciding which would be suitable. Coming to mind are 'On The Bumpy Road To Love', 'I Double Dare You', 'Boo Hoo', 'Hometown' and 'The Music Goes Round and Around'. It seemed so easy for Miss Uren to sit at the piano and play anything, sight unseen, and change keys to suit immature little voices. I was absorbing a musical knowledge that was to become invaluable many years later when doing choreography (I never could play piano). Although Miss Uren wasn't a good pianist, she would point and say, 'This is in 3/4 waltz time. This one is 4/4 (four beats in the bar), or 2/4. We won't use that second time bar, go straight to the coda, or back to the sign, tacit for 8 bars, double time the middle eight', etc.

During one Saturday class break, a tiny pupil had dropped a ball over the rail of the first floor walkway leading to the toilets. Being a big girl, fully seven years old, and adventurous, I would easily retrieve it. The ball had landed on the glass roof of a downstairs florist shop. The glass had wiggly patterned wire running through it and was made up of 2 ft squares bounded by metal. Getting over the rail was easy. Reaching the ball wasn't. It took three tentative steps before I went crashing through the glass. And because the underneath florist shop had a second ceiling made of wood, my descent was terminated at the waist. Strange how all the other children had suddenly disappeared. Which was more difficult, struggling back to safety, or stifling back the tears? And although I had many cuts on the inside of my thighs, there was little blood. I ventured back into the classroom sheepishly, hoping that

Alice Uren wouldn't raise the roof. I should have known her plan would have a much greater effect. With my cut legs stinging she said, 'now class, we will all do the splits'. I can still remember the pain.

The school thought the physical education needed a lift, and an exponent of the Highland Fling taught classes in the school grounds. Was it my fault that my feet were turned out, that I was doing the basics as well as the teacher! Even when the crossed swords on the ground were introduced it wasn't seen by me to be a challenge or that I might be showing off. I could just *do it*.

Later going home from school we were playing on a grassy nature strip.

'Now it's Valerie's turn to see who can jump highest over the rope!'

A jump seemed too ordinary, so I did a 'tinsky' over.

'Bet you can't go higher. Higher,' they chanted.

By now I was doing flying 'tinskys' and of course fell, and everybody disappeared. I couldn't see what had happened to my right arm, only that my school blazer was stretched approximately eight inches across at the elbow, and was an agonising dead weight. Holding this monstrosity at the wrist with my left hand, I limped home to my mother, and because she couldn't remove the blazer from its misshapen interior, she took me to the corner chemist. Strange that! Of course he bundled us off to the doctor's

surgery on the next corner. The doctor cut away the blazer and pronounced a dislocated elbow. It looked horrible—this ugly great bone protruding from the shiny, taut skin—it frightened me and my mother. A *broken* arm wouldn't have looked nearly so dramatic. Under anaesthetic I jumped from the table, landing on the offending elbow and, without knowing it, reset it myself. It never again felt 100 per cent though.

It took Alice Uren no time at all to teach me comedy songs, some of which were made famous by Gracie Fields. One in particular was 'Husbins', complete with a Cockney accent.

Now I've come to speak to the ladies,
We girls have been trod on too long.
It's quite plain to see, it takes people like me.
To find out what's right and what's wrong.
It's husbins—the riff raff
Men think that we're weak cos we're shy...

and so on. I was big at June Mills' community singing concerts. On a good day I got five shillings. A fortune!

Although my dancing teacher was grooming my stagecraft and even put the fees on hold, my surname Jelley, though an attention getter, *(Valerie Jelley with a hole in her belly)* wasn't exactly impressive for an entertainer. So Alma changed the second E to an A and I became Val Jellay. A name totally devoid of ancestors, and never to be found in a phone book. Of course my

father Jack always resented it but Alma vaguely claimed it was of French origin. By now Val Jellay of Valerie and Kevin Tip Top Tappers, The Melbourne Marvels and Comedy Songs and Dance had become a familiar performer at most of the venues in and around Melbourne—the Apollo then at the top of Bourke Street; the Kings Theatre in Russell Street; the Melba Theatre, also in Russell Street on the other side of Bourke Street, later called the Savoy; and the Garrick Theatre across Princes Bridge. The Hoyts circuit included the Padua in Brunswick, the Victory in St Kilda and the Park in Albert Park. The town halls also had many regular presentations and gave much employment to all kinds of performers. Our acrobatic troupe was very popular in these places because of the space available. Similar

venues like the Trocadero, the Windmill and Leggetts dance halls had the same advantage.

Community singing was popular everywhere—it was every housewife's ultimate day out. Whole audiences would sing with gusto songs chosen by the jovial compere, who guided them with a pointer stick tapping out the words projected on a screen. In every audience the loudest singer was always someone who knew all the words. I clearly remember every head wore a hat; it was strange really. So much poverty, yet an abundance of hats—and gloves. Knitting while singing seemed to be the stamp of the regulars. Among the intermittent acts my comedy song and dance routines were in great demand. This was possibly because the fee for my services was

▲ Modelling childhood fashion apparel – always out of season.

next to nil. Charlie Vaude and June Mills, as comperes, were tops in their field.

The Bijou theatre, just up from the Tivoli in Bourke Street, housed all sorts of entertainment from boxing matches to vaudeville. My very first performance was at the Bijou. It was a pantomime, and I was four years old, wearing a green tutu in the back line. We were to lie down and listen to the dialogue and singing, and exit in the black-out. When the lights came back on after the black-out, and everyone had made their exit, the stage was empty except for one little green fairy who had gone to sleep. How embarrassing!

During one performance at the Princess Theatre I had a quick change from a cellophane dress into an oyster grey and red satin gown. I had eight bars in waltz time to change, with my mother's help—side stage of course. The band played the eight bars in 4/4 time, and Alma ran on stage shouting: 'She can't change in that time!' Another embarrassment.

It never occurred to me that this way of life was unusual. I did, however, yearn for Saturday afternoons at the pictures like other children. My parents always enjoyed 'going to the pictures'. It was a big outing and a night out at the local movie theatre, the Regent Theatre in Johnston Street, Fitzroy, was joy. Once again, how could I know that more than a quarter of a century later I'd frequent

those same halls on a weekly basis for seven years in a television variety show called *Sunnyside Up.*

Opposite the Tivoli was a store called Mantons where I was a child mannequin. This was quite a different kettle of fish. I never could understand why I had to wear tweed coats, velvet hats, long socks, brogues and gloves in the summer, and skimpy clothes in the winter. I thought most of the garments were very plain and ordinary and though I smiled and tried to look as if I felt gorgeous, all I felt was either freezing cold, or boiling hot.

By now Alma was a fully fledged dancing mother, and when I was in revue Mrs Jellay was always in demand to make up the little ones and apply the stage white (leg make-up—cold white liquid like calsomine). Performing around the traps (theatres, town halls, ballrooms and all kinds of palaces) meant having to adapt to their facilities. The Melbourne Marvels, our acrobatic troupe, needed space and height and an orchestra who could play marches at great speed. Other sight and gear acts would need similar facilities while jugglers required height. Magicians don't like working 'in the round'— for obvious reasons. Singers rely on acoustics and dancers have a constant concern for floor surfaces. Although my father Jack had no interest at all in showbusiness, with his labouring skills he took pride in making portable tap mats for me. One was 6 feet by 3 feet, the larger one 8 feet by 4 feet. These were made of wood slats 1$^{1/2}$ inches wide, with the sides planed and bevelled, then held firmly together flat by furniture strapping underneath, with all nails countersunk. Sanded, then lacquered, the whole thing could be rolled up like a piece of lino. The special wood and manner of joins created a great resonant sound.

There were always smelly tins of paint about, including gold and silver for shoes, and a variety of taps to be skillfully applied to growing shoe sizes. House numbers painted on garbage tins seemed ludicrous—who'd want to steal them—but our house number would be painted on with silver-frost paint, left over from the constant painting of my tap shoes. Jack managed to make the odd billy cart for me in between construction of resin boxes, which were a necessity for acrobating.

My favourite outing was when my mother took me to the Tivoli Theatre. While J.C.W.'s theatres, including His Majesty's, were the home of musical comedy and book shows—with the majority of their dancers having been trained at Jennie Brenan's predominantly ballet school—the Tivoli Theatre was vaudeville at its most spectacular, and its dancers were required to be good at everything. It was two shows a day, every day, and people flocked there from all walks of life. Everybody accepted a visit to the 'Tiv' as the norm, just as later we accepted 'going to the pictures' before television altered everybody's views on entertainment.

When the live pit orchestra began the overture, my stomach wanted to leap into my throat from excitement and anticipation and I would strain to see the musicians, to count them and to read the headings and titles on their arrangements. They always seemed so calm and capable, unaware of the magic they were weaving.

We can all be reminded of something significant in our past by a particular smell. No memory can be stronger to me than the smell that would hit the front stalls of the Tivoli Theatre when the act drop (front curtain) was raised. That curtain was plush burgundy velvet, so rich and heavy with gold trimmed festoons along the top, and a two-foot deep row of sparkling gold tassels along the bottom. It kept its magnificent secrets intact until it was raised and another world was revealed. That first gush of air was a mixture of paint and size (canvas undercoat), the smelly taffetas, nets, satins and sequins, glue, make-up and decades of perspiration. All these smells together were foul, but to me, it was the perfume of ecstasy. There was never any doubt in my mind as to how I wanted to spend my life. Here was fun, laughter, glamour, and talented, beautiful people who weren't lonely.

The child

At what age should a youngster enter the world of performing arts? Doing something about it usually happens when the child is about four (must get in first, before academic schooling gets priority). Parents of an only child approach this new world with greater enthusiasm for obvious reasons. It's perfectly natural for parents to believe their offspring has a future in showbusiness. Most times it is a transferred desire, having missed the bus themselves. And what is wrong with that? Nothing, as long as the child is willing.

Once committed to the discipline required, it's usually the mother who works harder than the student to maintain daily practice sessions, offer constant encouragement and enforce strict lesson attendance with excuses not to be tolerated. Most parents, who by now have surrendered their own pleasures totally, find themselves dutifully taking notes (in their own vernacular) and even attempting the instructions themselves, anything, to reinforce their belief that they have given birth to a budding genius. Along the way, we parents do come to realise that it's the hard work that is the spur. Many a child has been born with natural rhythm, a fine singing voice, perfect pitch, or a feel for impersonating or joke telling, but without the professional know-how the art remains underdeveloped and another talent falls by the wayside.

Even after putting in the early years of study, many children lose the necessary dedication when influenced by other interests, which often involve their outside friends. Life is an adventure, and exploring it through a child's eyes can cause impatience when only one road is being travelled.

Nevertheless, all is never lost. A dancer who after the tender years successfully pleads for release will still carry with them a greater appreciation of dancers. The lessons in posture, in self-respect, in knowing how to sit, how to stand and how to mentally applaud others will remain with them all their lives. Whether it be a lapsed dancer, singer or musician, the grounding and even the learned confidence never diminishes. It is re-directed into how to hold conversations with strangers or conceal shyness in unfamiliar surroundings. The learned knowledge is never wasted no matter how far it is tutored.

Padding the parts

Receiving my Merit Certificate from Middle Park Central School, via 2nd Form, was quite a miracle, and relied solely on my abilities in Mathematics and English.

Heidelberg Hospital, later referred to as Heidelberg Repatriation Hospital, became the home of our war wounded. It housed a hall suitable for entertainment, and radio stars regularly performed there. Alice Uren, my teacher, supplied the production and its personnel. There were regular parties at her home, and my parents became friends of Max Reddy, Stella Lamond and Alwyn Kurtz who was becoming a star of radio, following in the footsteps of his famous father Donald Day. I was later to write a radio segment for 3XY starring Alwyn. It was a short-lived comedy contribution entitled XY's Wise Guys. Alice Uren's parties were notorious marathons, and strictly showbusiness. My mother, a non-drinker, loved the company, and my father, together with Max Reddy and the like, was always the life of the party. We children were sent to another room where we swapped ghost stories and fell asleep where we sat. Usually, we stirred to the smell of bacon and eggs being cooked for breakfast. They had staying power, that group of parents! Often the phone would ring and we children would hear, 'Stella—that was Toni. She said bubby's got the itches again'. Although I was older than Toni Lamond, I didn't see a lot of her during those years. She was usually taking care of her baby sister Helen. They were stepsisters, because of different fathers, Joe Lawman and Max Reddy. Both Helen Reddy and Toni Lamond became stars in different areas and no two people were prouder than Max and Stella. Both our families share a bond that doesn't require dialogue; it's just there, forever.

With the shortage of manpower and also womanpower, jobs were plentiful. And I was restless. I was desperate at age 13 to be involved in theatre, any theatre. Being tall, I was able to convince Hoyts management that I was 17. My enthusiasm and outgoing approach was probably the decider. Hoyts de Luxe was my first venture into being an usherette, a very prestigious occupation. Wearing a gold-braided uniform gave me a sense of authority and presentation. And wasn't the foyer's spruiker the most famous in the land: 'The Man Outside Hoyts'? Directly opposite was the Tivoli and its spruiker, spouting the joys of vaudeville. With their gloved hands holding pointers they added colour to the busy hubbub of Bourke Street with its many attractions. Uniforms of all kinds were everywhere, instilling pride.

I could watch the comings and goings across the street outside the Tivoli, not the least of which was 'poverty point' every Monday morning. Literally an institution in its day, actors would gather looking for work, making themselves available and doing deals with reps and small time

At the Capitol Theatre in 1941 with Olive – 14 looking 17. Back in uniform after onstage presentation with Valentine & Monty. The movie 'Forest Rangers' followed.

22

bookers. Humility is a necessary part of a performer's character, together with persistence and hopefulness, to cope with the disappointments of rejection. Showbiz stories would be swapped, as would money, with loans sometimes being repaid. Passing pedestrians would ignore the goings on, as the lingo was the performers' and was theirs alone.

I recognised a fellow dancer among the Hoyts de Luxe staff immediately. Not only did she have natural carriage, but she didn't bend her knees when she bent over to change shoes, a dead giveaway. Her name was Olive. Olive was transferred to Hoyts Capitol Theatre. I was transferred to Hoyts Plaza Theatre, an awesome time. The Plaza was underneath the Regent in Collins Street, and the young ladies, in my case very young, shared the same huge change room adjoining the theatres backstage. Because the Plaza was without a dress circle and stairs (very unusual), we were able to wear elegant burgundy and gold evening gowns that came down to the floor, without threat of tripping. The manager preferred hair to be upswept, adding to the air of elegance. I just loved to swan down the aisles with my long gown swaying. It was even better ushering latecomers, in the dark, as I could smile to myself, exaggerate my swinging hips and pretend all sorts of things. This dreaming would come to a sudden end when eventually, indicating vacant seats with my torch, I'd discover the patrons had chosen their own seating long before and disappeared into the sea of seated figures. How embarrassing. Sneaking back up the aisle, torch off, was done with furtive haste. They called me 'The Showgirl'.

I eagerly agreed to be part of the Capitol's stage presentation as a foil in a ventriloquist's act, known as Valentine and Monty. The featured movie was 'The Forest Rangers' with Paulette Goddard. At interval I would give out the pass-outs, then rush backstage, change from my tailored grey uniform into a gorgeous little glamorous stage costume and come on stage at a given cue, carrying a ventriloquist's doll. I daringly made the most of this entrance by working the doll's eyes and eyebrows as though reacting to something suggestive. Quite forward for an enterprising 14-year-old. We swapped scripted dialogue that I didn't think was funny but it always got laughs. Childhood experience had taught me timing, and how to make an entrance and 'milk' an exit. Getting back into the usherette's uniform, tearing tickets, smiling patiently at bad-tempered and sometimes tipsy patrons, wasn't nearly as much fun. But it was all a learning process.

Dealing with the public can make great actors of us all. I got to know the dialogue in every movie and would act out every part.

❧ *Parents' Party Time. One of Alice Uren's notorious marathons. Back row holding glass: Alwyn Kurtz. Third row From back: Mother (2nd from left). Centre: Teacher Alice Uren. Third row from front, far right: Max Reddy and Stella Lamond. Second front row, second from right: Father Jack Jellay. Front row: Large Rex (WACA) Dawe 'Yes What'.*

Musicals were my favourite; I'd know all the songs and all of Betty Grable's dance routines but Sonja Henie's skating was a problem. A special movie for me was *Orchestra Wives* about musicians on the road and it featured the great Nicholas Brothers, two fantastic black tap dancers and acrobats. They worked in tails with patent leather shoes and had great musical arrangements.

The Capitol Theatre had a huge upstairs foyer, which overlooked the stalls from its well-like structure at one end. This allowed the sound to fill the building at full volume. After the house settled for the feature movie, it was an opportunity for me to indulge my restless urges. Just being in attendance like a guarding sentry demanded extreme self-control when I could hear the musical soundtrack wafting up. It never entered my mind as I danced and whirled all over that upstairs foyer, that anyone would, or could, ever see me. The Nicholas Brothers were my downfall. After two years at the Capitol Theatre, the manager's patience

♣ *At 13. Due to the wartime manpower shortage, Hoyts management accepted my age as 17.*

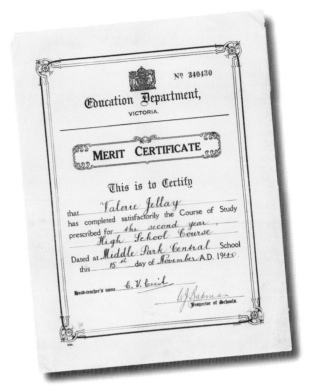

was exhausted when he walked in on my impressions of cartwheels, round offs, and worst of all—jump splits. He did however give me an excellent reference.

My older friend Olive had arranged for an audition at the Tivoli. She was an aspiring 'ballet girl'—a term used for being an exceptionally good but, of necessity, versatile dancer. She was nervous about her weakness in tapping and asked me to teach her a short routine. Of course I did, and I also went with her to the audition. Just sitting in the darkened theatre at the back of the stalls watching the vast, empty stage was thrilling. All my young life I had watched the Tivoli shows, and was now seeing it in a different light—literally. If I hadn't helped Olive, and gone with her that day ... who knows? Life is one big 'if'. But now I knew what was required for an audition. In the meantime, my Hoyts Theatres credentials and reference got me an excellent position at the prestigious Metro Theatre in Collins Street, opposite Georges. Promotion to the booking office and the adjoining switchboard should have

satisfied me, but no. It was through the Metro switchboard that I swung an appointment with Wallace Parnell, the managing director of the Tivoli Circuit. But it was David N. Martin who interviewed me and who put me in the hands of Ronnie Hay, the great dance arranger.

'Choreographer' hadn't reached the language of Australian theatre yet. On reflection it was an unacceptable audition by today's standards. I had the necessary shoes for demi-pointe ballet, also point shoes, tap shoes, and non-slip tumblers. There was just Ronnie Hay and myself on this huge, dimly lit empty stage. Beside a working light stand I obediently performed high kicks, cobblers, ballet basics and my own tap steps. Then I had to follow Ronnie with his steps. It was like a bad visit to the dentist. It ended when he said: 'We'll be in touch with you at the first vacancy'.

Back at the Metro movie theatre I personally received the call at their busy switchboard, to report for rehearsal the following Monday morning.

❧ *School certificates.*

26

Tivoli Theatre Melb. 1944. Age 17

Tivoli years

Tivoli producers were taking frequent trips to America to gather ideas for exotic and elaborate productions, find set designs involving moving staircases and technology from the Ziegfeld type shows (with revolves and showgirls being lowered from the 'flys'), and copy costume design and gimmicky props.

Various sight and gear acts were imported to tour the Tivoli Circuit and everything was of the highest possible standard. Entertainment was booming, audiences wanted escapism from the realities of war and my generation was accepting the situation as permanent — as the years rolled by we had adjusted to this way of life.

My years at the Tivoli were frantic to say the least. I was expected to do everything and anything, and it was wonderful. Most of the audience were regulars and receptive. I embraced that love with all my heart and soul as it swept across the footlights, and enjoyed flirting outrageously with the audience. Even now I know that I shift gears in front of a live audience—it has been a very long love affair.

Tales of stage door Johnnies have always been fallacies. The only things at the Tivoli stage door were rats. Huge rats would scurry about late at night after the show. They came from the many cafes facing Swanston Street. Of course they are no longer there (in case I get sued!).

With rehearsal time always limited, activity would be everywhere. As production numbers were being created and learned by the dancers, showgirls and principals involved, comedy sketches were being rehearsed in the upstairs dress circle foyer. I was often called away from the stage to attend comedy rehearsals. There was a big iron soundproof door leading from the stage manager's prompt corner to the front of house, via a passage behind the 'stalls-base', and a little staircase with its passage, behind the 'circle box' leading to the dress circle. Halfway back of the dress circle was a concealed door leading to the music room. In it was chaos. A library of music arrangements, full ashtrays, a very worn piano and a very worn piano player—Bernie Duggan. There were always melodies being learned, keys being set, harmonies being experimented with. Pencils, erasers and manuscripts, new and old, were everywhere. With its limited space, soundproof door and never being cleaned or tidied, the air was foul. Not the ideal environment for singers. To me it was mystical.

The music room was hallowed ground and only rehearsal principals would attend their respective calls. My early enthusiasm was poorly received when curiosity caused me to sneak a peek at what went on in the music room. An intent group was working on 'I Got Rhythm'. As the singer paused,

❧ 1944–45, War years.

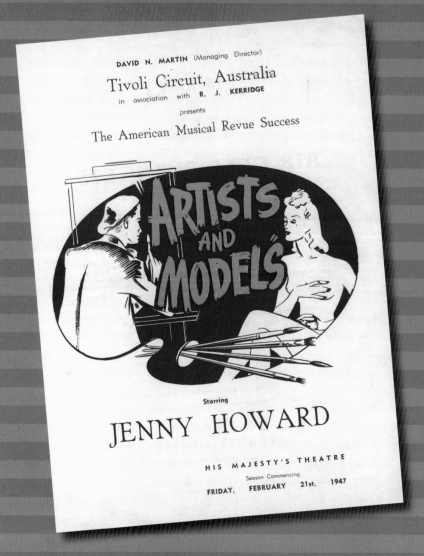

DAVID N. MARTIN (Managing Director)

Tivoli Circuit, Australia

in association with R. J. KERRIDGE

presents

The American Musical Revue Success

ARTISTS AND MODELS

Starring

JENNY HOWARD

HIS MAJESTY'S THEATRE

Season Commencing

FRIDAY, FEBRUARY 21st, 1947

I burst into the room. 'I know that song', I announced with great authority, and segued into the vocal, getting through to the first four bars, before I noticed everyone had spun around to see who was responsible for the interruption. The singer's jaw dropped in disbelief. I hastily backed out of the door, and wondered when I would ever control my enthusiasm.

The dress circle foyer comedy rehearsals were at first awesome. Jim Gerald, Syd Beck, Morry Barling, Roy Rene, Joe Lawman, Buster Fiddes, George Wallace and Will Mahoney were just some of the comedy greats I had the privilege of working with. Some had their permanent leading lady feeds but, mostly, more than one girl was required in their sketches. This situation gave me the

opportunity to watch and learn from the experts. Essie Jemmings was Mrs Jim Gerald. Sadie Gale was Mrs Roy Rene (Van Der Sluys), Evie Hayes was Mrs Will Mahoney, Doris Whimp was with Morry Barling and Joy Lawman worked with Joe. George Wallace always had Bubby Allen, and the great sketches of Edgely and Dawe were complemented by Edna Luscombe, Mrs Mick Edgely. These marvellous comedy performers had over the years polished and perfected every move, every word, every breath, so that their unique and original styles were beyond improvement. Taking over the lesser roles in these ultimate environments would have fazed the most experienced. They were very serious people. The discipline cancelled out my awe, and by jumping into the deep

Above: Tivoli programmes.

end, and receiving orders, criticism and getting yelled at a lot, I was mastering a very difficult craft. Comedians deserve the greatest respect. 'Laugh clown laugh' is such a succinct epitaph.

It didn't take long for me to grasp the importance of comics stealing each other's material. They were so protective of their scripts, to the point of paranoia. When scripts were handed out at rehearsals, I was never given a complete script. Usually it was just the particular lines I had to say preceded by the cue only. For example:

CUE: ... down the stairs

VAL: Be warned. They are very slippery.

And then, perhaps, I would have a missing page of dialogue with another set of dots leading to a cue that didn't make sense. Quite a difficult way to understand what it was all about. Mostly I received no script at all and was just told what to say, with the crucial 'business' and moves explained, then committed it to memory. Putting a foot wrong or giving a word an incorrect intonation would bring forth the wrath of God and I would be verbally jumped on. I was actually afraid of Roy Rene, Will Mahoney and Jim Gerald. They were stars and they deserved to have people around them who knew what they were doing. Their teachings were invaluable—I learned so much. The real meaning of discipline; the setting up of lines; how a breath or the flick of an eye could make or break the comedians' lines; never

do anything unless it was to their advantage; and the futility of one so-called comedian trying to 'top' another. Throughout those Tivoli years, whenever I had my hands on a complete script, I conveniently hung on to it. I wasn't quite sure why, only that all the devious cloistering meant that a script was something precious. Years later I was to learn why.

There was always so much activity. With morning rehearsals, matinees daily, and the second show nightly, gear and sight acts never seemed to leave the theatre. They were always in corners practising, or checking and repairing props. Eddie Gordon and Nancy was a typical act. He was an American trick-cyclist; a baggy-suited clown with a ginger fright wig. Magnificent tricks were done with gentle visual humour and very clever props. Nancy was the glamour foil. Then there was Jandy, an authentic European clown. He was always in the theatre three hours before any performance. That was the time he took to check his props, get made-up and dressed. He was immaculate, and a perfectionist. Vaudeville and variety demanded dedication. These clowns were very serious businessmen. Their act was their life.

One of the many gear acts in which I was assistant with Dawn Butler was that of the magnificent German juggler Elimar. It was essential that I learn to throw, catch and carry a variety of specialised props, in a manner that took many rehearsal hours. Elimar was so demanding of himself.

Whenever possible, he would rig his slack wire working for hours and if he missed a trick he would slap his own face with force and real venom, yelling and swearing in German. The result was a sensational act. The war years were unkind to him and because of his nationality he was shunned and made to feel an enemy. Even fellow artists would turn from him. Elimar was a gentleman, that was all I knew. Times were very confusing.

There were many overseas acts forced to remain in Australia. The jet age hadn't arrived. Travelling by ship was impossible and only warships sailed the seas, always in danger of being sunk by aircraft or mines. The Chinese were the best forward acrobats, the Australians the best backward acrobats. The Americans, like Gardner and Kane, were the slickest dancers, the Europeans the best gear and sight acts, due to their great history and circus background.

Dancers were the busiest, always learning new routines. The beautiful showgirls,

❧ *Pantomime.*

'To Val, the girl who gave me a lift', from Elimar 1946.

'To Val, the girl who gave me a lift', from Elimar 1946.

Tivoli stage door … Two shows a day, every day … with morning rehearsals.

although appearing to do little more than parade and pose in stunning costumes, actually faced the most hazards. Each opening night, which occurred every five weeks, they lived in fear of many things. Their magnificent headgear and assorted trappings were kept, elevated on pulleys, side stage, and the stage hands were responsible for lowering and raising these cumbersome and usually heavy adornments. Most of their entrances were made down staircases—steep staircases—which had very narrow treads. Their job was never to hold on to anything, always smile, and most of all, never, never look down. To not look down when coming down a steep set of steps is difficult in the best of circumstances. To walk erect with knees just brushing, feet turned out, legs straight, chin up, shoulders back, arms extended, heavy and huge headgear on, smile—well, those beautiful ladies were something special. One of their particular nightmares were 'revolves'. Each girl would appear separately on a 'revolve' which, on an opening day, would either stick and refuse to move more than half way, leaving the showgirl to straddle a gaping set piece like a truckie, or else it would spin around freely but reach its stop spot with a jolt that would send the poor girl hurtling off onto the nearest refuge. All of these hazards on stage, after having to climb up onto huge elevated sets back-stage via various odd boxes, step

ladders and rostrums, were part of their job.

When one of these gorgeous showgirls—Claudia—took ill, she had two important moments that had to be filled. Ginger James, the great Tivoli producer-director, decided I was to substitute. I was going to enjoy the showgirl parade down the huge staircase, featured alone, wearing a magnificent pale blue sequined full skirted gown. It was a floor length period-type gown, with an underneath hooped skirt, a rear train, a beautiful lace and satin bonnet, worn with long blue gloves and blue satin high-heeled shoes. All of it fitted fine. There were two male tenors dressed in white tails who sang 'Stay as Sweet as You Are' from microphones on prompt and OP (opposite-prompt) corners. The first problem was trying to get up the step ladder at the rear of the huge staircase, because of the hoop in the underskirt. Holding the hoop up at the front and pushing it down at the back didn't help—it just meant that I couldn't see where I was going. The same action in reverse meant that I put my foot on the hoop instead of on the steps. That hoop had a mind of its own. My head was to gradually appear on high as if from a cloud. I was lucky to appear at all, finally arriving as though I'd been shot from a cannon. I was alone up there on a huge staircase wondering how I could walk in time to this pretty ballad being sung to me. Were the steps actually there! According to that hooped underskirt I was meant to take flight. My efforts at smiling resulted in lips that were uncontrollable. I could feel them jumping everywhere with nerves. Reaching the stage finally, after what felt like an endurance test, I was to double time the walk to one singer. That was achieved, and then back to the slow walk across the footlights downstage, right across the front to the singer at the opposite side. There is an art in walking sideways elegantly, with one leg crossing the other while the body remains full on to the audience. Once again it was the smile that gave me away. Once getting the grin in place, the top lip wouldn't come down because my mouth and gums were so dry. Any anxious performer will have experienced the top-lip-sticking syndrome. Can an audience really notice? I wonder!

Claudia's second urgent appearance was even more hair-raising. She was a special showgirl who was paid more because she did the occasional topless reveal. The law at that time stated that the model must not move, at all, and was to appear for a few seconds only. The lighting was always perfect, and done with great taste. It was a boudoir production. The entire stage was a gold and white dressing table, with side draws and a large oval mirror centre, way up high. The dancers were dressed as French maids with cute aprons, caps and feather duster props. The showgirls paraded in elegant chiffon negligees and feathered boudoir gowns. The big finish was when the music swelled, the lights lowered, and the big oval mirror revolved with Claudia appearing topless. Blackout. Of course Ginger James knew I wouldn't appear topless, but someone had to be on that revolve, it couldn't just appear—empty. My dear lady friends in wardrobe found me a satin undergarment, known today as a 'teddy'. I couldn't wear Claudia's costume. There wasn't one. Only a g-string. I brushed my long hair over one side, like Veronica Lake, to cover my face. With only a tiny ledge for my feet, it was quite a balancing trick. Ginger James was having a marvellous time at my expense. And as I was waiting with dread for the thing to revolve, Ginger was still laughingly trying to make me appear topless. Even as it started to take me around, he was still calling up to me: 'I'll give ya ten shillings for one!'

I was sure Ginger James knew absolutely everything about the theatre. When Maurie Rooklyn, known as 'Mr Rooklyn the great illusionist', appeared at the Tivoli, he proved a big success with his spectacular show-manship. His complicated illusions were set behind beautiful white crushed velvet French action tabs. They had been especially made and looked magnificent. In front of these tabs I introduced Mr Rooklyn, with dialogue set to eerie rhythm and creepy sound effects, all done in blue light. My costume

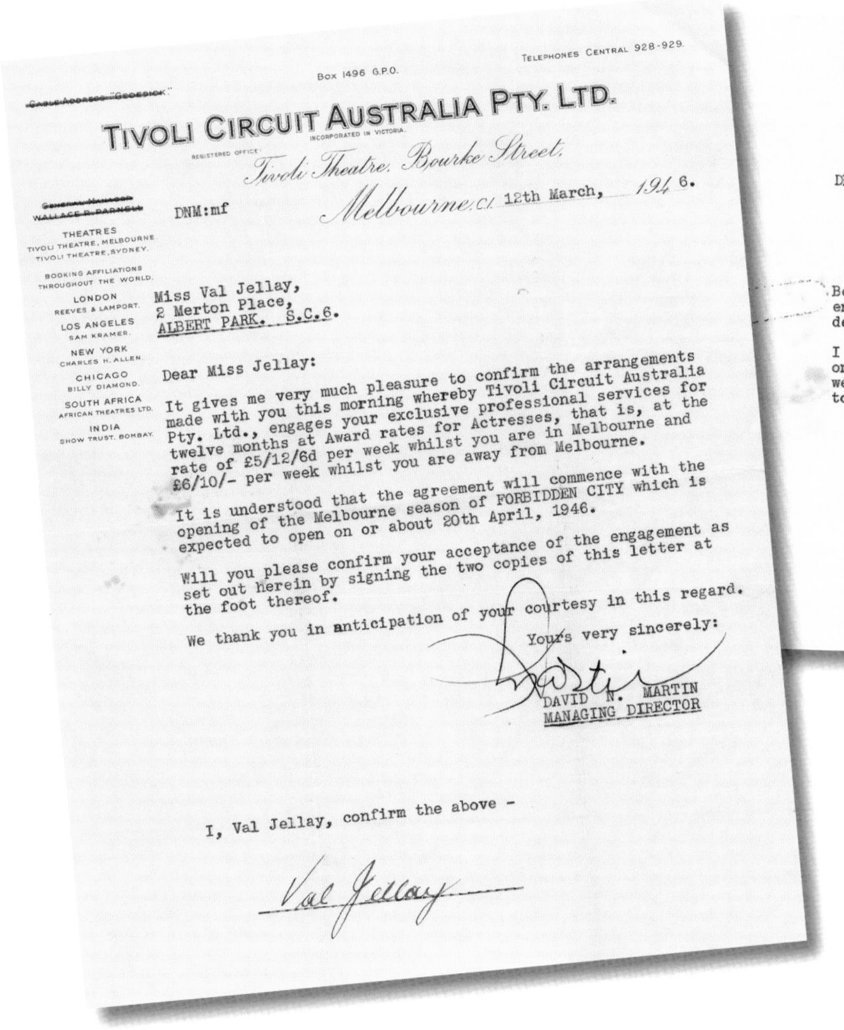

Telephones Central 928-929.

Box 1496 G.P.O.

~~Cable Address "Geosick"~~

TIVOLI CIRCUIT AUSTRALIA PTY. LTD.

Incorporated in Victoria.

Registered Office: Tivoli Theatre, Bourke Street,

Melbourne, C1 12th March, 1946.

~~General Manager Wallace R. Parnell~~

Theatres
Tivoli Theatre, Melbourne
Tivoli Theatre, Sydney.

Booking Affiliations throughout the World.
London – Reeves & Lamport.
Los Angeles – Sam Kramer.
New York – Charles H. Allen.
Chicago – Billy Diamond.
South Africa – African Theatres Ltd.
India – Show Trust, Bombay.

DNM:mf

Miss Val Jellay,
2 Merton Place,
ALBERT PARK. S.C.6.

Dear Miss Jellay:

It gives me very much pleasure to confirm the arrangements made with you this morning whereby Tivoli Circuit Australia Pty. Ltd., engages your exclusive professional services for twelve months at Award rates for Actresses, that is, at the rate of £5/12/6d per week whilst you are in Melbourne and £6/10/- per week whilst you are away from Melbourne.

It is understood that the agreement will commence with the opening of the Melbourne season of FORBIDDEN CITY which is expected to open on or about 20th April, 1946.

Will you please confirm your acceptance of the engagement as set out herein by signing the two copies of this letter at the foot thereof.

We thank you in anticipation of your courtesy in this regard.

Yours very sincerely:

DAVID N. MARTIN
MANAGING DIRECTOR

I, Val Jellay, confirm the above -

Val Jellay

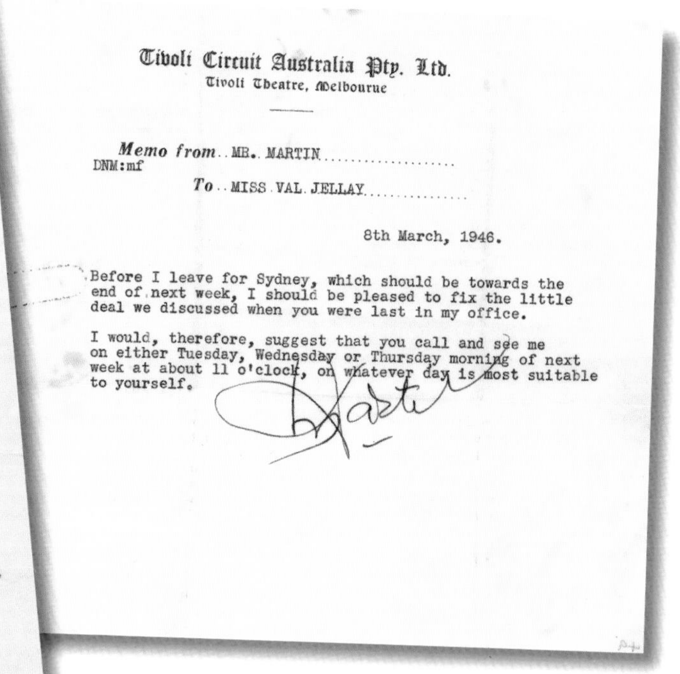

Tivoli Circuit Australia Pty. Ltd.
Tivoli Theatre, Melbourue

Memo from .. MR. MARTIN
DNM:mf
To .. MISS VAL JELLAY

8th March, 1946.

Before I leave for Sydney, which should be towards the end of next week, I should be pleased to fix the little deal we discussed when you were last in my office.

I would, therefore, suggest that you call and see me on either Tuesday, Wednesday or Thursday morning of next week at about 11 o'clock, on whatever day is most suitable to yourself.

From understudy to a front line girl ... to utility ... to soubrette. After two years of 12 shows a week, changing programme every five weeks, I was finally placed under contract to Tivoli Circuit Australia.

was white velvet, sexy but cute, with a huge white velvet bow in my hair. On opening day Ginger was his usual quiet, agitated self, watching from prompt corner and, as I was waiting to go on, I said, 'Excuse me Ginger, but my costume is the same colour as the tabs. I won't be seen clearly and I'll disappear into the background'. For a moment I thought he was going to explode. With his lips thinned he turned to me and said, 'Don't you worry dear, we'll have the tabs replaced'. What a sarcastic cynic he was; but funny. I thought he was the greatest.

After one matinee I was summoned, by means of the PA system, to come to the stalls. I donned my street frock, went down through the pass door to a small gathering of management who presented me with a marathon script to be learned by the next house. The show was under time, and they had written a two-handed routine to be done with Charles Norman (the suave English compere), directly after the big opening number. His opening dialogue would give me time to change. By now I was used to working in sketches and doing dialogue well rehearsed, but this was a different kettle of fish altogether. My scallywag friends Les Ritchie and Honest John, who knew all the tricks, assured me it was nothing to worry about. Over and over they ran it through with me in the limited time available. One of my lines was: 'I used to do the dance of the seven veils'. They told me to slow the line down and swing from hip to hip on the words 'dance', 'seven' and 'veils'. They told Wally Hind, the

drummer, to give me a bass drum beat with each hip movement. When my nervousness suggested I might forget some of the enormous amount of unfamiliar dialogue, they said don't panic, just say either 'whose turn to talk?', or 'where were we up to?' To this day Charles Norman and myself laugh about that first time we did the double act. There was no time to go through it together, so when Charles heard 'I used to do the dance of the seven veils' (with drum effects), his reaction was so funny it got a laugh and he asked the question again, and got the same reply. The rest was going well until my mind went blank, and I remembered my instructions and said: 'whose turn to talk?' Charles Norman just stared at this teenage stranger with a stunned look and eventually said, 'Pardon?' I then said the other emergency line, 'where were we up to?' He was meant to get me back on track but, instead, he broke up laughing. Later Charles asked how and where I learned to cover a 'dry' like that! Of course Ginger James had his suspicions—after all, he was of that ilk and thought the same as those other Aussie pros!

Ginger never let on if he knew about my sneaking into the back stalls on Sunday afternoons prior to an opening day, which was always Monday, to watch him light the sets. Sitting unnoticed in the dark, seeing the lighting magic being created was fascinating. Unseen voices would call back and forth as cues were marked, altered and re-marked, and I would mentally mark my rehearsals with the light cues. Same thing with Monday morning band calls. We were all called anyway, but not that early. I had truly found what I loved being part of—with a passion.

Every spare minute between entrances I was always observing. Mostly side stage where getting under everyone's feet didn't deter me from watching and learning from the greats. Another favourite observation look-out was from the darkened 'flys'. The constant clanging of the counterweight system fascinated me, as the fly man worked with the stage mechanist on constant cloth and scenery changes. Stage hands patiently explained how large flats were slid rapidly in quick changes by the balance and placement of their arms; one high, one low, with the elbow doing the balancing. One man to a flat, they were always stacked neatly in reverse order for their next use. I learned to 'toggle': throwing a rope line over protruding wooden blocks which brought two or more flats together and then 'tying off', which is a special knot that can be released with one tug. The names of coloured medium used for lighting had to be learned and electricians patiently answered all my questions. I learned to distinguish and watch the rigging of legs, borders, French action tabs, festoons, concertinas, and that all ropes must be pulled hand over hand.

❧ *Previous page: Mixing it with wartime 'blitz babies'!*

Theatre abbreviations

P.	Prompt side, the stage-managers corner.
o.p.	Opposite Prompt
BOZ.	Business
S.M.	Stage Manager
A.S.M.	Assistant Stage Manager
M.D	Musical Director
U.S.	Up Stage
D.S.	Down Stage
B.O.	Black Out
STRIKE.	Remove From Stage
THE HALF	Half Hour Call
W.U.	Warm Up Call

The wardrobe department held a particular fascination. With a change of programme every five weeks all of us were constantly being fitted. Madame Mackay would let me look at Angus Winneke's wonderful costume-design sketches, and when the wardrobe trimmers could find nothing for me to do they would let me pair up all the shoes in the large shoe area. Stage-struck? You bet!

It was probably a means of getting me out of their hair but the management arranged for me to have singing lessons. Allans' Collins Street music house had tiny tutoring rooms on its uppermost floor and my singing teacher was a little old fat man steeped in legitimate opera techniques. 'Diaphragm. Sing from the diaphragm' was his constant demand. I was interested in showmanship.

Back at the theatre one day, between shows when the theatre was dark, I went down to prompt corner, raised the centre microphone and turned on the volume, which I'd seen the stage manager Keith Johns do many times. Such audacity when I think of it. It wasn't meant to be devilment, it was an urge and opportunity led it to be satisfied. There was a George Wallace show on at that time, with Bubby Allen featured soubrette. She starred in a western production singing 'Cow Cow Boogie'. It had been recorded by the Andrews Sisters and was a big hit. So, standing alone in the darkened theatre I sang 'Cow Cow Boogie' totally unaccompanied, acting out my fantasy, pretending I was the star. It didn't matter to me that the sound was turned on and took my sudden invasion of silence to

every speaker in the building, including the management's office. People came from all areas, mainly from the dress-circle stairs, the rear of which was David N. Martin's inner sanctum.

'Who is that fooling with the sound system?'
'Who was that singing?'

The reprimands were, of course, well deserved. The fun actors I now knew well, calmed my apprehension and, like my other exploits, it became a storm in a teacup.

No matter when you looked to the orchestra pit, the smiling face of the wonderful Musical Director Hal Moschetti would be grinning back. Even when things would come unstuck on opening days and his shoulders weighed heavy with his own problems, a look to the pit and Hal Moschetti could dispel all fears; everything was perfect. Fred Gulliford, the ever-reliable pianist, would take over the baton when Hal Moschetti went to Sydney to open each show transferred to their Tivoli Theatre in Castlereagh Street. Together with Wally Hind, the greatest ever 'pit' drummer, arranger-clarinet player Dud Cantrell (who was Lana Cantrell's uncle) and their fellow musos, what a safety net we performers had.

Their so-called band room was under the stage, as it is in most theatres, along with the office of the mechanist Stan Carrodus and bulky laughing Mick Day and Jack from the Flies. The reason we girls spent time running up and down those stairs was because we were gambling on the races. Six-pence each way was quite acceptable and, because we never finished up in front, that SP book must have been a going concern, (again, no longer there of course, in case I get sued!). Thanks, or no thanks, to my father's training I was always allowed into the poker games. Stage hands always played cards. One was the handsome Durham Marcell who was on props. A quiet, efficient young man, he later married my good friend Pauline Stewart.

Always in the company of people like Buster Fiddes, Les Ritchie, Honest John Gilbert and the like, I received a very unusual education. On their way to Sol McDermott's actors' pub, the Post Office Hotel in Elizabeth Street (Ma Franks' Golden Fleece Hotel in Russell Street was also an actors' haven), they would walk me to the Collins and Swanston Street tram stop. This would often take quite some time as stops were made back and forth to buy vanilla slices and lamingtons (Les Ritchie's favourites), or else an hour would be taken up drinking a milk shake in one of the many late night cafes. Always, while waiting on the tram stop, we would swap tap steps. Honest John was a lovely soft-shoe dancer and Les Ritchie, with his wife Mavis, was one of the great dancing acts of that era. It's a wonder we weren't ever stopped by the constabulary—the laughter and noise were raucous to say the least.

All kinds of palaces. On tour.

I was to tour to Sydney's Tivoli Theatre with the other principals in a later show—an exciting time for me—when news came of a tragic fire having taken place there, backstage in the dressing rooms. The details horrified us all. It was winter time, and the showgirls had radiators in their rooms. Their net, feathers and sequined trains took but a moment to burst into flames as they accidentally brushed against a radiator. Two beautiful girls were burned to death, and survivors were maimed. The reality of the horror struck home as we arrived at the theatre and our dressing rooms were allocated. Two rooms and their corridor area were charred black, like a petrified forest. Water was still dripping everywhere from the futile efforts of fire hoses. The stench added to the morbid scene. It smelled like death. It was a situation we could not escape during the entire Sydney season. But the show must go on.

Back in Melbourne I was again singing and 'feeding' the many comedians we all loved. A book show, written by Buddy Morley called *Forbidden City* starred George Nichols, Steve Doo, and Bobby Le Brun as an American, a Chinese and an Australian respectively. When they supposedly visited Paris I was the French foil, speaking with a French accent. This was a wonderful company. We had so much fun. Little did I know that ten years later, when working for Bobby Le Brun, my life would change forever.

Another show to break totally with tradition was *Get A Load Of This*. It was a gangster story by James Hadley Chase, set in a nightclub. For the first time in the history of the Tivoli Theatre, patrons would enter to an exposed stage. There was no front curtain (act drop). It was designed in fact as two sets, one on top of the other. The top set was the office where the dramatic dialogue took place. Stairs from its side entrance door went down to the nightclub set, but weren't used until the end of the show. The band was on stage on prompt side and my feature soubrette song was an original, written by Hal Moschetti. He played solo riffs on clarinet as I sang the melody. My dress was red chiffon, with a pleated flared skirt. I was very proud to be on stage with the great Hal Moschetti—he was so respected. Everyone was anxious to be involved in this radical show and many out of work (or 'available') actors were employed as the patrons of the nightclub. They sat at tables throughout each performance as extras, reacting as required. The orchestra pit was also covered and tables and chairs with 'patrons' were seated across the front. Straight actors were brought over from Sydney—Eric Reiman, a young woman named Pat McDonald, and little Ronnie Shand who was cast as a cheeky crook. Our usual Tivoli audience were enthralled with the plot, and felt genuinely vulnerable when, at the climax of the story, uniformed police stormed through

With Dawn Butler and Kath Crawford in Christchurch, July 1947.

the back of the theatre with guns firing and whistles blowing chasing the criminals. *Get A Load Of This* was one of the biggies.

Cavalcade of Variety made use of the surplus of performers now in Melbourne. Instead of the especially written link music used in *Get A Load Of This* it was back to 'I Want To Be Happy' and 'Marie' (The Dawn Is Breaking). 'You' (Stole My Heart Away) was played loud and fast for play-ons and chasers in black outs. For years we sang eight bars of the American national anthem seguing from 'God Save The King' in the finales while, somewhere out there, Leonski was murdering young girls and sensitive issues about our armed forces were being fought over in the streets. One such incident erupted in the stalls of the Tivoli Theatre with Americans and Australians climbing over seats in an almighty brawl.

Showgirls were getting married. Margaret Siler married an American soldier; Elvie Reid married a Kodak executive; Pearl Schweig became Pearl Copolov when she married the illustrious furniture store owner. Gloria Williams married an Englishman and went with him to Lords where they managed a hotel; Tess Dennis married the manager of the Sydney Tivoli, Rudy Mann. And Jean Hunter married the compere-comedian Terry Scanlan, on stage, after a matinee.

Buster Fiddes was an unpredictably funny man. He and his dog Jake were inseparable.

Jake was allowed everywhere and slept under Buster's bed in many actors' pubs. Closing nights have always been an excuse to do the occasional fun thing but Buzzie took things a bit far during an elaborate pirate production. A big gold trunk was centre stage, supposedly filled with priceless gems. Each showgirl emerged from the trunk via a basement trap (lift) on cue, one bedecked as a ruby, another as an emerald, a sapphire, a diamond, etc. The last was to be pure gold but instead of the gorgeous gold, Buster slowly came up wearing a daggy dress and a tatty black wig. With him was Jake the Dog. He played it dead straight, doing the correct showgirl moves with Jake following.

I had been dressing on the ground floor principals' area for some time. Among my friends were Kath Crawford and Muriel Gardner, whose application of black face make-up was an education in patience as I watched her put large gooey black blobs on the tip of each of her own eyelashes. By contrast, Gloria Dawn would arrive at the theatre ten minutes before curtain, looking like a bedraggled street urchin. She would calmly get dressed and made up and stroll through the swing-doored passageway just as her intro was playing, and always timed it to perfection. She would light up the stage, always looking gorgeous. And what a performer. The greatest! Once, between entrances, she decided to bleach her hair.

❧ *Opposite page top: Don Williams of 'Williams and Shand', England 1953. Opposite page bottom: Muriel Gardner and Marvin Kane, 'Make it a Party', Tivoli 1946.*

🌿 *Buster Fiddes and Jake, Tivoli 1940s.*

With Kath Crawford, Ginger James and friends. The smile was soon lost to sea-sickness.

Napro was the emulsion used by blondes at that time. She soaked her hair in the thick milky coloured goo. Our next entrance was a Navy production, wearing cute navy and white satin costumes and French sailors' caps with a red pompom on top and ribbons down the back. While I panicked, she calmly removed the ribbons from her cap and interwove them into her hair, making one elegant plait down the back of her head. With the pompom cap plonked on top, she left the dressing room as her intro began, looking stunning. Nothing fazed her. Her mother, Zilla Weatherly, was a character to say the least and would never allow Gloria to work in sketches. Gloria would have been a big star overseas but, as Honest John said, she'd

rather have had a washing machine.

An eight-week season of pantomime each Christmas was not to be looked forward to. It meant three shows a day and it was hard work for everyone, including the stage hands and the musicians. Jim Gerald was the ultimate panto dame with the finest details of his make-up, wigs and wardrobe being attended to. Apart from always headlining a Tivoli show, Jenny Howard's famous forte was playing Principal Boy. She was another watch-and-learn experience for me and apart from my ever so many pantos as Boy for different managements, it was among England's traditionalists at Birmingham's magnificent theatre that I was able, thanks to Jenny Howard's influence, to hold my own in

Dick Whittington and His Cat.

It was presumed by the powers that be that sending a show to Adelaide would be accomplished with the least possible effort because we'd done it all before. Overlooked, perhaps, were the theatre's different dimensions and different musicians reading unfamiliar music. It was always a nightmare. On one opening night Maggie Fitzgibbon was to make a grand entrance down a staircase, in a beautiful flowered gown as the music played the intro to the elegant 'Jewel Song' from *Faust*. As she started to descend the stairs, the band burst forth into the Schnozzle Durante classic 'Umbriago' and they played it loud and fast with the musical director waving his baton with great gusto, totally engrossed in the music he was wrongly reading. Poor Maggie, we wondered what she would do. Calmly she stopped the music and spoke into the microphone: 'I do believe that you could be playing the wrong music—would you care to start again!' With all the poise in the world she won the audience, composed herself while the musicians shuffled their pages, and started again. Of course she killed 'em!

Adelaide at that time also had a theatre called The Tivoli, which was an independent. Harry Wren, the then very famous entrepreneur, booked an entire show and cast of Tivoli Circuit people to open in Adelaide, do a season there, then tour South Australia and Victoria. Once again it was chaos. We ran through sketches we'd done before. Terry Scanlan and I rehearsed *Night In The Garage, Two's Company*, and *The Dog Cemetery*. Meanwhile the scratch band was trying to sort out the manuscript music and the dancers and showgirls were standing around not knowing what was what. I started to lend a hand after Harry Wren asked me if I knew what music went with what production number! He said that all the music had been jumbled and mixed up in transit, and there wasn't anyone to explain the dance routines. On reflection, I felt sure he knew exactly what he was doing. Because of my enthusiasm and because I had been doing the routines previously I just fell into putting the whole show in place. It wasn't creative but I had absorbed procedure and knew what was needed and how to do it. From then on I was not only a soubrette and feed, but a choreographer. And I became creative. Mine was never an ambition to reach great heights; I never even thought I had that kind of talent. It was just a love that I couldn't get enough of. Perhaps my goal was to receive the same respect that I had for others. Maybe that's really *all* that most of us desire.

I managed to play Adelaide's other theatre before it too was usurped. The well worn Majestic Theatre was that city's regular vaudeville house. I did an eight-week season there, in pantomime, playing Little Red

49

LANDING FIRST N.Z. show Tivoli Circuit. Feb. 1947 FLYING BOAT AUCKLAND N.Z.

❧ *Members of the Tivoli Theatre, Australia, who arrived in Auckland, New Zealand, Wednesday, February 12th. On the first of two Sunderland Flying Boats. Right to Left: Miss Jennie Howard, Percy King, Robert Butt, Ralton James (Producer), Kath Crawford, Joy Dare, Elaine Dempsey, Victor Moore, Eddie Gordon, Nancy Gordon, Joan de Paul, Joy de Paul, Eunice de Paul, Louis Maxwell, Nancy de Paul, Biddy de Paul, Fay de Paul, Muriel Gardner, Marvin Kane, Dawn Butler, Elimar, Isobel McIntosh, Wally Hind, Mavis Wilkie, Val Jellay, William Benson, Doreen Greenfield, Donald Davies, Len James, Max Maxwell.*

Riding Hood as Principal Boy.

The war ended in 1945 but it took until early 1947 for things to settle down and for plans to take shape for some of the overseas acts to get back to their homeland. The Tivoli management were still responsible for their return and, as the journey to America was via New Zealand, a big show was mounted to play the R.J. Kerridge circuit of New Zealand.

Those who so chose could go on to America, instead of returning to Australia. By paying their own fare some Australian acts had already taken the huge risk of seeking fame and fortune in England. Rex and Bessie were in great demand, Les Ritchie quickly found a young English dancer, making Les Ritchie and Wendy a popular act, and the high energy act of Williams and Shand topped

❧ *Previous page: England 1952–1954.*

them all. The deadpan comic Al Reynolds ('you'll all be dead when that dress circle collapses') claimed that Bill Kerr initially achieved English recognition by doing Al's gloom and doom parson act. If he *did*—good luck to him I say. Bill did have the talent and fortitude to take it from there—besides, nothing's sacred. Why should singers have all the best writers? Rob Murray the juggler did the same with Rebla's act—music and all. The huge show being taken to New Zealand was to break new ground, virtually virgin territory. Gardner and Kane would go on home to America, as would Eddie Gordon and Nancy, joined by Clifford Guest. The Musical Macs and Babs McKinnon returned to Australia as did the Flying de Pauls and Elimar the juggler. The Maxwells were two young gymnasts from Adelaide who did clever, fast balancing and 'aero' tricks. Eddie Gordon spent that entire New Zealand tour moulding those two boys into an act that was world class. He had the experience from Europe and America and enjoyed imparting his knowledge. It took months of patience and hard work. First he changed their dress. Tailored suits were made with too-short sleeves, too-short trousers and too-short jackets, but perfectly matched with shirts and ties. Each wore a little pork pie hat of the same fabric as the suit. They looked well dressed but comical. He put them in white make-up. And they never smiled! Each trick was slowed to a

snail's pace, looking like a slow motion film. After each trick, made to look more difficult by the extremely slow pace, they would stand where they landed and stare deadpan at the audience. This always drew a big round of applause. The Maxwells were always grateful for the marvellous guidance from Eddie Gordon that made them successful in America and all around the world. Without that presentation gimmick they would have remained just another gymnast double, which proves it's not enough to be just an excellent singer, or dancer or whatever. It's all in the showmanship and the effort to work up an act with an angle that makes it especially entertaining. Like the song from *Gypsy* says—'Ya Gotta Have A Gimmick'.

The big show that was to go to New Zealand also featured Kath Crawford, Buster Noble, Victor Moore, Bobby Butt, Jenny Howard and Val Jellay, with experienced dancers, showgirls, spectacular productions, a big pit band and I remember Wally Hind was the drummer. We had accountants, managers and all sorts of back up, plus the indispensable producer-director Ginger James. We were all booked to travel by ship on the *Wanganella*. Also on board were to be all the scenery, musical instruments, wardrobe baskets, a massive amount of props, personal wardrobe trunks, tabs, cloths, large stacks of flats, rostrums and lighting. Both countries' managements were sent into panic when the *Wanganella* sank on its way from New Zealand to Australia while crossing the Tasman Sea!

Here was one huge problem. We had dates to meet as the extensive New Zealand tour had been planned down to the finest detail. Everyone was stunned. I must confess to a lack of sympathy for the crew and passengers of the *Wanganella* and the returning Americans were even less sympathetic. Commercial air travel was not yet underway—the jet age was very far off. So when two flying boats were chartered, as an emergency transportation alternative, it created huge media interest. Flying boats are just that; flying boats. They fly then land in the water like boats. The two massive whale-shaped monsters were able to solve our problem. I have never grown out of the embarrassing condition known as travel sickness. To this day even almost motionless revolving restaurants cause nausea, and before I've even read the menu! The flight across the Pacific Ocean was the bumpiest journey imaginable—these machines were not built for comfort. It took six hours and I was violently ill. As we approached Auckland's seaway I was so grateful that it would all soon be over. When the lumbering aircraft hit the water it was like crashing, and it was almost another hour before we were able to escape. It taxied back and forth in the water, rocking like a rocking chair

so I was seasick on top of being air-sick. In anticipation of disembarking we were standing, instead of remaining seated. Not wise. There was no escape. Claustrophobia set in like an epidemic. When we all tremulously stepped onto a long pier which was hard up to the plane and in line with its doors, we were met by a media barrage. They naturally took their time having us pose in long lines along the pier beside the hideous aircraft. The New Zealand press were polite and thrilled with their coverage. We on the other hand were doing our best to smile and thank everyone for making the arrival possible. No wonder performers are lumped under the one title—ACTORS !

The long tour of New Zealand was wonderful. The theatres were large and traditional. We played all the major cities, the semi-cities, and had a short pack for smaller towns. Adaptation was made easy by having three changes of programme. The New Zealand people were warm and hospitable and I don't think that situation has changed.

A six month season in Perth gave me a different kind of education. We played almost every city and town with a population of 600 or more. Survival was our key aim. Inland to Kalgoorlie and Coolgardie, south as far as Albany and Norseman and all points north. Western Australia is a big state and outback people travelled hundreds of miles to an event. The heat, dust and endless travelling

should have dampened my enthusiasm but I saw it as a challenge and selling the tickets out front (with make-up on) then rushing back for the show was sort of exciting.

Then it was across to Adelaide. A season at the Majestic Theatre, once again, then off again on another tour of South Australia. Off to the German grape growing towns of Tanunda, Canunda, Eununda, Port Pirie with its train down the main street, and every other town with a population of more than 600. I was more than familiar with the trauma of 'one-nighters'. Is today's connotation of that term a throw back to vaudeville? Just like 'I never knew you could have so much fun without laughing' (courtesy of Jenny Howard).

With an invitation to join Barton's Follies and its Sydney season, prior to a tour of New South Wales, it was again time for travel.

Barton's Follies had been run successfully for many moons by the Barton family, a touring company loved by the populace of New South Wales. Tibby Roberts, brother of Roy Barton, was the lead comic. Norm Berrigan, husband of Bonnie Barton was also a comedian supported by Jerry Keough, Buddy Morley and Jandy the musical clown from my Tivoli days. A girl named Clarice worked in the dance line and had a very unusual contortion act presented as Clarissa. She was in fact, a great contortionist. Charlie Sleet, the pianist-musical director, and Clarice were to go in different directions. Clarice became the specialty dancer in *Kismet* where she met and married its star, Hayes Gordon. Later she was in an Australian movie and married its imported star, James Mason. Known as Clarissa Kaye she became a lovely actress. Charlie Sleet transferred to Sorlies Revue.

Val in pantomime, Majestic Theatre, Adelaide 1950.

54

Slaughter at the Tatler and other Sydney nightclubs

Queenie Paul was putting a show into the Tatler Theatre in Sydney and once again I was responsible for feeding the various comics, with Morry Barling being semi-resident. Frank Strain was my main counterpart. Choreography was now always a part of my input. A new dancer by the name of Judd Laine was also encouraged to create and put together a show-stopper that did my heart good. It used the Rodgers and Hart sensational composition 'Slaughter on Tenth Avenue'. The movie *Words and Music* had featured it but in live theatre we hadn't the benefits of cuts in editing or stunt people or bloodied make-up. Judd's radical, sexy dance style was a joy to perform. When he shot me (with blanks) as I stood at the top of a centre staircase, the crescendo as written for the moment inspired a fall down that staircase that called on all my childhood acrobatic experience. I crashed and rolled and bumped down the stairs, with total disregard for my safety. Then Judd would dance with my supposedly dead body to the most beautiful, melancholy part of the music. Forgive my indulgence. Both Judd Lane and Val Jellay had to take curtain calls when we stopped the show nightly.

Nightclubs had been thriving in Sydney through the war years. Golds late-late club was the musicians' favourite. Sammy Lees featured Bobby Limb's band and The Roosevelt was hugely successful for many years with the gorgeous Rosie Sturgess as one of their dancers. Sheila Cruize was putting on shows at Chequers where Jan Adele was one of the lovelies. Lorrae Desmond was killing them everywhere with her nightclub act. She was a lovely singer, with an even more beautiful figure. Englishman Joe Taylor was the city's favourite nightclub comic and Keith Peterson, an Aussie, was also killin''em. A young blonde doing Danny Kaye songs in the style of Betty Hutton was setting Sydney's nightclub scene alight. Her name was Dawn Lake. With so many successful clubs in Sydney it was survival of the slickest.

The Celebrity Club was a classy nightclub, importing American stars. I was asked to produce and choreograph the Celebrity Club Shows, answerable to Queenie Paul, and enjoyed the sophisticated challenge. My old friend Rosie Sturgess was always there for me, referring to herself unflatteringly as 'your old Auntie'. Kings Cross then was a far cry from its image of the 1990s. In the 1940s it was full of fun and wonderful characters. Bohemian was its worst label. Rosie and her darling husband Peter McMahon (brother of John) would often play host in their Kings Cross bedsitter. She taught me how to cook a roast dinner on a one jet stove (which was under a staircase) and a communal one at that.

Back in Melbourne a little elderly gentleman was about to expand his horse breeding interests and invest in showbusiness. Mr. L.O. Menck enlisted Val Jellay as choreographer-soubrette, and

Prince Charming in Cinderella, Perth early 1940s.

The Herald, Sat., Dec. 22, 1951—Page 11

PLAZA-NORTHCOTE
Testro Bros. Pty. Ltd. by arrangement with Plaza
Management, present Hal Lennon's

DAILY AT 2.15 P.M. NEXT WEDNESDAY DEC. 26th NIGHTLY AT 8 P.M.

CINDERELLA
PANTOMIME

Mother! The Children can see it for 1/-
Prices 5/, 4/, 3/ Plus Tax (excl. Sat. & hols.)
BOX PLAN AT GLEN'S, THEATRE, MITTY'S

22 Glittering Scenes — Cast of 60
See the Fairy Dell, the Transformation
Scene, Cinderella's coach and
ponies, the Baron's Castle, Alice
Uren's Ballet of 40

together we launched the Plaza Theatre in Northcote. Over the years that theatre was like an iron lung for vaudeville performers. The first pit band there was the Horrie Dargie quintet—augmented. A very funny young comic, Joff Ellen, and his partner were early successes (later, when television arrived he was in the right place at the right time). Al Mack and the fine straight man Len Rich had a new lease of life and Jenny Howard also found new audiences. Already displayed in her performances as a seasoned artist, the talent of the teenager Toni Lamond was to reach full bloom. We shared a fun dressing room. Frank Wilson's youth and versatility were put to good use, as were Frank Rich and far too many others to mention. There were

hectic program changes every two weeks. In partnership with Rex Testro, an old friend from Perth, we financed and presented a Christmas pantomime, *Cinderella,* and the Plaza Theatre twice daily had turn-away business. Its outstanding success financed my departure to England, sailing first class on the liner *Orcades.* Running true to form, sea sickness prevented me from appreciating the distinction. It was four weeks of misery. The Plaza Theatre remained successful in others' capable hands with many fine performers appearing there. One such act was Skit and Skat, who were to come into my life in different circumstances. Meanwhile the dreary port of Southampton England was looming as the 'Land of Oz'.

❧ *Tivoli 1945. Can you put names to faces?*

Appearance

Never wear flat shoes unless absolutely necessary — they don't flatter the legs.

Always, at any age, take time to apply a little lipstick.

If you have good hair, avoid wearing hats.

An actor doesn't 'go to work', he 'goes to the theatre', or 'to the studio'.

Never lower your voice at the end of a line, give each word equal value.

Greetings from

"SKIT
and
SKAT"

RYTHM
HARMONY
COMEDY
SOFT SHOE

Late of
"CHECQUERS"
PALLADIUM
A.B.C.
CELEBRITY
CLUB
Sydney, Etc.

—o—

AGENTS—

Home Phone

DUBLIN

England, Ireland, Europe, Syrup, Jollop

London, February 1952. I was 24 years old. My first reaction to London was excitement at seeing the board-game of Monopoly come to life. But the happy names like the Strand, Trafalgar Square, Marylebone Station and Piccadilly Circus from the game were, in reality, part of an overpopulated mass of streets inhabited by strangers who were living a sunless existence, accepting the fog and freezing conditions as their lot. The war had been over for seven years but food and fuel rationing was still strict. Evidence of the frightful blitz that the country had endured was everywhere, particularly in London's east end, but the sturdy English were getting on with their lives and theatres were thriving. I was getting the same question from the dozens of agents whose doors I forced open. 'What is your act?' Resumes and write-ups meant nothing. Being experienced in vaudeville, revue and pantomime was brushed aside—'but what is your act?' they persisted. The successful Australian acts in England were totally visual. This made them employable everywhere as the many English dialects and accents did not have to be integrated. Who among my friends from Australia's Tivoli days were in demand in the top theatres? The Ashtons; Warren, Latona and Sparks; The Bridges Sisters; Rex and Bessie; the Horrie Dargie Quintet; and Williams and Shand, of course. Not one comedian. Radio had embraced Kitty Bluett, Joy Nichols, Bill Kerr and Dick Bentley, and the velvet voice of Charles (Bud) Tingwell was heard in English films. Australia's great George Wallace Snr. tried his luck in England. Admittedly he went there too late, and with his guttural delivery becoming even more so as the English weather took its toll, he was rejected. This broke his heart. Buster Fiddes also had problems. Dear Buzzie. Diction never was his strong suit and his verbal pace was always rapid fire. He laughed when he told me he couldn't shake hands with anyone because the cuffs of his overcoat were so frayed. Removing the threadbare coat wasn't a consideration because he was always freezing. Years later, back home, everyone in the business was glad when Buster found a new lease of life in television, the visual medium. He was a unique comic.

Combining tapping, harmony vocals and 'aero' with a wardrobe change that transformed me from a glamorous showgirl into a pesky child, I put together a very strong 12-minute act. Most of the dialogue was done by the kid character. Using a Cockney accent and prefacing each line with 'eeah!' spoken slowly and deliberately it worked well. Thanks to Iris Shand's information, my glamour wardrobe was made by the best and band arrangements were perfect. No awkward props and space was never a problem. Playing the wonderful Moss and Stoll theatres for the feared Cissy Williams was a personal high! Next to the West End, that circuit was the ultimate. Often topping the bill I was on, were Max Miller (who couldn't be coaxed to Australia), Joyce Grenfell, Donald Peers or

⤚ Green buses in Dublin.

Ronnie Ronalde. All the names escape me but, oh, those theatres! For over two years I soaked up their ambience and acoustics.

Some of the very old theatres were the most traditional, like the Metropolitan in Edgware Road in London which I played several times. An act had to remain the same and if you were booked to do 12 minutes you could not do 12½ minutes or 11½ minutes. Precision and polish was acquired by performing the same act in the hundreds of theatres throughout the country (television soon put an end to that). Meeting new acts in different theatres each week was always businesslike, never personal. I was quite unused to this style of operation but as they say, 'when in Rome ...'

Performers arranged and paid for their own transport—distances are so short in that tiny country and the rail system was very reliable. Accommodation was recommended by each stage manager who received my letters regarding our intended arrival on a Sunday. The list of preferred 'digs' would grow in personal diaries—often they were private homes whose owners made a living renting out a spare room. They usually needed the money—badly. The rooms were spotlessly clean, with meagre furnishings polished with pride. Meals were provided and it was unwise to say that something was 'very nice'. I made the mistake of complimenting one landlady on her junket and was, thereafter,

served junket with every meal. On arrival at Birmingham for a pantomime season, bacon was served. It was so delicious! It was served in every way possible at every meal. I wondered how they could afford such luxury. It turned out the husband worked at an abattoir for pigs! And as for another host's speciality ... I'll just say I never want to see another can of macaroni cheese as long as I live!

At Christmas time, the high standard of English pantomime afforded it to be shown nightly as well as daily. Otherwise, it was variety twice nightly, usually at 6.00 pm. and 8.30 pm.

So much travel, so many theatres. Probably because one's first impressions are more significant, my fondest memories are of playing the inner London theatres—the Chiswick Empire, very large and often used in film locations; the Empress, Brixton, a No. 1 date then; the Empire, Shepherd's Bush, a joy to work and later converted to a television studio; the Finsbury Park Empire Theatre, with its scary musical director; and the unique Metropolitan in Edgware Road. I had rushed to these theatres to see the English performers, eagerly gauging the audiences, the presentations, formats, standards, staging, lighting and all those things that had always interested me. English musicians are, or were, the best sight readers. They had to be. Often the older (that's extremely

❧ *They call her 'The Shape From Downunder'. Egypt.*

THE ASTON HIPPODROME

AN F.J.B. THEATRE
Manager:
F. J. STUDD

BIRMINGHAM
ASTON CROSS 2341
BOX OFFICE OPEN
DAILY 10 a.m.—7 p.m:

COMMENCING BOXING DAY, DECEMBER 26th — FOR A SEASON

MON. to FRI. at 2-30 & 7-15 SATS. 2, 5 & 8

(NO FRIDAY MATINEES AFTER JAN. 15th)

SPECIAL CONCESSIONS FOR PARTIES (Consult Manager)   REDUCED PRICES FOR CHILDREN (AT MATINEES) —

RALPH BARBER & F. J. BUTTERWORTH (Productions) Ltd.
in association with TOM MOSS **present this year's** ———— SPECTACULAR COMEDY PANTOMIME

DICK WHITTINGTON

THE FUNNIEST, GAYEST AND MOST ENTERTAINING PANTOMIME TO BE SEEN IN THE MIDLANDS.

FEATURING
EVERYBODY'S
FRIEND

TOM MOSS

as
IDLE JACK

AUSTRALIA'S DASHING
"PRINCIPAL BOY"

VAL JELLAY

as
DICK WHITTINGTON

PANTOMIME'S
JOVIAL DAME

Hal Lennon

as
SARAH, THE COOK

ERIC V. MARSH ALDERMAN FITZWARREN   **RINGLE BROTHERS** CAPTAIN and MATE

GAIL HARVEY ALICE FITZWARREN   **GUY HOLLOWAY** KING RAT

AL BRANDON THE EMPEROR   **VALERIE** THE FAIRY

JACK COOPER'S BIRMINGHAM Babes **Peggy O'Farrell** "TOMMY" THE CAT   JACK COOPER'S Corps de Ballet

ALL THE
TRADITIONAL
CHARACTERS
AND SCENES.

REAL UNDERWATER BALLET
with DIVERS, SWIMMERS AND COMEDY ACROBATS IN THOUSANDS OF GALLONS OF WATER ON THE STAGE

PRESENTS FOR
THE KIDDIES
AND LAUGHS
FOR EVERYBODY.

CSE tour.

old), smaller theatres were more impressive than the larger, ornate kind. One particular charmer was at Leeds. Called The City of Varieties, it was later made internationally famous through a music hall style TV show *The Good Old Days*. I just loved that theatre. The more ornate Empire Theatre, Leeds, was then starring Laurel and Hardy.

The journey to Ireland across the Irish Sea meant travel sickness for me at its worst. The Theatre Royal in Dublin ironically opened its weekly seasons on Sundays, so acts travelling from England were unable to attend Sunday morning's band call. With my band parts in order, I was assured that the Irish musical director was very familiar with this situation and that he only needed a verbal run through in the dressing room prior to curtain. A hair-raising situation indeed. When the percussionist hit his 'timps' and the overture began it sounded like the Philharmonic Orchestra. My stomach did a Big Dipper plunge. The musicians must have done a triple read of my standard 12-piece band parts and it sounded magnificent with each section, including a beautiful string section, playing the never-seen-before charts—perfectly. The next tummy dip was

when I saw the auditorium. The theatre had a capacity of 4000. That's right, 4000! My first appearance before such a huge audience was overwhelming. The great act Wilson, Keppel and Betty was on the same bill and at one performance I ventured out front of house to the very back row, wondering about the view from there. Wilson, Keppel and Betty looked like three little dots on another planet. I guessed those audiences must have been used to it. No wonder the orchestra had a large personnel with such a big sound. Max Bygraves tells the story about the confident stand-up comedian who presented the Dublin musical director with one sheet of music for 'Happy Days are Here Again'. The musical director said, 'But I have 32 musicians, they'll all need a copy'. Without batting an eye the comic said, 'Let them all crowd around'.

It was a pleasure travelling north to Ireland's famous theatre in Belfast—the Grand Opera House. Syd and Max Harrison topped the bill and business was capacity. How fortunate I was—a tap dancing kid from Fitzroy—to have played so many lovely theatres. The stories they could tell! At the Hippodrome Theatre, Bristol, I

Dick Whittington poster, 1953.

66

breathed the same air as Frank Sinatra. The show preceding me at the Hippodrome, Birmingham, had starred Judy Garland and a new sound system had been installed for her. Flowers were still all over the place.

Newcastle's Empire Theatre was exciting, as was the Theatre Royal Portsmouth. Bournemouth's Royal Theatre was a change from the industrial cities, as was Brighton. And so it went on. This jumping all over the country was not unusual; it was what all established acts did.

I was living in a bedsitter near Hyde Park when a devastating smog descended on London. It was then recorded as the worst in history. The death toll rose every day with the elderly, those with respiratory complaints, and little babies fighting a losing battle. People being confined in London's fogs had traditionally accepted physical guidance from blind people who knew their way around in the dark. Conductors on buses were accustomed to walking slowly in front of their bus, guiding the driver by shining a torch along the gutter. The problems with visibility were not my main concern, however, as the foul air was making me truly ill. The timing was just perfect when I was invited to join a BBC cast who were to tour North Africa, Tripoli, Benghazi, Cairo, Fayid, then fly to Europe and play Italy, Austria, Germany, Vienna, etc. We flew to Malta where the tour began in the capital, Valletta. Most

of us spent the first week getting our lungs back in order. In this Riviera-type setting the thick black lining on our lungs was soon purged while, back in London, the fog was continuing to take its toll. I swear that had I spent another week there I would have joined the list of departed.

Under the heading of 'CSE presents' (which stood for Combined Services Entertainment), 'Radio Bandbox' was a talented company of BBC performers. They were totally professional and eager to allow me to guide them through an appropriate opening and finale which I had been asked to direct. It was a once-in-a-lifetime experience travelling through the much yearned for warmth of North Africa, then on to Austria's snowy alps and its story book cities.

Impressions of Europe gleaned from American movies had made their mark on me and, due to Australia's geographical isolation, the sights of Europe were particularly exciting. This was the early 1950s and the jet age had not yet made the world accessible. In Vienna the hotel lifts were of the gold cage variety and very noisy, just like in the movies. The Danube wasn't blue but the Vienna woods were there, and I danced myself a waltz. I rode on the vertical carousel that had housed Orson Welles and posed beside the tall round concrete structures that led to the sewers, both of which were part of the intrigue in *The Third Man*. Fluffy doonas,

so light, were standard warmth for bedding (why did they take so long to reach us in Australia?). Hotel bathrooms all had bidets alongside the toilets, perhaps *never* to reach us—pardon the innuendo. The Viennese cake shops were straight from Fantasyland. Visiting the birthplaces and homes of history's famous composers was a must.

Italy was also high on my list of impressions to be made real. Beautiful hotels once again. Trieste's huge square, which transformed into a bustling market, was totally Italian as was the red wine automatically served with all meals (as water is served in America). It was usually a light rosé called 'Vol-poli-cello'. It was mild enough for the whole family—that is if you were Italian. The winter clothing was beautiful but

expensive. They told us the fine wool was imported—from Australia.

Germany recovered quickly from the war and, apart from the many bombed areas which were still in ruins, everything was spotlessly clean and very organised. Of course the locals knew 'nothing' about the concentration camps and, with the Nuremberg war trials soon to begin, the war was a no-no subject. I played beautiful theatres in cities like Düsseldorf, Oldenburg and Celle, in contrast to theatres in Egypt which were makeshift and built by prisoners. In Egypt travel was by bus with armed guards. In Europe it was in huge air force bombers. The flight crews thought we were a novelty. On land we were always being questioned by uniformed guards at boom gates. There was always a feeling of apprehension at these times. In the zoned occupancy of Germany, the Russians gave our company a really hard time and the heavy snow did nothing for our spirits. The audiences consisted of our various forces' personnel who were stationed at crucial flash points. Officers were predominant and, whenever our show was presented, we were treated royally.

Concertina bands in downstairs cafes really did exist, as did sauerkraut and sausage served with large mugs of over-frothed beer. I noticed married couples didn't walk arm in arm. The men always walked slightly in

front of the women and I never saw men open doors for ladies or help them off a tram. That's pretty common everywhere these days unfortunately. The German people were uniform-happy, with the most menial wearing uniforms. The garbos looked very formal and the paper boys on street corners were easily confused with high ranking military officers, wearing boots, caps, cape, shiny buttons and belts. I had a photo taken with one of these young men but, of course, he didn't understand a word I said. In every country I managed to learn the bare necessities of the language to get by. 'Where is the toilet?', 'How much is it?' and 'Please write it down'. Shopping was always a nuisance (besides, I couldn't afford it anyway) but I did want to buy a black suspender belt (it was before the days of the pantyhose). In German I practised hard and learned 'Swartza kleiner hooft girdle bitte'. I was so proud of myself, right up until I walked nervously into the lingerie shop and the assistant said: 'May I help you?'—in English!

On return to England I had a marathon hard working weekly-change residency at Barrow-in-Furness and then 'The Aussie Show' did a busy provincial tour. It featured many Australians including Slim-de-Grey (who wrote a song for me called 'Up From Down Under'), Rex 'Waca' Dawe, The Shipway Twins, Les Ritchie, Buster Fiddes, and many more. The dancers were, naturally, a line of

Previous page: With undernourished English dancers, 1953. *In England singing 'Up from Down Under' in The Aussie Show.*

Cast of the CSE tour.

🔸 *Hanover-Germany March 1953.*

English girls. Buster and a pretty brunette were a couple for the tour and married and had a large family on their return to Australia.

After a Nottingham season, I was invited to entertain American army personnel who were stationed at various camps scattered throughout the Midlands. Transport was provided.

Rex Testro was in England with his wife Joan and their three tiny daughters, all under school age. The eldest was Lexie (Alexandra), then came Stacey (Anastasia) and the new-born Mandy (Amanda). Because Mandy was born in England, Rex called her his English rose. Stacey Testro is now an established theatrical agent.

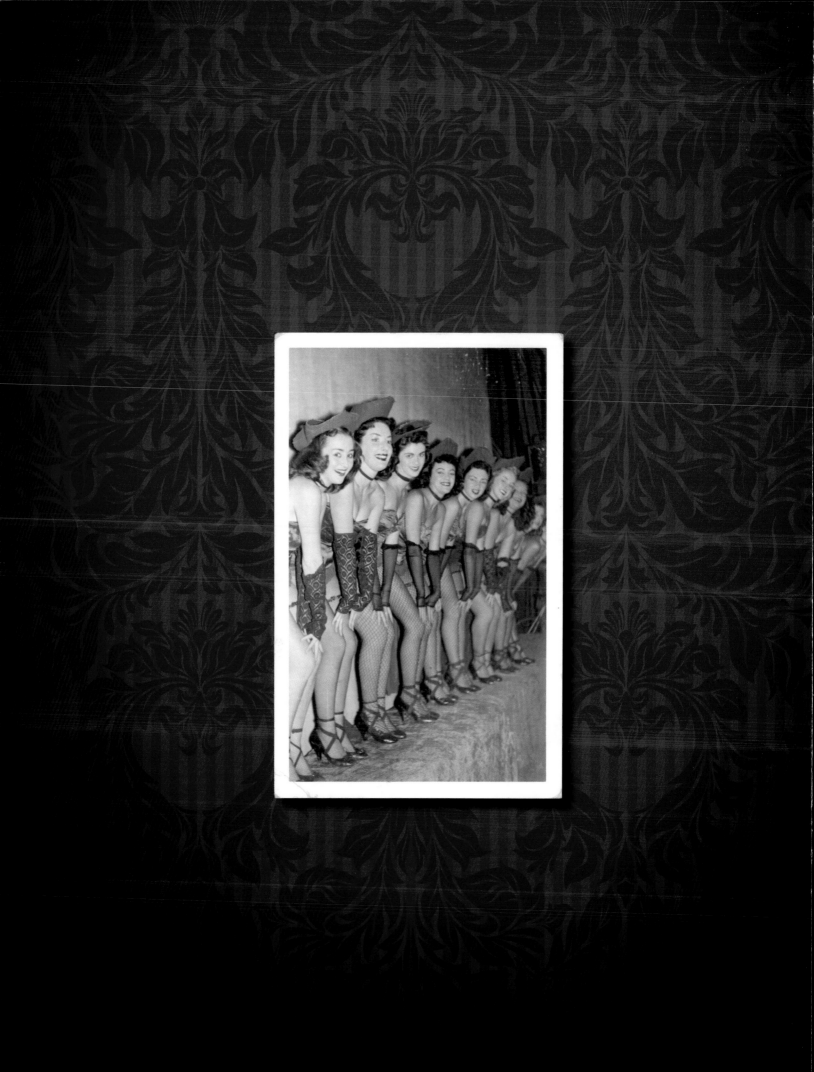

Sorlies and the show train

My old friend Bobby Le Brun, from *Forbidden City*, was now owner-partner of Sorlies Revue, together with George Sorlies' widow, Grace. Bobby had already communicated to me an open invitation to join his company at any time. Now was the time—I jumped at the invitation. My parents were at Port Melbourne to greet me when the ship berthed.

With but a week at home in Melbourne with my parents, it was time to do a performance at the Chevron Hotel. Ginger James, whose Tivoli credits gave him his correct name, Ralton R. James (the R was for Roscoe), was producing a farewell floorshow tribute to Winifred Atwell. My quick change was done behind the Maitre D's podium, which amused Ginger, prompting his dimples to surface. It was good to be home.

Sorlies rehearsed for two weeks in an upstairs hall in Goulburn Street near the Tivoli end of Castlereagh Street, Sydney, prior to opening in Newcastle for a December-January season. After that it was 'on the road'. Newcastle was where all the hard work and planning took place for the coming year while we did a pantomime each afternoon and a revue at night. The mornings were filled with frantic rehearsals, preparing three complete programme changes. In Newcastle the shows changed weekly. On tour it was changed every second night and most dates were for a week. And, of course, it was pantomime every Saturday—except for school holidays when it was matinee every day. Short packs (programmes with fewer props and less production) were planned for split weeks.

Bobby Le Brun was a great businessman as well as a strong comedian. His filing system could tell him exactly when he had done each sketch or gag routine, and in which town. With Sorlies having been a success for so many years, such detail was essential. Gracie Le Brun was a whiz with wardrobe and she was always able to dress my production ideas. Part of Bobby's system was to plan the comedy first, then I would ask him who I could use in the production numbers, according to his running order. Charlie Sleet was pianist, musical director and arranger.

Being versatile was essential. A specialist, like a singer only, was unemployable. Each year the star acts, of which there were usually four, were booked direct from the Tivoli Circuit. Bobby would approach these overseas acts with the explanation that a tour with Sorlies was the only way to see the real Australia. Of course they would jump at it. Those who didn't want to travel on the show train would buy a second hand car. One charming Frenchman by the name of Phillippe Andre had a lovely puppet act. He bought a sturdy old sedan in which to travel and also to sleep in. He kept food in the boot and with the lid of the boot up, that's where he ate. He was content, until mice

❧ *The Sorlies years, 1956.*

got in the upholstery and began eating his food. One day he decided on a solution which brought us all to attention. He went to a local pet shop and bought a snake—a logical solution he thought. The victim of an enterprising Aussie salesman, we thought!

Accommodation for the annual Newcastle season was, by tradition, supplied by the owners of the Beach Hotel, Greenhalgh and Jackson. They had been the 'Barnum' of Australia's 'freak' shows, importing big attractions from around the world. These acts were stars; they relied on being exhibited and were treated accordingly. Jo-Jo the Dog Faced Boy, the Bearded Lady, the Three-Legged Man, the Tiniest Couple in the World, Little Titch and many others were Greenhalgh and Jackson imports.

Their framed photographs were all around the hotel bar causing many a discussion. When the hotel was being painted, Duffy the Giant painted the ceilings without using a ladder. A team of midgets followed behind him, painting the skirtings. The law then was six o'clock closing for bar trade. When it was close to closing time Duffy the Giant, with his big, long arms, would lean across the bar when the publican wasn't looking and, with one finger, turn the big hand of the clock back ten minutes. With our odd hours, an understanding publican made life a lot easier. Drinks could be had at midnight, with everyone on the honour system. Sunday lunch was an event, the only real time we got to eat properly, and it was always a fabulous roast dinner. We had a choice of wholesome soups and roast lamb, pork, beef, or chicken, with vegetables galore. There were a variety of sweets like golden syrup pudding, wine trifle and bread and butter pudding, all served with thick, whipped cream. The dining room would be packed with actors having fun and being fortified for the coming week.

If the Tivoli acts that joined Sorlies Revues could do more than just their act it was a big plus. Gordon and Colville, a comedy double from England, were typical of this. They had several strong sketches that had been polished to perfection in England. Vic Gordon's wife, Josie, worked in the ballet line and Peter Colville's wife, Vikki Hammond (they were later divorced), worked in the production numbers—singing, dancing and generally looking gorgeous. The two girls gave strength to the other comics' sketches as well as Vic's and Peter's. They stayed with Sorlies for two years and Vic Gordon, to this day, says it was the most wonderful two years of his life. Later his wife Josie passed away, a victim of cancer, and he met and married Jeannie while they were both working for Crawfords. Vikki Hammond played Principal Girl to my Boy in many pantomimes, including *Puss In Boots,* many years later at the Princess Theatre. We have been friends for forty-five years. She and her handsome

Princess Theatre, Melbourne, with the ever beautiful Vikki Hammond – another performance, another Principal Boy.

Sorlie's Theatrical Enterprises.

Aussie husband Bill now have three gorgeous sons, and being a wife and mother gives her all the happiness she ever wanted.

It was during a NSW tour, when we were playing Wollongong, that Bobby Le Brun told me of an act he was going to put in the show for one night as an audition. The act were up from Sydney playing one night at the Wollongong RSL Club. They played musical instruments so they wouldn't need a band rehearsal, only a chaser on and off. Bobby asked me to watch them to see what I thought. It was a double act—two fellas. One was shortish and stocky, the other tall and slim. They wore large checked blue and white zoot suits, red shoes, red panama hats, and one played the trumpet, the other the banjo. They called themselves Skit and Skat. When Bobby asked me what I thought of the act, I remember saying; 'Their music is great, the blend of the vocals excellent, but their gags are lousy':

1st man: What's a four letter word found in the bottom of a birdcage?
2nd man: Grit
And
1st man: ... and he crossed the street in busy traffic
2nd man: Did he get across?
1st man: Yes, a big white marble one.

and so on.

Under the black-face it was not possible to see what they looked like but I told Bobby I thought they could be useful in the show.

After the show that night I met them. The short, stocky one was a smiling curly-headed blonde named Kenny Bowtell. The tall, slim one had blue eyes, dark hair and was very shy. His name was Maurie Fields.

Skit and Skat slipped into Sorlies system like a hand into a glove. Apart from their act, they were doing things they had never done before. They were funny in the sketches and added vocal class to the big production

79

numbers. Getting them to rehearse was often a problem. Kenny because he found it difficult and Maurie because he found it too easy. If Ken was having trouble mastering a move at rehearsal he would just toss it in and walk off. Maurie was used to Ken's mood swings and would co-operate in every way, as if over-compensating. He never requested keys to be changed—he'd find alternative notes. He danced with ease in the Hope-Crosby style. Ken would wear funny hats and black out his teeth to be funny but Maurie could do it with a look or an intonation, instinctively.

Both of them enjoyed playing and singing, especially at the regular wind-down parties after the show. Ken had worked hard to achieve his standard of trumpet playing. He was self-taught and sometimes got angry with himself for not having that little extra that would make performing easier. He found solace in alcohol. Maurie's older sister had taught him basic piano and ukulele chords, and his great 'ear' did the rest. For their black-face double act Ken, ever the go-getter, 'acquired' a banjo for his partner and continued to 'come across' a variety of that instrument, with Maurie just accepting whatever came his way. Ken dearly wanted to be talented; Maurie didn't know how talented he was.

When the pantomime *Mother Goose* was cast, Ken played the part of the goose. The goose-housing prop, with its wire frame, was uncomfortable for the wearer but somebody had to do it (Iris and Ron Shand's father, Ernie, always played the goose for the Tivoli Circuit and elsewhere). It was the most important part of that pantomime, yet, because there was no dialogue, Ken treated this responsibility with great disdain. He had to wear yellow stockings and special web-footed shoes. Being bandy added to the character, which had to be done in a bent over position—very uncomfortable. In one scene the 'Dame' coaxed the goose to lay the golden egg and the audience got involved in the encouraging. The fun was when the goose first laid a cabbage, then a bunch of carrots, then a house brick and, finally, the marvellous egg. If Kenny didn't feel like going through all that, he'd waddle on, drop the lot in one bundle and waddle off. It looked like he was totally disembowelled.

So Kenny was always coming up with gimmicks for the Skit and Skat act. He had iron stilts made that would make him taller as he blew his trumpet higher and higher. When he tried this one night he grew taller and taller but hadn't figured how to get down. It took four blokes to tip him on his side and drag him off in a blackout. The heavy iron stilts were carried around for months while a solution was being worked out until, one day in a black rage, Kenny hurled them into the dusty distance, never to be mentioned again.

Another brainstorm was to have smoke come from his trumpet as he played hot jazz. He had tried this before in Max Reddy's Follies at the Theatre Royal at Hobart in Tasmania. Ken had a balloon filled with talcum powder and placed it inside his shirt. Meantime, Maurie had a piece of wire around his ring finger with a sharp spike on top. He was to throw open his arms on cue, burst the balloon on Ken's chest and the white smoke would come up. Instead, it went straight down inside his trousers all in one fell swoop, leaving him with a stunned look on his face. His 'sausage and two veg' received quite a jolt too. With determination he tried it again. This time he filled an enema bulb with talcum powder. Em Reilly was the pit pianist—she was prim and proper, devoid of humour and always with a tight finger-wave hairdo. Ken, this time, had the powder-filled enema bulb under his armpit with the tube attached to his trumpet under the valves. He was to create the steady flow of white 'smoke' as he played faster, by pumping the rubber valve with his arm. It worked all right; except, instead of coming from the rubber tube, gradually it plopped out in large lumps—all over Em Reilly's head. When they looked down Em Reilly was glaring back with her head covered in white powder, looking exactly like a scone.

Poor Ken, he could never get anything quite right. Much later he returned to Sydney and had a lot of success around the clubs with another partner, calling the act Big Red and Bojangles. A mixture of alcohol and drugs was his final downfall and we heard that he had died while making love. If it was true, it's exactly how he would have wanted to go.

With all the touring companies following the agricultural show-days in each town, it meant a feast of entertainment. Apart from Sorlies Revue Co. there were Barton's Follies, Coles Varieties, Les Levante's Magic Show and, later, Max Reddy's Follies. The circus was always popular. Wirth's always did well, as did Sole Bros, Bullens, and Perry Bros. Over the decades there were many.

The show train provided transport for all who were without their own means. The showground folk, showies, and tent 'warbs' were a passing parade. Showground families like the Pinks and the Greens had been in the game for generations, similar to circus folk. Des Whittingslow's family still present the fairground's finest. Jim Sharman's boxing troupe was always part of a countryman's big day out and Jim junior conquered the changing tastes of time. The show train could be treated as fun or else extreme discomfort. On a scale of priority in the running of the railways, it rated nil. Sleep was virtually impossible due to the shunting back and forth during the night as we were diverted to sidings. The limited water on board would

dry up within an hour, depriving the end carriages of water for our basins and toilet flushing. Discovering a water tap near the lines always caused excitement.

It wasn't easy but, eventually, I was able to put a deposit on a second-hand FJ Holden.

It was a start and boy, was I proud. Bobby Le Brun paid petrol money to those with cars, plus extra per passenger; it was a system that helped everyone. Some of the cars were more than suspect and not up to the gruelling hours of motoring on corrugated roads. The overseas acts that had come from the Tivoli circuit to see the 'real Australia' got a lot more than they bargained for, getting themselves involved in all sorts of dramas.

Guus Brox and Myrna were from the Netherlands. They were a wonderful act and a big asset to Sorlies Revue. Myrna

was six feet tall and elegant. Guus was a tiny little fella, very funny and a multi-instrumentalist. They did unusual comedy, such as him climbing up her arm to retrieve a harmonica she held up high out of his reach. His English wasn't the best and he had trouble making himself understood. His instruments were invaluable, with an antique European accordion his prized possession. When he bought a second-hand Terraplane car in which to travel, we wondered about his choice. Guus was a sweet little man who loved his wife and little daughter and it would have been cruel to dampen his enthusiasm. One journey between Moree and Goondiwindi was in doubt because of heavy rain the previous week. There was quite a convoy of cars and caravans by now—all banked up and stranded. The ever-

🎵 *Skit and Skat – Kenny Bowtell and Maurie Fields, 1957. The tall one was so shy.*

resourceful Bobby Le Brun hired a tractor to go on ahead and steer us through and to tow those in bother. It was hazardous and the churned up road had covered us all with mud but we knew from experience to stick to the crown of the road. The sides of the crown may have looked solid but they were indeed a quagmire. When the tractor driver had done his guiding duty he turned back to Moree, passing Guus and his family who were straggling along at the rear. He didn't understand the Aussie tractor driver's instructions and, being so short, the large steering wheel of his big old Terraplane restricted his vision. What he could see on the track ahead was frightening to the little Dutchman; he wasn't going to attempt to drive through bumpy, muddy terrain. The sides of the road seemed beautiful, all smooth and solid looking. So that's where he steered the car and the trusty Terraplane sank, right up to the axle. Guus just sat there crying. His wife Myrna had heard about chocking the wheels to get traction so,

wading through the mud back and forth, she placed leaves all around the area of the submerged wheels, one leaf at a time. No one had told her she would need half a gum tree. The Brox family had been the last to leave Moree and we didn't hear of their plight until later. The three of them were in tears when a furniture truck finally came along, travelling in the same direction. Guus waved down the driver and, mustering his best attempts at the English language, begged for assistance. As it happened, the driver of the furniture truck was also a Dutchman and excitement mounted as they embraced and jabbered away in Dutch. All the gloom and doom had disappeared. What a heaven-sent rescue! His new friend would tow them out of the treacherous trap with a big chain he kept specifically for that purpose. He wound the chain around the front bumper bar, put his own truck in gear, gave the engine a couple of revs and, with a burst of speed, took off in his truck ... along with the entire front of the Terraplane. Inside the car the Brox family

Some of Sorlies Ballet girls, Josie (Mrs Vic Gordon) at centre back.

remained dumbfounded.

On another occasion our harsh climate was to bring about another travelling problem for Guus. Extremely high temperatures had caused his motor to overheat and, not being mechanically minded, Guus ignored the signals and the motor caught fire. With flames coming from the bonnet the car filled with smoke and Guus panicked. He jumped out of the burning monster, ran around ranting and proceeded with a rescue in order of priority. First he went to the boot and got his costumes out, then from the back his accordion, then his daughter and then lastly—his wife.

Sunday travelling was also our time for barbecues along the roadside and drinks at friendly country pubs, with unplanned parties developing at any time of the day or night. It was on a cold Sunday that a group of us gathered at a very cosy pub to relax. Guus just loved the Aussie beer; he couldn't get enough of it and was a very happy drunk. This day he was well away and long past his capacity, singing and dancing around. When he fell into the flaming fireplace he was still singing, not at all concerned that he was on fire. We had to roll him around on the carpet to put him out.

Heavy beer drinkers tend to have temperamental bladders that demand relief at inconvenient times. The biggest problem with caravanning was finding somewhere

to plug in for power, especially at showtime when the caravan parks were booked out. All sorts of people got approached in the hope of getting permission to park in their backyard. A newsagent obliged the Brox family and allowed their caravan to park and plug in at the rear of the shop. The newsagent had been handling our box plan and advance bookings and was a friend of the boss, Bobby Le Brun. The following day's editions of the daily newspapers had been delivered in the early hours of the morning and were all outside the shop's back door, together with all the weekly magazines. It was still dark when Guus, inside his caravan, had an urgent need to 'undrink' and relieve his bladder. He had no idea where he was and just threw open the caravan door and aimed it straight out. Instinct told him he shouldn't leave a puddle outside the door, so he sprayed it from side to side, like a fan, back and forth—all over the newsagent's new magazines and papers. There was big trouble over that one. No one person could 'pass' enough to ruin all those stacks of paper—but Guus did. He was so upset and apologetic that Bobby couldn't be cross with him for long, but another agent was found for the booking plan.

Partying on led to many a sobering outcome. Many great jugglers had enjoyed the conviviality of touring and my Sorlies years had seen many. Rex Allison, head of the famous Allison family, was then a very young man who joined the Wirth's circus pack-up party one Saturday night. It went for hours, with Rex falling asleep in the centre ring. Next morning he woke up in an empty paddock with the sun beating down on him. They had expertly packed, cleaned up, moved on, and he hadn't heard a thing.

When Ken joined Max Reddy's Follies as a single act he was given other responsibilities. He was put in charge of the big attraction: The Great Water Tank on stage featuring, underwater, the gorgeous Margo Clancy (The Girl In The Goldfish Bowl). It was a huge prop and the monitoring of the water pressure was crucial. Even more crucial was the levelling and bracing of the various stage sections as the weight of the filled tank was tremendous. It was in Bathurst that Ken got careless and didn't level or brace the front section of the stage. When the tank filled with water, the front of it slowly sank down into the stage, tipping its tons of water straight into the orchestra pit. It was a deluge. Margo Clancy could not continue and was left floundering around the stage like a goldfish out of water. Fortunately no-one was hurt and a very wet group of musicians did their best to play for the rest of the show from side stage, swapping and sorting out bits of soaking wet manuscript.

Max had plenty of strength around him. The best feed in the business, Stella Lamond,

his daughter Helen Reddy who was no slouch, and Frank Sheldon and Toni Lamond made it a real family affair. It was nice to see Toni and Frank on a Queensland tour. They could often be seen strolling in the sunshine with their baby son Tony in a pusher.

In a touring company, theatrical pros become very close; it's inevitable—the constant packing, unpacking, the formality on stage, informality off. The illnesses that must be ignored, the urgency of getting from one show to the next, ovations, deflations, heat, cold and a minimum of clothing for both. The dreams and ambitions remain private but emotions are always close to the surface. A Sorlies Tour meant a minimum of one year's commitment. With some it was for three or four years. In my case it was seven.

During the years there was only one time Bobby Le Brun took me to task. It was because of my passionate love of animals, which had gotten me into trouble before. A man named Frank was the owner of a dog act—a truly great dog act. The dogs were of mixed breeds but most were fox terriers. After his act one night, I wandered outside for a breath of fresh air and there in the dark Frank was beating the dogs. He had them by the back legs and was belting their heads against a lamp post. The yelping and crying couldn't be heard inside. I was revolted by the sickening sight. With a barrage of abuse I verbally attacked this cruel monster. His

act was nightly receiving rave reactions: 'Aren't the dogs clever?', 'Aren't they cute?', 'You can tell they love what they're doing', 'Look how he pats them' (they would cower while he twisted their ears), and 'He deserves the spontaneous applause'. The sight of those dogs getting their heads and little bodies smashed against that lamp post is a memory that remains as clear as if it were yesterday. Frank of course went straight to Bobby Le Brun about my actions. Bobby had no option but to call me into his dressing room and tell me to mind my own business. 'You have no right to interfere', he said. 'How dare you speak to one of the acts that way. We're in the middle of a tour and I have a show to run'. Bobby Le Brun was, himself, the kindest man in the world and was in a difficult position. Frank, master of the dog act, later asked me several times to join him and his wife for dinner. I sometimes visited, just to see how he was treating his dogs. They were always well fed and seemed happy enough, wagging their tails and anxious to do anything to please him. That's the way a dog is. Forever forgiving, always without a

grudge, loyal no matter what.

In England, my caring about animals had got me into trouble with a big time animal act called Vogelbein's Bears. They were kept in a jail-like cage back stage, with bars that allowed a fist to punch between. Those bears received powerful punches to their heads after every performance. With their spirits broken and dignity destroyed I felt so sad. It was so frustrating to be unable to help them in any way. My disapproving words resulting in a dressing down by the management, but they'd heard it all before. Everyone turned a blind eye and a deaf ear.

Skit and Skat were to solve the expense of accommodation when they decided to buy a tent. Between them they mastered the put up, and two single stretcher type beds close to the ground were the extent of their furniture. Settling down for the first night in Parkes, Kenny's eyes began to open wider and wider as, by the light of their hurricane lamp, he watched a snake slowly slither under his stretcher bed. Snapping himself out of his trance-like fascination, in one leap he was in the air and came down with his

Maurie with our second-hand FJ Holden.

🎋 *Backstage in Hawaii with Maurie, old mate Helen Reddy and her children Tracy and Jordan.*

feet landing on the wooden slats on either side of the bed. The sudden impact broke the wooden supports and he landed on the ground. Of course the snake vanished in the commotion, with Ken vowing to get a .22 rifle the next day. Moving to Forbes the tent was once again assembled, with an invitation to Warren Kermond to join them in the great outdoors. He had a sleeping bag. Warren was a meticulous 20-year-old, with his clothes pressed, his shoes always shined and his car gleaming. His thoroughness in his work and daily living kept him in a constant state of agitation. He stuttered badly and was always nervously twitching—he needed the calm of an evening outdoors. With Kenny Bowtell? Impossible! While the others talked themselves to sleep, Ken was drinking himself to sleep. The hurricane lamp had to be extinguished, but how? He wasn't going to get out of his bed. So, with the newly acquired .22 rifle, he took aim at the lamp and fired. Warren Kermond sat bolt upright—speechless. The noise of the shattering lamp and exploding rifle did little for his nerves. He wisely invested in a caravan.

Skit and Skat persisted, yet again, with their investment and the tent was erected alongside a river—an ideal position. During the next night the river rose; not enough to reach the tent, but enough to cause the evacuation of a million caterpillars to higher ground. This particular species of caterpillar travelled in single file, nose to tail, and were fat and furry. When Maurie woke the following morning all he could see were caterpillars. Not one speck of canvas was exposed; they were wall to wall, all over the interior roof and the two beds were moving in slow motion. There was no space to tread. The caterpillars were in Kenny's hair and all over his face and he was still snoring thanks to a liquid supper the night before. That was the last straw—and the end of the tent. As they said later; 'We threw it to the shit-house'.

Expert tips for young players

Auditions

Your agent will have made an appointment for your audition (unless it's an open audition, unkindly referred to as a 'cattle call').

You will approach someone at a makeshift reception desk in an audition room, and be handed a form. The form will ask your age, your singing range, if required, and your height, weight, and maybe recent experience.

Your agent will have already sent in a head shot photo, but take an extra one just in case.

For musicals, a pianist will be supplied. You must take your own piano music, marked clearly, especially with any tempo changes, and it must be in the right key. Audition pianists are not required to transpose from sight.

It's money well spent to invest in your own pianist (get quotes). Then rehearse before the audition.

Singers are usually required to sing a fast and a slow ballad, and nothing from the show in question. There are no microphones. Don't be afraid to move, if you are a mover.

Make a short list prior, of everything that you do well. Incorporate your strong points into the few minutes available. Dare to be different.

Wear clothes that mirror the character you hope to portray.

They may say, 'tell us something about yourself!'

So that they hear your speaking voice and see your style, ask questions. Be confident. When does the show open? How much time in rehearsal? Will the show tour?, etc.

And 'Sparkle'.

Rehearsals

Being late is unforgivable and will not be forgotten.

If dialogue is involved, arrive to rehearsal having learned it thoroughly, and be word perfect. The director may coordinate moves and the use of props that will prohibit the actor from holding and referring to a script.

Look your neatest, have early nights. First day, first impressions. Hair groomed, minimal make-up. Leg-warmers distort leg shape. Cardigans tied around waist do not disguise a large behind!

Have an 'overnight bag' that contains scripts, shoe changes (character, tap and ballet shoes) if likely to be needed.

Bring a hand towel, water, snacks (nuts and fruit) for legitimate ten minute breaks.

Don't put bags on chairs, but always somewhere away from rehearsal area.

Don't chatter. When not working, watch, listen and learn. Nobody knows everything.

Remember names, particularly the director, choreographer, wardrobe and props masters, stage manager and assistant stage manager, cameraman or musical director.

Never leave the area without asking the stage manager or assistant director for permission.

Eating in the working area is unprofessional.

Be alert and co-operative and save questions for an appropriate moment.

Be energetic, pleasant and humble.

Good luck. You already have the part!

Props

Always rehearse with props, no matter what they are. Have your agent request it. The stage manager, or floor manager will always oblige.

A walking stick may be too long or too short, make sure it's comfortable.

A suitcase may refuse to open or shut. It may be too big or too small to move around a set. Get used to using a preferred hand, from day one.

Wear prop glasses at rehearsals, they take some getting used to.

A hat can sometimes help in finding a character. With a man, he feels totally different wearing a bowler to a straw decker (not on the back of the head please!). And a hat is not a hat until it is tilted.

Find an unusual character by rehearsing in the chosen hat—always.

Papers, pens and any other hand props should always be set out at the beginning of rehearsals.

Ladies, when filming, a handbag is a wonderful place to store a script. Pockets are also handy.

Actual props always work better than fake ones. Beer must be freshly poured beer. A cream pie must be a cream pie—shaving cream just doesn't work.

Try not to trip over the counterweights and electrics.

Wardrobe

Your measurements may be asked for by phone, including shoe size. Have a complete up-to-date list sitting by the phone. Be prompt at any wardrobe calls, so nothing is left until the last minute.

Be careful with hats and caps. They will create a shadow on the face, especially in the theatre with its dome lighting. Avoid brims when possible.

Learn how to tie a bow.

Always rehearse actions like putting on or taking off an apron, shoes, a hat or a coat, etc. Then you know how long it takes, and where to put the wardrobe item. Make sure nothing can fall off, especially a hat.

Don't wear florals, stripes or patterns of any kind on television. Red is too dominant and it 'flares'. Pastels are safe, and usually photograph stronger. Nothing white unless advised otherwise.

Avoid clothing that pulls over the head; it will ruin your hair and make-up.

Make sure your feet are comfortable; you will be on them a long time.

Wardrobe departments will check the colour of background sets, so that you don't blend in and disappear.

Whenever there is time, hang up your own clothes and pair up shoes after use. Wardrobe staff have a hard enough job as it is.

Resist wearing sunglasses. The eyes are any actor's asset.

Suggesting wardrobe items of your own for a problem situation will often be appreciated.

Don't sit around in crushable clothing.

Enjoy being somebody else. Flaunt it!

Make-Up

In television, on arrival at the studio or location, go first to wardrobe then to hair and make-up. That way everything will colour blend. Unless playing a character like a rugged bushy or an old wigged lady, television make-up is based on a natural look. Glamour is achieved by subtlety.

In theatre it's the opposite. Glamour is achieved by eyeliner, lip liner and false eyelashes. Base colour should be tanned rather than natural. Theatre lighting drains the colours. Don't forget lip gloss for glamour effect.

Television rarely notices shoes, so dress for comfort. Theatre is the opposite—everything from top to toe is relevant.

In theatre, the performer does their own make-up. Be sure to blend base into chin-bone line to avoid a mask like effect.

Television will notice if the hands don't match the colour of the face, a common oversight.

Have in your personal make-up case a magnifying hand mirror (for false eyelashes, lip liner etc.); make-up removal cream; hand towel and soap (a must). Don't overdo the eye shadow (less is more). Spare tights (from wardrobe). Hair brush and spray. And don't forget the deodorant.

Display those pearly whites—smile!

Shooting film or television

Sit down whenever possible. There is a lot of standing around in film and television, especially between set-ups.

If skimpily dressed, keep a jacket handy—a wardrobe person will care for it, and you.

Remove all your scenes from the master script, mark the scene number in the top right hand corner, together with shooting order, and a reminder if a wardrobe change is needed.

You will be required, constantly, for polaroid photos to be taken on set. These are necessary for the continuity person and the director when cutting the film.

Keep all your day's scripts together, nearby, for a needed check, but not on the set. They can be looked at when the crew is busy with setting, or re-setting. When you're in a scene but not involved with the main action, the director may instruct you to 'look after yourself'. This means that it's up to you make sure you're 'in shot', i.e., not standing behind someone or something. If you can see the camera it can see you—therefore you are 'in shot'.

Hitting your 'mark' is absolutely essential. It's a mark on the floor or ground that the camera has lined up. Avoid looking down by mentally noting the equivalent in your eyeline, i.e. a vase, a mantelpiece, photo, sugar bowl, anything.

Mark your dialogue on scripts with highlighter or any see-through text liner. They come in many colours.

Remove delicate wardrobe for meal breaks. Wear a gown from wardrobe. Crew eat first, as they are back to work first.

If outdoors—pray for good weather!

Moves

In television, keep the work small. If a scene ends on a long freeze, don't move. The mood can be altered by a slight tilt of the head, or lips pursing, a frown, blinking, with drawing a breath. Keep it small. Let the audience do the work, by wondering.

Don't move quickly when sitting down, the camera needs to go with you.

To hit your mark after a long walk in an exterior scene, rehearse the dialogue by walking in reverse. Start at the mark and keep walking until you finish the required dialogue. That will be your starting point, for the eventual shooting.

Theatre performances can often be larger than life, depending on the subject and the director's wishes. Trust him, let him do his job.

Don't forget little presents and cards for fellow cast members on opening nights. Leave gifts in their dressing rooms—surprise!

Go out there and come back a star! (42nd STREET)

Maurie Fields

Skit and Skat had been with Sorlies for about a year when I found myself enjoying the after show get-togethers more and more and began eagerly looking forward to the Sunday barbecues and pub relaxations. It's hard to stop pros working when they are among their own kind, and Ken and Maurie never needed coaxing to play and sing. I found myself watching Maurie's hands. He played Banjo then—it had a better sound for theatre. His fingers fascinated me. I'd seen him and others bump in and bump out; he was strong and straight and yet his fingers could deftly glide over the banjo strings, finding the chords as though they invented the instrument. His left hand seemed to caress the stringed arm and the finger tips found the right positions with the smoothness of an Hawaiian dancer. I noticed he never looked down at them—his hands just seemed to know where to go. He loved singing blues and he knew so many songs, all written long ago. I never tired of watching and listening. Maurie was always quiet and shy, except when he relaxed with his music. There was so much emotion; it came from his whole being. It fascinated me, I was intrigued. After a while my interest progressed from his hands and up to his face. The blue eyes set wide apart beneath a high forehead were kind and they were embarrassed by being stared at. My interest was more than aroused. He didn't talk much but, when he did, it was usually bright and funny. I began to notice that Kenny's excessive drinking and mood swings would cause Maurie to leave many a gathering. They knew each other so well, he knew what was coming and would walk away from impending trouble. He had had years of defending Ken, physically, and had tired of joining his battles, and yet there was a brotherly bond between them stemming from childhood and their mutual love of music. When they sang together it was magic—and I was a fan. Maurie would sit at a piano and play and sing for hours, just because he enjoyed it and not to attract attention. But he always *did* and people stopped, listened, and gathered around, loving the old blues songs they'd never heard before. His self-taught piano style was just like him; not technical but full of emotion, with light and shade, expressive and caressing.

It was some time before he noticed me staring at him. In the midst of an attentive crowd, eventually our eyes met and he was singing just for me. Getting him to talk to me—that was a lot harder. For a long time it was the old adage 'eyes, across a crowded room'. And, without smiling, it can be a powerful means of communication. I began to notice him standing side stage when I was 'on'; he'd be watching me from the wings. If I looked in his direction he'd move away. When Skit and Skat made their entrance for their act, they came straight through centre tabs and, because they were carrying their instruments, a smooth entrance was difficult. For a year I'd not bothered about

❧ An early Maurie and Val act.

Everyone has the potential to do amazing things.
It takes energy, occasional encouragement and hard work.

this problem. All of a sudden I was there, every performance, holding the upstage overlap so they could walk through cleanly. It was a chance to stand alongside Maurie, close. He was so straight and tall and I would stare at his black-face make-up, which was so professional, like his music. Kenny was always nervous and toey and always tuning up— 'Give us an "A", Moch; give us an "A"'. Moch was his nickname for Maurie, like 'Much' with an 'o'. We never talked. But I'd always be there.

Knowing how to walk through centre of a set of tabs, without disturbing them, is an essential art. The trick is in the rear overlap. It still disturbs me to see centre tabs flung apart on an entrance. It shows a total disregard for what they are concealing.

On Sunday nights the country golf clubs and RSL clubs would sometimes have a dance for their members and, with typical Aussie country hospitality, any members of Sorlies Revue were always welcome. Maurie and Ken would often sit with the local musos transforming the old Pride of Erin and barn dances into happy jazz. Inevitably, Maurie would also sit in on drums. When he did, I would tune out from everything else around me. What else could I discover beneath the surface of this quiet man? The rhythm of his drumming style seemed to have more 'filling' than the drummers I had heard. For instance, his right foot playing the bass drum always played every beat in the bar, no

matter how fast the tempo. In those days it was customary to take a drum solo at the end of a number, then all in for the coda. A lot of drummers would become intimidated by the responsibilities of a solo and would race the beat, getting lost and out of time. With Maurie that was impossible. Once again his style was unorthodox, like his piano playing. He held drumsticks down beat style—like Buddy Rich.

He was just as talented a singer. He couldn't sing out of tune and found singing harmonies as easy as singing melodies, and in any key. No matter what some bands were able to manage, it never ever bothered him. He had an unusual range and a unique ear.

At one of the Sunday country dance nights he quietly approached me and, without a word, gently took my hand and led me to the dance floor. Ballroom dancing was something I had never done. When I was very young my father would *never* let me go to a teenage dance. He always said; 'Boys only go there for one reason'. So forever more, if it wasn't stage dancing, I avoided it. But now Maurie was leading me on to the dance floor. He could have led me to a raging bush fire, I wouldn't have cared. But I *was* nervous. On a dance floor! What was I doing? The little band was playing a show ballad; *that* was going to show me up even more.

With a fast tempo I could swing my way out of it. But it didn't matter; Maurie was

95

❧ *A publicity photo. Handsome huh!*

holding my hand. I looked up into his gentle, blue eyes, and he slowly put his arm around my back and we were swaying to the music. Not a word was spoken. With my left arm on his shoulder I was looking over it, at nothing, thinking how straight and strong his body was (we were both in our twenties and very slim). He must have sensed my nervousness and, as we swayed to the music, he gently drew me closer—so slowly. A warmth just swept through my entire body, from the top of my head right down to my toes. We stayed like that for some time and then his hand on mine pressed firmer and gently squeezed. That's when it happened, that indescribable moment. It was electric and we both knew, at the same time, we were on an emotional journey of discovery.

We didn't share our thoughts, verbally, but we still gazed at each other and, for a while, it was enough. In crowded rooms he sang only for me and we communicated through the lyrics of composers we never knew. In groups, we had lots of malted milks and toasted sandwiches in old country cafes with cubicles, until finally we found ourselves alone. It was over malted milkshakes that we eventually had private conversations. But it was a slow process.

He was so painfully shy. I found it very appealing. He was strong and athletic and he could make things and mend things and, in the company of men, he was popular. To me he was sensitive and a gentleman, with kind eyes that would melt your heart.

In Queensland, the coastal towns added much to the leisure side of a busy touring company and we all spent as much time as possible on or by the many lovely beaches. Maurie and I began to enjoy each other's company, exploring natural habitats around the rocks as the waves lapped over our feet. He always knew the names of the little creatures that lived in the rocks and would tell me how they all survived, and he knew the names of all the different birds and plants. He made me aware of things I had never really taken notice of before.

Maurie at the electric piano that refused to revolve. It was bought on time payment at £2 a month.

As time went by, we were having more fun together—more parties, more laughs, more barbecues. Nothing was ever planned. I had a constant responsibility with the show and was forever worrying about new presentations with the necessary programme changes. I tapped into everyone's talent, drawing from them every bit of ability that might otherwise have lain dormant. Maurie became a sort of challenge. There wasn't anything he wouldn't attempt. I began to write double acts for us. He never resented me explaining fundamentals, like how to handle props, and different ways of making an exit or an entrance. How to explore the comedy by altering the delivery or a move, and the importance of setting up a gag and when to let it hang before pulling the tag. Always open strong, finish strong and experiment in between. Have a hand-pulling exit. Don't take your eyes off the audience when taking a bow. Don't move when others are talking. Learn how to listen. There were a thousand things he wanted to know. He was

eager and only needed to be told anything once.

This was the 1950s. It was a wonderful time of slow discovery and each day was becoming more filled with affection. Romance was a totally new experience for me. We even dared to hold hands at the movies. It was in Albury and Doris Day sang 'Que Sera, Sera' in a Hitchcock thriller (to this day, that was *our* song). It was well into the movie before Maurie dared to nestle closer to me. In the darkened theatre we were staring at the screen but didn't see any of it. We were so aware of our closeness. We were on the verge of trembling, when Maurie's hand closed over mine. It was warm and comforting. A big, strong hand, enveloping, so gentle and I couldn't help wondering if the rest of him would feel the same way. As my hand turned so that our palms were touching, I remember thinking how clammy we both felt. And it was winter.

Some of us were staying at a private guest house in Albury and the kind landlady woke

❧ *The other half of the electric piano act.*

us each morning with tea and a biscuit. Actors are notorious for sleeping late, but one morning I was up and about earlier than the rest. The landlady was at Maurie's door with his tea (with two sugars) and I asked her to let me take it to him. As I crept in, hoping he was asleep, I wondered why I was sneaking about. Was it to find something about him at his most vulnerable? Probably. He was sound asleep, gently breathing deeply. No snoring, no slack jaw, and I could see he was wearing a white singlet. Why was I standing by his bed staring at him? Did I want him to stir and see me? It wasn't very ladylike. So I left. Anyway, he never did like his tea to be too hot.

Our first commitment to each other was in Griffith, high up on a mountain overlooking the twinkling lights of the town below. Together for the first time, we seemed wrapped in light and tenderness, scarcely daring to touch. How I had longed for him to hold me, for us to be in each other's arms. Before dawn we declared our eternal devotion to one another. And the unattainable moon turned into the glowing sun.

❧ *Gundagai – returning to Sorlies once again.*

❧ *Opposite page: A vaudeville double act in the 1960s.*

 Television

While I was managing to cook many meals (illegally) in hotel rooms on a primitive metho primus stove, television was erupting across Australia. I had always written home several times a week, and now my mother's letters were filled with news of who was appearing on television. Some of my Tivoli friends were adapting to the small screen and some of the less experienced theatre people were becoming overnight stars. 'Material' of every kind was in demand, as one performance immediately became passé. Studios were being run by newspaper executives and sports commentators. Established radio performers were now required to work without scripts. It was 1957 when Maurie and I were invited to appear on Bert Newton's variety show on Channel Seven. Bert was TV's teenage sensation—all smiles, and wearing a straw decker hat. He took time, even then, to make us welcome—as he has always done with everyone, over the years. I've always felt that Bert makes everyone feel safe. And he just loves 'pros'.

Sorlies had three breaks of two weeks throughout each year, when most of us headed for our respective families. Maurie and I had polished various double acts on the road and we were in great demand. Doug McKenzie was an old friend from my Princess Theatre and 3XY days. He was producing variety shows for Channel Seven and would put us on, sight unseen. When we left Melbourne to go back to Sorlies as scheduled, Doug McKenzie was often on my mother's doorstep asking: 'When are they going to be in town again?' Dear Doug, he must have got pretty frazzled trying to keep up with the demand. Straight drama, with its supply of actors, was as yet untapped by television but it was waiting in the wings—as Dorothy Crawford and her brother Hector were about to develop it in a big way. Meanwhile, on our next break from Sorlies, we appeared on Graham Kennedy's *In Melbourne Tonight* on Channel Nine. The next week we did a different act on Channel Seven, not realising the barrier between the two channels was so strong and the rivalry so fierce. When *In Melbourne Tonight* heard about us working for Channel Seven we were informed that we had 'done the wrong thing'.

We were married at Albert Park's Baptist Church on Easter Monday in 1960. I wore a pink taffeta cocktail dress with a matching pink hat. Honest John said the dress looked like a bedspread. We went back to my parents' home in Albert Park after the wedding and an act from Sorlies (The Flat Tops) took home movies of us and captured our excitement. They didn't have the heart to tell us they couldn't afford a film for the camera, just as we couldn't afford an engagement ring. We were in love; it didn't matter. We only wanted each other. Forever.

Nobody ever really knows another human being until they live with them. The love Maurie

⤴ *Various pregnancy disguises on 'Sunnyside Up'.*

❧ *Maurie and Bert Newton.*

had for me was all the things that I'd never known. He was by my side caring for me, always protective. I knew I'd never be lonely again and that if I never worked again I could depend on him. It's greater than all the money in the world.

During one lay-off time I did a season at the Theatre Royal in Brisbane. Laurie Smith, who had a harmonica act at the Tivoli when I was there, had been managing the Theatre Royal for some time. He went overboard with the publicity announcing my arrival. I was direct from everywhere. Direct from Europe. Direct from England's leading circuits. Direct from Harry Wren's tours, Sydney nightclubs, Sorlies famous revue. And the cast were

going to see a real soubrette. Thanks to the hard working Doris Whimp, I wasn't required to do any choreography and the weekly changes of programme were a real pleasure.

The dedicated George Wallace junior was a wonderful comedian. For years he kept grinding out what appeared to be a never-ending supply of new sketches due to his ability to recycle old gags. Young George was never far from his typewriter, localising comic situations, keeping up with the news items and writing them into sketches. He had a clever brain and he used it. Scripts were handed out, then one morning's rehearsal was all we got. Of course those in charge of props, scenery and wardrobe were on a

permanent merry-go-round. George Junior was funny like his dad and never strict like the old guard of Jim Gerald, Will Mahoney and Roy Rene. He had the speed required to learn and get those shows together, and his know-how was depended upon. Young George delighted in breaking us up into laughter and Eddie Edwards was always the first to 'go', setting everyone off, to the point of agony. We did *Red Riding Hood* pantomime and the jovial Eddie Edwards was, as usual, perfect playing Dame (the first to use two baby's dummies as ear-rings). Of course I was Principal Boy again—never, ever, Principal Girl.

Today, the young TV stars go to England to play in pantomime because of their television fame. I am stumped for an answer when they ask if I have ever been in a pantomime. It's an example of the sort of questions often asked of far more experienced people than myself.

During the Brisbane season, Maurie came there to take care of me. If ever we were apart he wrote to me every day (I still have the letters).

In my early days with the Tivoli Circuit, Honest John's reputation was unusual. He knew all about everything but couldn't do it himself. Management employed him to keep the actors happy. Offstage, he was the greatest comic ever.

Television opened a brand new door for him and the knowledge of a lifetime found its outlet. A new variety show had begun on Channel Seven called *Sunnyside Up*. The station's chief executive was from *The Herald and Weekly Times* and the producer of *Sunnyside Up* was previously employed at 3DB as was the compere—Bill Collins. All these managements came under one ownership.

The old 'Tiv' comics had long gone to God. A new breed of funny people were about to adapt to the wonderful new medium and old hands like Honest John were listened to with anxious respect. Thank goodness. When Honest heard I was in town he recommended me for the comedy team in *Sunnyside Up*. My past television appearances in earlier endeavours like *Club 7* and *Hold Everything* carried no weight. I was needed to work in the sketches and I knew them all. Material was precious. A Sydney comedian who had been knocking around the clubs had a cheeky style, which was ideal for visual comedy. He called himself Seyler Heylen.

Maurie and the new caravan.

104

When Channel Seven flew him each week from Sydney to Melbourne his success was immediate and he used his given name—Sydney. Early billing was 'Sydney from Sydney'. That was dropped when the commuting each week became impractical and the show became more demanding, resulting in a permanent shift to Melbourne. Syd, Honest, myself and Bill Collins were the comedy team. The show went to air— live—every Friday night, at 7.30 pm. The

coped with limited everything. Limited working area, limited rehearsal and limited scripts (none!). Our skeleton comedy team sometimes drew on the singers in the regular cast when an extra person was needed. Val Ruff, Shirlene Clancy and Billy Fowler always obliged but were never happy about it. I had become used to Syd's unpredictable style and could pull him out of sticky spots. That's the job of a 'feed' but the usually composed singers found it nerve-wracking. Among

Becoming a star is not what matters most. What really counts is being prepared to commit to a dream, and do whatever it takes to make that dream come true.

early time slot made it an ideal family show and children became the boss of the TV in every household. Fish and chip shops did a roaring trade as families had their evening meal on the lounge room floor in front of the television, watching *Sunnyside Up*. While we were pioneering at Channel Seven, similar things were happening in a later time slot at Channel Nine. My old friend Rosie Sturgess was adding great strength to the sketches with Joff Ellen and the marvellous Graham Kennedy. Comedy was the strength of these shows, supported by singers and dancers. Now it's the other way around, with the dancing line disappearing altogether.

For almost a year, at Channel Seven at Dorcas Street in South Melbourne, we

the males who often stepped in were the four Thin Men—three of whom were Neil Williams, Ron Lees, and the dancer Jack Manuel. One sketch caused a big hitch when a tag required a man dressed as a cannibal. It had to be done in black make-up. Because the show went to air live, there wasn't time for anyone to get into and out of the make-up. I had the perfect solution: Maurie could do it. At this stage Maurie wasn't a complete stranger to Channel Seven—he had been picking me up after the show at 8.30 pm every Friday. The next week he made his debut in *Sunnyside Up*. With complete body make-up, a bone through his nose, hooped ear-rings, a fluffy black wig, and wearing only a lap-lap, his head appeared over the

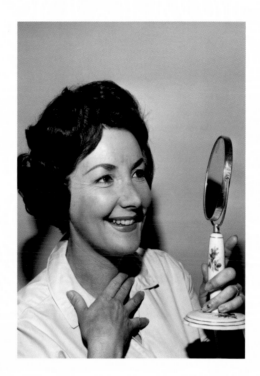

top of a screen and he uttered that never to be forgotten tag: 'DEE-L-I-C-I-O-U-S'. Somehow, an extra man seemed to be needed in every show and we *both* became regulars.

Studio space was stifling production and the old Regent Theatre in Fitzroy was taken over. The rear of the stalls was transformed into a control room, accommodating the affable Dick Jones in the director's chair. The Regent's upstairs foyer was transformed into dressing, make-up and hair dressing rooms, with the charming Randal Worth staff coping with the chaos. The show got to air like a well-oiled machine. It was a strong, successful team with the biggest influence coming from the photographic mind of Bill Collins. He never used cue cards and could step into the breach in any emergency and remain totally unruffled. My calming influence was always Maurie. If ever my tolerance was tested, he would catch my eye and give me a look that said 'let it go, we know what's right'. Those wonderful eyes could always do it for me.

I was 33 years old and Maurie 34 (he was the elder by 14 months), when I informed him and my parents that I was pregnant. This news floored the lot of us. I stayed in *Sunnyside Up* until I was seven months pregnant and publicity had fans sending in the usual gifts and good wishes. The wardrobe department used every disguise possible and most sketches were done in overcoats, smocks, or loose dressing gowns. Syd Heylen still continued to rough me up, as was his style. Shirlene Clancy and the singer Maria were forever telling Syd to 'be careful, she's having a baby'. His reply was; 'Nar, it'll do her the world of good'. So over the back of a couch I'd go, or get thrown out of a bed. Totally unrehearsed of course. Bill Collins ran a book on whether my baby would be a girl or a boy and the dear man, because of my condition, allowed me to share his toilet-sized dressing room side stage so I could avoid the stairs to the upstairs foyer. It was a hilarious squeeze with us both being each other's dresser. Ivan Hutchinson's band

played live behind the scenery in the comedy area. He couldn't avoid witnessing many a drama but usually he sat with his head in a book, one ear listening for music cues. A great musician and a lovely man.

With their radio backgrounds, it was inevitable that Crawfords and Channel Seven would form a successful working relationship. My old friend Alwyn Kurtz had been compering *Raising a Husband* and Crawfords' new action series *Homicide* had been successfully launched. A very youthful Ian Turpie starred as a criminal doing a bank heist in the first episode. A circular was sent to us at the teletheatre inviting auditions for drama, and those interested were to attend at Crawfords' offices in Collins Street in the City. With variety shows on television proving popular in every state, lots of performers treated the drama request with an 'it'll never last' attitude. But not Valerie Jellay. What could I lose! I did a reading and received a 'don't phone us' reaction and an explanation that girls were plentiful and they needed

male actors as the roles being written were mostly for men. My first episode of *Homicide* was called 'The Last Enemy'—about a priest who gets murdered. The day it was to go to air, a priest was actually murdered and it was headline news. Because of the religious sensitivities involved, the episode never went to air. On the day of my audition for Crawfords, Maurie waited for me in the coffee shop on the ground floor of that rabbit-warren-type building. I suggested to the very serious deliverer of the 'anti-female' explanation that my husband Maurie Fields was downstairs and that he was a very experienced stage and television performer. I dragged a bewildered Maurie away from his coffee. He auditioned—and became, in the words of a Crawfords casting official, their 'resident mongrel'.

This new form of entertainment dealt a severe blow to live theatre and cinemas. J.C.W. theatres survived and movie houses were later to make a huge resurgence by taking advantage of modern technology.

❧ *In hospital with newly-born Martin Fields, 1961.*

MAURIE FIELDS as JOHN QUINNEY
in BELLBIRD   ABC-TV

Melbourne's sophisticated nightclub scene had been flourishing and, before television sounded the death knell, the clubs had kept me particularly busy. Both Maurie and myself were going in all directions. The diversity of work was overlapping but not a great deal of money was changing hands. I was putting on floor shows at Marios, Ciros, The Roaring 20s, and the Chevron, while still doing *Sunnyside Up* and guest roles for Crawfords, as well as the occasional commercial. Maurie was busier. Band gigs, *Sunnyside Up* and Crawfords kept many an actor from lamenting by-gone days. Pleasant Sunday mornings at various football clubs kept our many double acts dusted off, although they became mini versions and topical. Fitzroy, South Melbourne and Hawthorn couldn't get enough of Maurie and Val. They were informal and fun to work and we often raced from one footy club to another, fulfilling commitments.

When answering a call for a TV job we were so anxious to accept that we often said 'yes' before inquiring what the part involved. This eagerness often led to unexpected developments. A 'Post early for Christmas' commercial sounded very sedate when Maurie was asked to attend a location near the beach at Sorrento, and to wear a smart business suit, shirt, tie and hat. Of course he wore the appropriate accessories, including a brand new pair of shoes. He needed them anyway. It was a cold windy day and Maurie was escorted to the end of a jetty where the director of the 'Post Early for Christmas' commercial pointed to a tiny dinghy, 5 ft by 2 ft, containing only two oars. 'We want you to row the dinghy straight out into the bay. Off you go'. Of course Maurie obliged, rowing frantically, with the director waving him on. Suddenly the entire crew started waving. Maurie had rowed himself so far out, he was in a shipping lane and a steamer was bearing down on him. Manoeuvring the little dinghy into reverse was achieved with added speed. The shore crew were still waving him in. The director called for Maurie to by-pass the jetty

Maurie as John Quinney from Bellbird.

on the way back and step out onto the sand, which he did. Unfortunately he was on a deceiving sand bank surrounded by a twelve foot drop. When Maurie smilingly stood up in the dinghy and took a step over the side, the dinghy moved away and Maurie took a sudden vertical plunge and disappeared from sight. When he surfaced, it was minus the smile. His only suit and new shoes joined our growing list of used props.

Port Phillip Bay was to catch many an unsuspecting actor off guard. Water played a big part in many of Crawfords' dramas. An episode of *Homicide* entitled 'Double Cross' initially involved a two-hour call at Port Melbourne. Maurie and the marvellous stunt man, Peter Armstrong, were to play criminals, collecting drugs from a cargo ship as they sped past in a small outboard. A film crew waited on the opposite side of the big ship, with one of them ready to toss the parcel of drugs as if it came from over its side. Maurie and Peter were to appear in their boat from around the front of the cargo ship. The scheduled big ship failed to appear on time and left both smaller boats at anchor for some time. After the two-hour call became four hours, and after three visits from curious water police, the big ship arrived. But it was a different ship and nobody had informed the Captain of what was going on. It was now or never. In their sudden haste to 'get the show on the road', Peter Armstrong

couldn't get the outboard motor started. It burst into life later than planned, making their cutting across the front of the ship very dangerous. 'We're gonna dead heat with this thing,' Maurie yelled, whereby Peter veered away at the last minute, leaving the boats on either side of the big cargo ship. Everyone forgot about the bow wave. The two little boats became airborne as the ship glided by. Maurie asked Peter: 'What if we had ended up in the water with the Noah's Arks?' (sharks). Peter produced what looked like a hinged nail file and said: 'Don't worry, *I've* got a knife'.

Another boating story had Maurie cast as an illegal lobster fisherman. He was to be looking up at two gorgeous girls on a jetty while he suggested they invest in his catch. The props weren't put in their basket until the 'take' when Maurie plunged his bare arm into dozens of live, spiky crustaceans. 'Make-up!!!' (never mind the infection).

Fishing for eels with Max Cullen during another Crawfords drama became an hilarious invitation to pneumonia for all involved. But it was all in a day's work. A glamorous business!

The Britannia Hotel became a gold mine for its mentor, Milton Kruger, when he decided to tap into TV 'names' and present floor shows with a ballet line, showgirls, Maurie's band, comedy by Syd Heylen, celebrity singers, and the big draw card— Exotic Dancers. Everything was class with beautiful wardrobe and lighting. Syd and Maurie did comedy doubles with songs and dances. The Exotic ladies were just that— they were actually imported. This show was a first. The only time I felt my standards were lowered was when Milton Kruger, wanting to expand the success of the night shows I was choreographing, asked me to put together a lunchtime fashion parade. That sounded acceptable; he had done a deal with a fashion house and the models were professionals. I gathered up appropriate band arrangements, mostly standards, and then discovered the clothing was lingerie of the briefest kind and that he wanted me to compere the show. That didn't sound like a big ask, except I was six months pregnant. His attitude to that was 'it will add to the presentation'. I did one 'performance' but never again. It shamed me. Besides, he didn't get the 'monied business men' audience he had expected.

Helen Lorraine was also infanticipating and, at seven months, both of us were farewelled by Bill Collins during the finale of that special *Sunnyside* episode in September 1961. We had strict orders for us both to return to the show in 1962. The birth of Martin Fields made newspaper headlines; the power of television was already in place. Syd Heylen took advantage of the situation by organising his own press crew and invaded St Vincent's maternity hospital

empty handed. He stood by my bed after grabbing flowers and gifts sent by others and pretended he had brought them all himself. The sincere, smiling comedian posing beside his workmate and her newborn baby looked all heart.

All mothers know the frustration of those last couple of months before giving birth. Billie Fowler was always on the phone to me. She had been pressed into service and was working in the *Sunnyside Up* comedy sketches. Her calls were always stressful; sometimes she was crying, always pleading: 'Please hurry back, I can't take any more ... When will you be back? ... How do you stand it?' Poor Billy, she sure welcomed my return. I had been waiting it out by doing my usual paperwork. I wrote out sketches in longhand, with the prop lists and wardrobe required attached to a rough sketch of sets. During the confinement even the 'business' had to be written out, all in longhand. It was a pleasure to be still contributing. Having learned never to discard those old 'Tiv' and Sorlies scripts, I joined the league of those all too willing to have their brains picked! *Sunnyside Up* ran for seven years, always live to air. Many things happened during those years. Betty Pounder regularly contacted us with offers of musical-comedy roles in Williamson's stage productions but, because of other commitments, we always declined. Without brothers, sisters, aunties or uncles, there was

❧ *Opposite page: Maurie with a young John Farnham from Bobby Dazzler.*

 Maurie in 'A Town Like Alice' with Gordon Jackson.

 From 'The Music Man'.

a lack of baby-sitters for my son Martin. Apart from *Sunnyside Up* each Friday evening, when he was with my parents, my answer to work was 'no'. When he began school I insisted on being released by 3 pm so he wouldn't come home to an empty house. Our house, incidentally, is the same one we bought in 1961. A piano was bought before the baby arrived. Whether a boy or girl, the child, no matter where in the world, would always have a friend with the universal language of music. I encouraged my son's piano studies with a passion.

The ABC was taping a drama series that was scheduled to air only five weeks after studio, making it tight for editing. A new character had been written and the actor (well known) was unhappy. He was very pucka English and the part called for a businessman type, well dressed but essentially Australian. The conflict held up production. Maurie was sent for. He arrived at the ABC studios in Melbourne expecting to be interviewed or, at the most, to give a cold reading of something. Instead he was taken to a 'live' set and was asked to read with the rest of the cast. Then he was bundled into wardrobe and back to the set for a take.

Fortunately he had the right temperament. Overnight he learned a further eight scenes which were taped the next day. He gave the character an elegant but likeable arrogance and John Quinney, stock and station agent of *Bellbird,* was born. It ran for ten years. Who says it only happens in the movies? Unlike the commercial stations, the policy of the ABC did not require its artists to be exclusively theirs. After, say, five to eight weeks work there would be several weeks off. Still in the hands of the writers it allowed for other work to be accepted, keeping everyone fresh and on their toes. While Quinney became a favourite that everyone loved to hate, Maurie was able to benefit from the many successes coming from Crawford Productions, various film houses, variety appearances and, later, Grundy's drama successes. Amid all this, his band had become known as Quinney's Quintet. Not only did the original pucka English actor lose his job, it was the beginning of the true Aussie accent being accepted as credible. All of a sudden, managements wanted a Maurie Fields voice. Agents have told me, even now, that clients ask for a 'Maurie Fields' accent.

Amid the diversity of work that kept the

❧ Helen Morse as Marion, Paul Petrie (Davy), Martin Foot (Ron) and Martin Fields (Neil – 'Stinker'), from the ABC show 'Marion'.

adrenaline pumping, were many challenging stage-plays. At the Alexandra Theatre he played Willie Loman in *Death of a Salesman*. A huge role. He took over the lead role of Jock from Frank Wilson for the return season of *The Club* for the Melbourne Theatre Company. When casting took place for the movie, I don't believe David Williamson had seen Maurie play the part. Several times Graham Kennedy and Maurie have been thwarted from doing drama together and that was one of them. A play called *The Next Greatest Pleasure,* about gambling and the racing game, was also a successful challenge as was his initiation (apart from school efforts) into Shakespeare. It was *Macbeth,* at the Athenaeum for the Melbourne Theatre Company.

Shakespeare's dialogue coming from various parts of our house during rehearsals even had our dog sitting and staring in wide-eyed confusion. I remember saying to Maurie; 'What do all these words mean?' 'Buggered if I know', he replied. 'I just learn the bloody thing'. The result was not a bad effort, from an old banjo player.

Many of Crawfords' successful productions were created by the distinguished writer Terry Stapleton. He had great respect for comedy-actors; he knew they were rare and Maurie was his favourite. The marvellous father and son relationship he created for Johnny Farnham and Maurie in *Bobby*

Dazzler proved a winner. Dear John still calls him Dad. The role of Barney, the best mate of my old friend Alwyn Kurtz, in *Last of the Australians,* fitted Maurie like a glove. Maturity was adding another dimension to his work and he eased into parts with polish and a confidence that directors could trust. The mini-series *A Town Like Alice* cemented Maurie's acting versatility.

According to the management, *Sunnyside Up* was suddenly terminated after seven years because the dancers had been instructed to strike for principal pay rates. Shows closing have never surprised me; not after a lifetime of good and bad. They all end sometime. Nothing lasts forever, so don't ever leave a show; eventually it will leave you. Maurie's philosophy was: 'Don't aspire to stardom, try to be a 52-weeker (never out of work). That way, when a show goes well you can go up to the star and say: "We killed 'em didn't we?" And if the show happens to go down, you go up to the star and say: "What happened to ya?"'. Besides, if you've got star quality, you're going to be one anyway.

With both myself and Maurie guesting in anything that was happening—*Cop Shop, Solo One, Matlock, The Sullivans* and, later, *Carson's Law* and *Prisoner*—we also managed to do an education series on music for the ABC. Together we had lead roles in an ABC comedy series called *No Thanks I'm On A Diet*. Tristan Rogers, now starring in an American daytime soap, played a cameo guest part in one episode. Also together, we had a marvellous time in the lavish ABC versions of popular musical comedies. We did *The Music Man, Kiss Me Kate, Guys and Dolls* and *The Pyjama Game.* The ABC even had our young son in many programmes. Martin clearly remembers, as a four-year-old, walking around all day with a saucepan on his head. Destined to be a 52-weeker. Later, as a 10-year-old, he *did* advance to playing the lead character of Stinker Ferguson in the lovely series *Marion* starring Helen Morse. Filming in winter school holidays around a creek bed encouraged his conservatorium piano studies. Staying at Brighton Grammar School until reaching 12th Form and HSC (which he did) also held greater appeal at that time.

One night we were at home in our pyjamas watching the Logie Awards on television. We were pleasantly relaxed and watching the proceedings with mild curiosity when nominated for best supporting actor was ... Maurie Fields, for *The Banana Bender.* He jumped out of the lounge chair as if to go up on stage, pyjamas and all. It was such a surprise, he felt he had to do something. A short clip with John Hargreaves was shown. *The Banana Bender* had been one of many guest roles he had gone to Sydney for and forgotten about, an experience probably shared by many a busy actor.

During a moment of pondering I asked Maurie if he would prefer to be *good* at many things or absolutely *great* at just one thing? His reply was: 'Can I have an easier question?'

A Pram Factory play, written by Jack Hibberd, broke all running records when it transferred to the Chevron Hotel banquet room. *Dimboola* ran for a year and a half, with a great cast headed by Rosie Sturgess and Maurie Fields, both of whom were doing the TV comedy series *Last of the Australians* during the day. Taping took place on alternate weeks. Rosie began to feel the pressure and asked me to share her *Dimboola* role. So, for the long run of Melbourne's version of the play, Maurie had two wives, alternating weekly. Under Burt Cooper's direction the arrangement worked fine. It was a pleasure to be with a live audience again; that feeling of manipulation and its responses was like a tonic. And, of course, Maurie and I had always felt so comfortable working together. With every house packed, it was often more than dangerous to be sitting close to where Maurie made his entrance. The drunk gate-crasher, Uncle Horrie (Maurie), enters the wedding breakfast during the formalities, complete with ankle bicycle clips and riding a two-wheeler push bike. At several performances Maurie fell off the bike and landed in somebody's lap. Trying to keep a path clear for that bike was impossible. Also, the character of Father Pat falls asleep at a critical moment in the play.

🌿 *Maurie and James Coburn on the set of 'The Leonski Incident', 1985.*

The gentleman playing Father Pat admitted a preference for vintage champagne but when the cast repeated their cues for him to wake up, only to discover him totally passed out, it was revealed that he had long imbibed anything from methylated spirits to French perfume. During the *Dimboola* season there were several Father Pats.

It took years for my mother's rheumatoid arthritis to eventually confine her to a wheelchair. Daily visits from me, whenever possible, could not aid her misfortune but prevented her from being concerned about the housework. She did her best to smile and be bright company throughout the years of pain. 'Nobody wants a moaner', she would say. My father did his best for her but I knew

his pushing of the wheelchair, and her dependence on his compassion, was demeaning them both. Lymphosarcoma was also to strike and bad news was expected from the hospital. When my father, Maurie and I were told to wait by the phone, the outcome became inevitable and cancer took my dear mother from me.

Personal questions: Revealing answers

The trio of Fields was a close knit family. We never did anything unless it was the three of us together. Many times Maurie and I were offered prestigious work that would have meant being apart, but it was without appeal, especially as being with Martin was our first priority.

So many times we were asked the secrets of staying together and having a happy marriage. The answers were never simple and of course impossible to disclose in formal interviews. Nothing is cut and dried, especially in a show-business marriage. Perhaps now is the time to disclose some threatening situations and how to handle them. Firstly, we did not believe in the old adage 'absence makes the heart grow fonder'. Of course circumstances can necessitate separations but many a show-business marriage break-up results from being apart, especially when it's been on a regular basis over a long period. Also 'mixed' dressing rooms can pose a problem. Sometimes this situation is unavoidable, especially when filming on location and a caravan is the only change room for everyone. When dressing rooms are available and there is a preference for 'all in together', unless both partners are in the same show, it can spell trouble. Depending on how you look at it.

Experience teaches many things. Often at gatherings I spotted Maurie from far away staring at me. 'I like to keep an eye on ya', he would say. When that same situation was reversed and Maurie had an admirer my female mind reacted differently. I approached the young lady and said; 'Why don't you let me introduce you to my husband! It's no good making signals from afar. What is your name? Do you have an autograph book with you?' By then I have brought her face to face with Maurie and said; 'This is Florrie (or whatever). She's very anxious to know if you're available'. Well, anyway, it worked. There wasn't a scene, only exchanged pleasantries which sent them scuttling off. Of course that situation could have had a stronger reaction if on the way to the face-to-face intro-duction I had said; 'He likes his underpants and hankies washed by hand'. Men are far more gullible when it comes to flattery. If women can accept this as a fact the blatant approaches can be easily counteracted, if given thought. Devious? No; perhaps more intelligent. Neither Maurie nor I ever stood for our love being threatened. In that area we wouldn't be messed with.

Obvious episodes are not the long-term worries: it's the little things. Sometimes a man finds his ego fed by constantly putting his partner down, especially in company. 'Don't ask her, she wouldn't know', 'She's the worst driver in the world', 'Keep out, this is men's talk', and so on. How could such a man expect to be loved. And from a woman: 'What time are you going to be home?', 'He never mends anything I ask him to', and 'All he thinks about is football'. It's easy to slip into that kind of rapport, believing it's the banter of married couples, and life can become a contest of one-upmanship. A lot can be learned by observation. It's obvious that smart alec dialogue will never replace 'please' and 'thank you'. It's no good demanding that a husband be home at a certain time. He's got to want to be with you. What's the good of having him home at a certain time when he'd prefer to be somewhere else? As for mending things, start on the job yourself. He will always say: 'Let me do that' and then it's set up for him to preen as you say: 'What would I do without you?' As for football, or golf, or bowls, or cricket, or whatever he enjoys that you don't, go to the trouble of learning the terms even if you hate it. That way he will want to tell *you* all about his day, rather than some stranger in a pub. If he invites you to join him, never say no. He may never ask again. If he comes home and has something to tell you, stop what you are doing, whatever it is. Sit down, listen and be sincere. It's called 'loving someone'. It can also come under the heading of 'working at a marriage'.

It doesn't take a professional marriage counsellor to tell you: keep yourself nice. When using the toilet, close the door. Always keep that private. Use the same manners as when you first met. Good manners and consideration should be a natural instinct, not just because you're 'out'. Like passing the pepper and salt without being asked for it. Let your partner know how precious it makes you feel to be hugged. Touch each other a

lot. Maurie was forever kissing my hand, or my cheek. I liked to run my hand down the back of his neck, or across his shoulders. His silky skin felt special to me.

If something mundane needs doing, whoever notices the need does it. Like washing up, making beds, putting out the garbage, watering plants. It's nobody's job. If you really love someone with all your heart your desire is to do everything for them, and it becomes mutual. If you are fortunate to find a wonderful someone to love, say so. Constantly. If there's a need to be critical, do it gently, constructively, with flattery. For example: 'How do you feel about the blue shirt with those pants? You always look so handsome in blue'. Corny stuff! Maybe so, but it worked for us and I am still asked the same old question: 'What was the secret of your happy marriage?' It's no secret. Ask anyone who knew us or has worked with us. Then again ... life is a lucky dip.

Opposite page: 'Versatile Vaudevillians'.

On the boards, as ever

The 1960s came and went, and during the 1970s work continued to flow in. TV shows also came and went.

The first, and most successful, theatre restaurant in Melbourne was Tikki and John's Music Hall in Exhibition Street. A marvellous plan slipped into place. During the three long school holiday breaks Maurie and I did a vaudeville-type show. For the rest of each year Tikki and John presented a Music Hall show. Ernie Bourne, Vic Gordon and Margo Clancy worked in both. A later inclusion was Judith Roberts and even later, Tikki and John's very talented offspring Paul Newman added a new dimension. Paul was also a capable manager during his parents' absence. It meant that the restaurant and its popular presentations were keeping their regular patrons treated to a constant change of programme, for 52 weeks every year. Once again Maurie and I were working together and loving it. Tikki knew I wouldn't leave my son at night, so she also created a back stage job for Martin, on his school holidays so I could be available. Many years later he appeared without us, as an adult in the cast. For over a decade we were employed at Tikki and John's. It was probably the most significant ten years of our lives. We were treated like members of the Newman family. It was a busy time but all the outside work, including television, never conflicted and we always had fun.

Unless you have worked for Tikki and John, you may never know the constant revelation of your own true potential. John has the creative mind of an eccentric genius. Bringing his brilliant ideas to fruition never ceased to amaze. In perfect partnership Tikki has always unselfishly and patiently drawn unexpected talent from many a grateful performer.

Over the years, with special wigs, make-up and costumes, Tikki wrote and produced a variety of single acts for me. One elaborate production based on the life of Ethel Merman was a real stretch. Then there was a very authentic Charlie Chaplin. Ginger Rogers was easier, but I remember Barbra Streisand, complete with prop nose, being both funny and a vocal challenge.

The most dangerous thing for an actor is to refuse to listen to anyone else; to feel you know more than anybody. You become your own worst enemy. Perhaps it's a manifestation of insecurity? It takes a great deal of security to say 'I don't know' without feeling embarrassed, or, 'What does that word mean?' or 'I don't understand'. Most insecure people will say: 'Yes—I know all about that', thereby closing their minds to learning. They are the losers.

❧ *With John Newman (at Tikki & Johns in 1979).*

Ernie Bourne & Maurie as John Travolta & Olivia Newton-John from 'Grease'

❧ *Tikki & Johns.*

❧ *With Maurie and Bob (Bridie) Murphy – creator of wardrobe for The Particular Inc., Torville and Dean, Val Jellay and Maurie Fields Stage Productions, Barnham, South Pacific, The King and I, The Wizard of Oz, Anything Goes and, of course, many Tikki and John productions.*

Running the TV gamut

It was 1984 when Crawford Productions included Maurie and me in the prestigious cast of a new mini series, based on Australia's unique medical service to the outback—the Flying Doctors. The six-hour mini series was to have the title of its fictional town—Coopers Crossing.

Channel 0, later to become Channel Ten, had successful drama series with the Sydney-produced *Number 96* and the Melbourne-produced *The Box* about the behind-the-scenes goings-on in a television station. Once again I managed to get a guernsey guesting. The boss of the fictional TV station was played by the New Zealand actor Fred Betts. His character was stern and sombre. When they needed a network boss, a fearful supremo, Maurie was cast as the dreaded wielder of power. The way Maurie played that role proved, once again, that he could make an audience believe he was the toughest villain in the world. Leaning over Fred Betts, eyes filled with hate, faces almost touching, poor Fred could only wilt under the towering, fearful strength of the portrayal. I'm probably most proud of Maurie's roles as the heavy, because I know what a gentle man he is. It proves the absurdity of wearing sunglasses: the eyes are an actor's greatest asset.

Channel Ten was again on a winner when *Prisoner* took off. The women's prison subject was to create lots of work for actresses. Over its years of success I was several times cast as a mean-spirited landlady, who harboured criminals, stole from them and beat up old ladies. 'Baddies' are far more interesting to portray than 'goodies'! Maurie once again played a menacing prison warden. His part was the worst kind of stand-over villain. Wearing a warden's uniform his position of power allowed him to tread on girls' hands, break noses by slamming doors on the unsuspecting, rape the female prisoners and, with Maggie Kirkpatrick, he had the best all-in fist fight in the history of television—between male and female that is! Maggie as The Freak made it an evenly matched punch up. As with all good performers, they both had a good time making the drama convincing.

When the *Coopers Crossing* mini-series was completed I went into a semi-regular role in *Prisoner* as Mabel, a retired prostitute. My clientele would have had to be very exclusive as I wore the best of clothes and fine jewellery. The sets for Mabel were ornate, creating a contrast to the prison sets. For this part my hairdresser, Terry Worth, dyed my hair blonde. Much mileage was got out of my aiding escapees.

Maurie and I had no idea what lay ahead for us when we signed what we thought was a short-term contract with Crawfords. After the best part of a year, *Coopers Crossing* was to be picked up by

Maurie and Val on set in 'The Flying Doctors'.

❧ *'The Flying Doctors', 2ⁿᵈ edition.*

❧ *Sophie Lee, Robert Grubb, Lenore Smith and Maurie and Val with baby 'Scarlet'.*

Television abbreviations

MUTE.	Silent	V.O.	Voice Over
T.V.	Television	M.O.W.	Make Own Way
B.G.	Background	Travelling	Request is on its way.
F.G.	Foreground	P.U.T.	Pick-up time
W.S.	Wide Shot	O.B.	Outside Broadcast
C.U.	Close-up	LOC	Location
E.C.U.	Extreme close up	INT	Interior
F.X.	Effects		

CRAWFORDS
AUSTRALIA

3rd December, 1991

Ms. Val Jellay
57 Page Street
ALBERT PARK 3206.

Dear Val,

How pleasant it has been to see your smiling face coming along the corridor or entering the studio, for with it came the knowledge that the show would be done well. Over the years we have worked together you have consistently turned in excellent work, consistently known the words, consistently hit the marks and consistently left the set as you entered it - with a smile.

Thanks for the opportunity of letting me see you work - it has taught me so much. I hope we can do it again.

Regards,

BRENDAN MAHER
PRODUCER
"THE FLYING DOCTORS"

The Stars of
THE FLYING DOCTORS

MAURIE FIELDS & VAL JELLAY

Maurie Fields and Val Jellay are recognised throughout Australia as being two of the most professional and entertaining people ever to "tread the boards". Maurie, a multi-talented musician and quick fire gagster, is also a fine character actor, having played in several top movies during the past few years. Val, a dancer, choreographer, songstress and comedienne, is equally famous for her work, both on the stage and on film.

Three years ago they made their debut in the popular television series, The Flying Doctors. They are quickly recognised as Vic and Nancy Buckley, who run the Majestic Hotel in Coopers Crossing, the Royal Flying Doctor Service base in the television series.

When Farndale Limited asked Maurie and Val to appear at the Royal Flying Doctor Service Benefit Dinner, both were quick to reply... "Wouldn't miss it for quids."

the Nine Network as a series, to be called *The Flying Doctors,* the name of the actual service on which it had been based. Our roles as the publicans, Vic and Nancy Buckley, would become part of our lives for eight wonderful years. Under pressure to produce it on video tape and not film, Hector Crawford remained adamant throughout its entire run and *The Flying Doctors* retained its excellent quality, mainly through the exacting process of film making allied with great scripts, star quality guests and attention to detail in every department. As for Maurie and myself, while

working harder as Vic and Nancy, it became a progression of mischief, mirth and madness.

After three quarters of my career had been spent on the stage, I found real pleasure in transferring the joy of contributing to the ongoing success of *The Flying Doctors.*

We had the happiest times and also the saddest. Our dear friend and wonderful writer, Terry Stapleton, would die. Hector Crawford's passing would rob the industry of its founder and guiding light. I would become hospitalised and Maurie would have two heart attacks.

❧ *Previous page: Nancy and Vic from 'The Flying Doctors'.*

❧ Clockwise from top: 1. With Hector Crawford (The greatest mentor to Australian Drama) & Glenda Crawford. Lunch Break on location with 'The Flying Doctors'. 2. Maurie and Liz Burch, 'The Flying Doctors'. 3. With Toni Lamond. 'Write it down it's the best therapy'. 4. With Pat Evison, John Michael Howsen & Robert Grubb. 5. Amidst three very different humourists: John Blackman, George Kapinaris and Max Cullen.

Love

When a heart attack alerted Maurie to his mortality, he took a keener interest in his physical health. It was a scare that shook us all, and the need for each other could not have been felt more deeply. A second attack occurred on a long plane flight and was diagnosed as heart failure. The second hospitalisation meant more adjusting, which amounted to common sense. Gone were sugar and salt, along with the obvious. He became an advocate of light beer for his daily chat with 'the boys'.

A third Vaudeville tribute by the Fields family was a success at the Concert Hall.

As *The Flying Doctors* became more popular, and fan clubs in Europe and England were keeping the publicity department busy, Maurie accepted accolades for two successful vocal albums. Thanks to the enthusiastic persistence of Alan Zavod, an old friend, Virgin records distributed *Cheers* and then *All The Best,* thereby permanently recording all those wonderful songs that Maurie was singing when we fell in love 35 years earlier—the great blues classics and happy jazz. Alan Zavod added the family touch by including Martin's compositions—'There's So Much Of Australia' and 'Tell Us A Joke, Maurie', based on a segment in *Hey, Hey, It's Saturday*. My small input was a touch of vaudeville.

Basking in Maurie's shadow has always made me proud. Very soon it will be forty years since Bobby Le Brun of Sorlies threw us together. It was a loving life together. Maurie's talent was beyond question but only I know how utterly kind and caring he was. Our son Marty is aware of life's pitfalls and has his priorities in order while experiencing family life and the sweet sound of applause.

In 1993 *The Flying Doctors* ended its life of eight years. Gone were the early calls and the hard working days with so many close colleagues, all of it sprinkled with large doses of fun and gaiety. Eventually every show comes to a close—it's the nature of the game. For me it means leaving a part of myself behind.

Fan mail is always answered and requests for personal appearances continue. I am always ready for the unexpected. Life is like that whatever you do.

Due to changing times many things come under the heading of entertainment—but I will always be thrilled by attending the theatre. I will be seated earlier than necessary, so as to watch the house coming in and assess the respect the audience has for the performers by the clothes they wear. I will continue to stare at the front curtain (the act-drop) and anticipate the magical secrets it conceals. I will enjoy wondering about the moods of the actors. Are they nervous? Are they pacing? Are they making last minute make-up and wardrobe checks? Will the stage-manager be reaching his final call over the P.A. system: 'Overture and beginners please'? My interest will have me looking for the sound console, counting the spotlights on the lighting rigs, checking the angles of their

The two wonderful men in my life on 'Hey Hey It's Saturday', 1993.

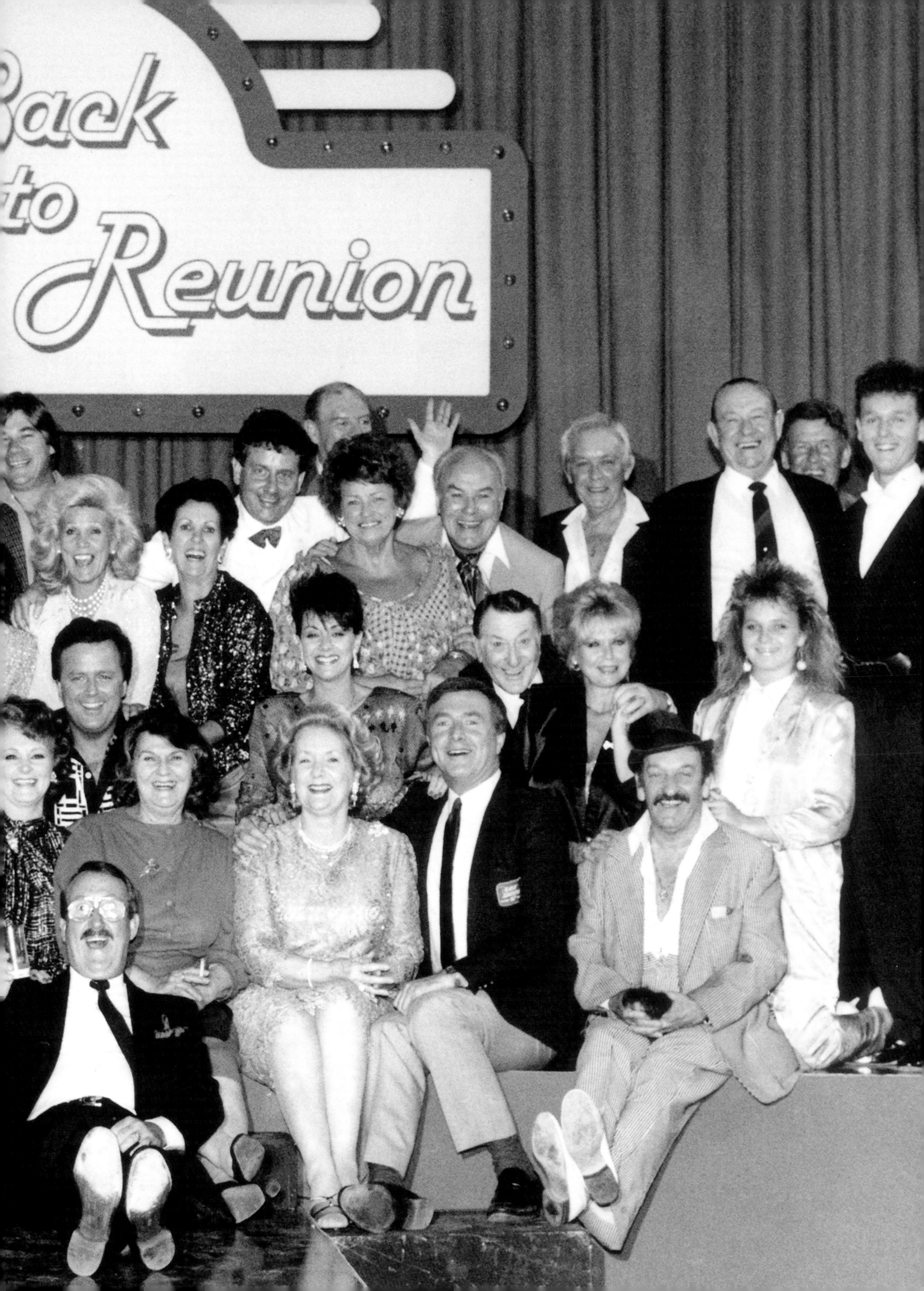
Back
to
Reunion

throw. As the orchestra enters the pit from their private world beneath the stage I will stretch forward and endeavour to count the sections and how many musicians are in the band. As the act-drop rises I will, for an instant, recall the beautiful odour of paint, size and sweat that swept over the Tivoli audiences. The impressionable times of my sweet youth!

❧ *Only I know how kind and caring he was.*

139

'A likeable man'

You couldn't call him a butch looking bloke. That conjures up burliness and a gruff manner. Gruff he never was, unless playing a part. It was Ernie Sigley who said, *'Maurie, you always looked like a toff'.* Which of course he was far from being. Looking like 'you've got a quid' is an old ploy of actors. The prosperous and busy facade is a leftover from the old vaudeville days when appearance off stage was as important as on stage.

He was indeed six feet tall with dark hair and blue eyes. One hundred per cent Aussie, with a voice to match, identifiable anywhere. There were no airs and graces. Sincere when he called everyone mate, and patient with persistent fans, answering the most frequently asked questions as though it was the first time, and laughing at jokes they insisted on telling him, pretending he hadn't heard them before.

Maurie died in 1996, leaving behind a legacy for showbusiness folk to forever treat as a beneficial.

Born in 1926, Maurie was the youngest of four children. Apart from being the birthplace of an Aussie icon, Fairy Bower at Manly in Sydney still remains a famous landmark.

Toasting bread over an open fire was a family affair, and great fun while listening to the new invention called 'the wireless'. Compulsory listening was 'The Lux Radio Theatre', 'Dad and Dave', 'Martin's Corner', 'Yes What', and the spooky 'Mystery Club'.

Over the years Maurie's temperament has become legend. Directors loved him for his naturalness and ability, his need to please, and avoid confrontation.

The family home in Camden Street, Fairfield, Sydney, seemed huge to the youngest member of the family, but in fact was a two bedroom, single-fronted weatherboard cottage. Its occupants were six, plus the dog—a fox terrier who answered to the name of Skipper. This was a Catholic family and Maurie's mother's maiden name was Hourigan; Eileen Mary Hourigan, and she married Esmond Bede Sheil whose six years spent studying for the priesthood came to an abrupt halt when he met Eileen. Three of their children were aged 15, 14 and 12 when the youngest was born. His arrival made the older three feel they were a separate generation. Esmond and Eileen called the unexpected newcomer Maurice Alphonse. The waiter-like Christian names caused many a giggle throughout the innocent babe's future life. He sided with the teasers by suggesting that his mother must have fallen for a French man.

Music was the main source of joy in the family. Mother Eileen shared her piano playing ability with her eldest daughter Joan who had learned the 'Shefte Method of Pianoforte'. This system certainly belonged way outside the curriculum guidelines of the conservatorium. Nevertheless

Being prepared to commit to a goal, whatever that goal, is the way to achievement. Do your duty to your destiny, and you too can bask in the good times, and never give up in the lean times.

the whole family's musical ability never relied totally on tutoring. Each had an 'ear' that was God given, a feel for rhythm and harmonies that was like an extra sense to them. Maurie learned to play ukelele and piano from his sister Joan. Being fifteen years his senior probably enabled her to instil some discipline into his musical education. Professional lessons in tap dancing were acquired by attending the dancing classes of a Miss Boss at Sydney's foremost School of Stage Dancing. Because the school's pianist for lessons was Eileen Sheil, her youngest son Maurie received free tuition.

This was the 1930's, and vaudeville was thriving. Theatre skills were being taught to lots of boys and girls as outings to the local live theatre were standard family entertainment. Standards varied, with the Tivoli Theatre being the ultimate. The Tivoli Theatres in Melbourne and Sydney each had two shows a day, at 2.00 pm and 8.00 pm. There were no four letter words, (one 'bloody' was allowed), but the naughtiness and shock tactics served their purpose. Vaudeville relied on visual presentation. All the comedians were multi-talented by necessity. Versatility made performers valuable; being a specialist limited their value in these shows, which were very elaborate and clever. Maurie's childhood teachings were to be invaluable as he found out many years later when he was thrown into every theatrical situation imaginable.

Towing the line (No Laughing Matter)

The father of the family, although very strict and without affection, was not a bible basher. After studying six years for the priesthood he could have imposed his Catholic teachings on all and sundry, but he wasn't one to quote the Scriptures or damn his children to hell if they were disobedient. He was just not a communicator. Marrying the bubbly outgoing young girl he had met during final leave before taking the vows of a priest may have been too far removed from his earlier plans of a different dedication. In any case he distanced himself from all family love, and when a stroke disabled him permanently, his physical involvement with the family was also forcibly reduced.

Esmond's wife Eileen remained bright and very musical, as did their four children. Joan the eldest was a singer and piano player like her mother and she could also belt out a mean tune on the ukelele. Then came Vince who possessed a fine tenor voice and declined an invitation to join the Australian Opera Company in favour of joining a wartime concert party, spending the war years entertaining Aussie troops. Melba was a champion ballroom dancer in the days when going to a local dance was comparable to today's addiction to television. The youngest child was to benefit from the talents of all his siblings.

Maurie was a shy child and that side of his nature was to remain part of his personality forever. Shyness however, was no barrier when it came to the dance floor. His sister (the champion ballroom dancer) had instilled the many techniques into the youngster's natural feel for rhythm.

Maurie was patiently taught piano as well as drums. This began by practising on saucepan lids and various noise producing gadgets from the kitchen cupboard. It progressed to taking over brother Vince's drum kit totally when later he too played in his mother's band. He was too little to see over the top of the drum kit and dancers would see a flash of sticks only. Just one drumstick would keep the rhythm going when he took over the vocals from his sister, singing through a hand held cardboard megaphone. Microphones were for the very sophisticated and not yet acceptable. Besides, being able to project one's voice was essential.

Mixing business with pleasure was everyone's recipe for survival in these tough times. Moving pictures were still a novelty with the die-hard live theatre goers being reluctant to let go of proven pleasures. The common solution was to mix the two entertainment forms. Two full-length movies were standard fare for decades, with the movie after interval being preceded by live entertainment. Maurie explains, 'I remember one picture was called *Over the Hill*, a real tear jerker. Then after interval me and Mum did our "turn" to a huge local following before the main feature came on. It was all about the First World War and the German ace pilot known as the Red Baron. The movie

❧ *Maurie Fields, 15 years old. Great straw decker hat.*

was called *Hell's Angels*. Management was also promoting the next attraction. It was some Indian flick and they gave every kid a cardboard Indian headdress. It was a great advertising gimmick. 'Course us kids all wore 'em to the movie, couldn't wait. Trouble was they were about two and half feet high, and when we all sat down no one could see the screen'.

Facing live audiences began very early in the life of Maurie Fields. The entire Fairfield State School was to face him every morning at assembly when they marched into their various classes to the beat of a lone kettle drum. The opening solo varied before the march off. Ra-ra-rum. Ra-ra-rum. Then came the showy bit, and off they'd march. Of course the drummer was the very last one to march into the school and by the time he put away the kettle drum and the sticks he would miss at least five minutes of the lesson every day. There have always been perks in life and there always will be.

Maurie liked singing in the school choir. 'My voice was still in soprano range and to break the monotony I'd try different harmonies, causing the strict choral teacher to turn bright red with exasperation. For some reason the rest of the kids would giggle and disruption would take over. For a quiet kid, I always seemed to take the fun way out, and take everyone else with me. Corporal punishment they call it now, but I remember it as "Six of the Best". We all copped the strap at different times for a variety of reasons, with one of the Brothers marching us off to the office of the Brother Superior. One hand had to be placed on top of the other hand, with both palms facing up, and each hand getting its share of the dreaded strap. This punishment was always received in a kneeling position, allowing more force into the impact. Winter was the worst time to get the strap. I can recall my hands blue with cold and stinging with pain. Often it would be snowing outside, and I'd be told to go to the chapel and pray for forgiveness. I dunno about the prayers for forgiveness. If God was listening he wouldn't have been too rapt in my mumblings.'

Record holder in Hop-Step-Jump.

When the school play went into rehearsal it meant studying something by Shakespeare. When a musical production was on the school agenda, it was usually something by Gilbert and Sullivan. From what I hear these days, that system hasn't changed. Midsummer Night's Dream could have been called Midsummer Night's Nightmare, when Maurie spent many a night learning the marathon speeches of 'Puck', the lead comedy character. A very sketchy recollection:

I know a bank where the wild thyme blows
Where ox-slips and budding cow slips grow
Quite over canopied with luscious woodbine
With sweet musk roses and with eglantine
There sleeps Titania some time of the night
Lulled in her slumber by dances and delight
There the snake throws her enamel skin
Weed wide enough to wrap a fairy in
And with the juice of this I'll streak her eyes
And make her full of hateful fantasies.

Titania on waking is to fall in love with the first person she sees. It eventuates as the unfortunate 'Bottom' who is wearing a donkey's head because of another play supposedly being learned.

Maurie failed to get the part of 'Puck' and finished up in the role of 'Bottom', who turns into a donkey (wouldn't ya know). An early lesson in showbusiness rejection?

A production of H.M.S. Pinafore was staged at a proper theatre in the main street of Katoomba. A picture theatre in fact. Maurie remembers all the regalia on his naval uniform and feathered hat. 'I remember one entrance after meeting the Captain's daughter with a view to wedlock. I tripped on the rail at the bottom of the door, went arse-over-head, rolled up on to me feet, faced the audience and loudly proclaimed, "I don't think she'll do." It got the best laugh in the show, plus a severe reprimand when the curtain came down. I can still see the script and the songs. One in particular, and the parts marked ALL. When everyone yelled at once it sounded more like a football match.'

ROLE OF SIR JOSEPH PORTER, ADMIRAL K.C.B.
(Knight Commander of the Bath)

When I was a boy I served a term
As office boy at an attorney's firm
I cleaned the windows and I swept the floors
And polished up the handle of the big front door
ALL
And polished up the handle of the big front door
SIR JOSEPH PORTER
I polished up the handle with a hand so free
And now I am the ruler of the Queen's Navy
ALL
He polished up the handle with a hand so free
And now he is the ruler of the Queen's Navy.

Loss of innocence

Years later Maurie met up with an old school friend, Ken Bowtell, who played trumpet and had a wonderful collection of records. Ken liked songs like 'Moonglow', 'You Made Me Love You', 'Basin Street Blues', and on trumpet he played them beautifully. Ken, unlike his young brother Colin, was a very good singer and his record collection included lots of Fats Waller, Bessie Smith and Ella Fitzgerald. Maurie spent many hours listening to these jazz greats, learning phrasing and the many styles of jazz music, and he fell in love with the blues.

When Maurie and Ken started playing music professionally around the traps, their band, known as 'The Backroom Boys' was a big part of the very popular jazz scene. Drugs were unheard of, but it was a carefree merry-go-round of cigarettes, whisky and wild, wild women.

'The Backroom Boys' consisted of Jack Allen on piano, Don Harper on trombone, his brother George Harper on bass, Keith Silver on clarinet, Ken on trumpet, Maurie on drums, and Brian Anderson played guitar.

The Wentworth Hotel Ballroom near Wynyard was the 'in' place to go, with Harry Brown's band being the best of many bands around, and there too young Maurie was the drummer and featured vocalist.

Jim Gussy was renowned for his famous ABC Dance Band. It featured the top drummer Tommy Fisher, and when Tommy's many commitments conflicted, Maurie was his substitute. They were heady times.

Tom Fisher was also a teacher and had his own rooms among many other music teachers in the large ABC building, which catered for music education. Here Maurie took lessons in reading music, specifically drum music.

He also spent some time in war-torn Rabaul, New Guinea, that only amounted to about four months. Many things left a lasting impression. One discovery after the war was at Tunnel Hill where the Japanese had stored a massive supply of machine guns, search lights and all kinds of artillery and ammunition. Most of it was still in crates, untouched. The surrounding mountains of Rabaul had been classed as impregnable, and the harbour impossible to regain. So with a warning to the locals, the Americans and Australians mounted huge bombing missions. It was the only way to recapture the island, by almost destroying it themselves. At the time it was presumed that more bombs had landed on Rabaul Harbour than on Berlin. With the aid of the American surveyors the many sunken ships were built over, filled with concrete and made into wharves.

Captain of the Athletic team – Maurie in the centre.

Maurie however, was finding that his job as a retail hardware salesman was not looking like a wise career move, although the learning experience did stay with him. He struggled with nail and screw sizes, saws, hammers, paint colours and a million and one other gadgets and tools involved in hardware. The day job was augmented by a night job as a tally clerk. He was one of three young men who checked the bags of copra being carried by trucks on to a weighbridge before being loaded on to ships. Some New Guineans would sneak heavy dirt into the bags for filling and if caught would stare wide-eyed with fear when warned about the D.I. (District Inspector). 'Him beaten you—no kai kai (food). You gammin like that you looking blong D.I. You stop along house blong D.I. (jail).' Imagine Maurie Fields threatening anyone! Not likely.

Due to the Americans who were supplied with jazz music in the form of V-discs with compilations of the jazz greats, he spent hours listening and learning old obscure songs like 'Go Back Where you Stayed Last Night', and 'If You're A Viper'. Party tunes which later would bring comments like, 'Where did you learn those!' And he just smiled. Of course he also learned that he wasn't overwhelmed by baseball, and always a beer drinker—his dislike of whisky would never change.

'Can you ride a horse?'

Casting agencies would frequently ask the question when selecting actors for their movies and television shows. Is it best for us not to know what our future holds?

In 1945 the war had ended, families were being reunited and people were on the move.

Maurie was always willing to do anything. For a while he lived in wool sheds; his job was as 'rouseabout'. Transportation to anywhere was by horseback. There were no roads to and from the jobs required of a rouseabout, and after a couple of years horse-riding became second nature.

Maurie quickly learned the many skills of a bushy. It was survival time, and very tough. Replacing old and putting in new fencing was a daily duty. He learned to shear sheep and do wool pressing. Crutching sheep was never-ending. Some would already be fly-blown, but it was all part of the job. He often took over as shearers' cook when the regular cook passed out cold—not from the heat but from rum. Old Soldier was the brand of rum and sheep station workers in the outback drank it like water.

Maurie talked about it; 'I remember thinking I might as well get into the rum like all the other blokes; it didn't seem to

❧ Group photo – Backroom Boys (Maurie far right, Ken third left. Later to become 'Skit and Skat').

151

affect them. Until there was a fire on a big property called *Ballindigie* and I fell off the back of a fire-truck. The fire-trucks were blitz-buggies left over from the war and painted camouflage green and brown. They were big heavy trucks with huge tyres and had the sides removed. They transported big water tanks and with petrol pumps we fought the fire. I remember the boss yelling orders, "save the stock and fences and let the bastard burn". I was on the back of this big fire truck with a bottle of Old Soldier rum in one hand and a hose in the other. It was on a bush track and the truck suddenly hit a bore drain. I flew through the air like a gazelle. The bottle of rum reached the ground and smashed before I did. That was the first time I dislocated my shoulder. The same shoulder got dislocated thirty years later when I tripped on my cape at the Athenaeum Theatre, Melbourne, during the run of Shakespeare's Scottish play for the Melbourne Theatre Company. I upheld the long superstition of Macbeth being a theatrical jinx.'

That large, remote property burned for three months. Quite a disaster, but not uncommon in the vastness of outback Australia.

Maurie's fencing skills and shearing should have left him stooped, but to the day he died he walked tall and straight with a back that was broad.

Whenever Maurie stayed on at that town's pub he borrowed a guitar. The locals soon forgot he was a shy young bloke and encouraged his passion and pleasure in entertaining. Some of the shearers were thinking of heading south, so he too made the decision to return to the big smoke. Inevitably here he would meet up with his old friend Kenny Bowtell, the trumpet playing jazz fan.

Kenny Bowtell and Maurie Fields, 1957. 'Skit and Skat.'

154

'There was this poor mongrel

Until the war years from 1939–1945, Hollywood had hoodwinked the rest of the world into believing that all Americans were movie stars. The geographically isolated Australians were probably the most gullible.

Sydney, Melbourne and Brisbane catered for the money influx, with Sydney being the most influenced by the opportunities of a fast buck. Each city had its share of bohemian style areas, like Sydney's famed King's Cross, which had until then been filled with real characters, quaint shops and specialty delicatessens. Adelaide had been labelled the City of Churches, Melbourne the heart of theatre and the arts, while Sydney was regarded as being the nation's playground.

When Maurie returned to Sydney from the Queensland outback town of Dirranbandi and its dirt roads, horses and hard work, the war was well and truly over. Sydney was not as he remembered it. His respect for anyone in authority had deepened, and taking one day at a time had also been reinforced. Being ambitious or pushy was foreign to him, and his daily needs were few. This casual approach to life in the now swinging city of sophisticated Sydney could have seen him drift along in no particular direction. But he found his old friend Ken Bowtell, a live wire who shared Maurie's love of music, and together they did something about it.

The nightclubs that flourished during the war like The Roosevelt, Sammy Lees, Golds, Chequers and The Celebrity Club were renowned for presenting lavish floor shows. Some went on to even better productions, catering for a more sophisticated audience who had until the war years, been entertained by the Tivoli vaudeville shows and JC Williamson's Musical Comedies. Wartime concert parties had of necessity turned amateur performers into professionals. They now joined the ranks of acts appearing on Sydney's busier and more diversified showbiz scene.

Electronic musical instruments were becoming popular. Youngsters were discovering electric guitars and jeans. Big bands that relied on reed and brass sections were being replaced by smooth trios, with jazz bands performing for traditionalists in selective venues.

Both Ken and Maurie were excellent vocalists, with natural ears for harmony and a note range that never presented a problem with keys. This was just as well, as neither of them could read music well enough to write it. Listening to Ken's large collection of recordings by jazz greats during their teen years had definitely influenced their choice of music. With Ken's *other aptitude* he 'acquired' a banjo and a ukelele, which Maurie's elder sister Joan had taught him during his school days. Using a capo the fingering was the same, but of course it had a fuller, louder sound, and equally important, it looked showy and theatrical. Kenny's trumpet playing had gotten even better and he never went

❧ *Another television commercial.*

anywhere without it. A spare mouthpiece would always be in his pocket, like some people carry a pack of smokes.

He lived with his parents above a shop, while Maurie's accommodation was provided by sister Joan and her husband Jack. Ken and Maurie solved the rehearsal room problem by practising every day in the huge open space of the public gardens in Fairfield. What better place for the very noisy goings-on than a park bench!

Sydney was buzzing with available variety acts. The boys needed a presentation with a difference. The vocals were thoroughly polished with strong intros, varied tempos, perfectly blended harmonies and well rehearsed movement that was subtle. Even gag routines that allowed for audience communication were incorporated. Their appearance was the final gimmick that made them Sydney's busiest nightclub act. They had suits personally tailored from blue and white check wool fabric. The style was exaggerated, with very long jackets and

pegged trousers, known as Zoot Suits. Their shirts were white with royal blue satin floppy ties. The kicker was broad brimmed bright red hats and bright red shoes. Their music was a straight pinch from the American south, with scat riffs and tight musical accents, and they spoke their gags in a southern Negro accent. What made the act so different would be totally unacceptable today and considered racist—they worked in Black Face. It was a terrible inconvenience. The black make-up was exactly like the professional standard of Al Jolson and Eddie Cantor. Once established in that get-up they were stuck with it. They called the act Skit and Skat, and the audiences loved them.

Maurie's family name was Sheil, which had always been a problem for others to spell and pronounce. Fields was easier and near enough to Sheil. It was later legalised by deed poll. New names, new outfits, new act. Maurie Fields, typical knockabout Aussie, didn't have any idea he was on the verge of an all consuming professional career in

❧ *Maurie's book 'Leave 'Em Laughing'.*

showbusiness.

The hours and days spent rehearsing the act was a bit of fun for Maurie. He found it all too easy and it was never his style to worry a great deal about anything. It went against the grain to make his presence felt; he would always let things fall into place without much effort. It made him happier than those who worried, and he was fun to be with. Summing up—he didn't give a 'bugger'.

Skit and Skat played every date possible in and around Sydney. Poker machines were the new craze and some venues, like Granville RSL, which began as tin sheds, evolved into plush gambling complexes. Interstaters were made to feel privileged when allowed into clubs, only after being scrutinised and proof of domicile was presented. Non club members residing in NSW were barred. What did it matter, all they wanted was your money. The rules did make the clubs more intriguing and desirable. The buzz was always, 'How can I get in? Can you get me in? Lend me your driver's license. Cop this fiver mate. You're in!' Everyone wanted to go to the flashy clubs and didn't care how much they put into the machines. Booking agents commanded exorbitant fees for their artists. Management never minded; they knew whatever they paid out would go straight back into the one-armed bandits, so called because the first machines all had a long lever on the side, making the player feel it

was the lever that decided the outcome. The payouts were usually no more than a couple of coins but at least it jingled into the tray more often. With a few coins you could have fun for hours with no harm done. How times change.

The early club managers were drawn from all walks of life. Some were actually returned diggers, some were showbusiness drop-outs working in cahoots with the booking agents, and some were ex-pub bouncers. Most were never without a beer in their hand.

The clubs put on shows for their members at weekends on Friday, Saturday and Sunday nights. It was boom time for all the local Aussie acts. Everyone played the clubs and nightclubs. They included Frank Ifield, Will Mahoney and Evie Hayes, the great juggler Lloyd Nairn, The Flat Tops, Slim De Grey, The Discords, Frank Strain, Jenny Howard, Billy Brady, Keith Peterson, Barry Ruggles, Syd Heylen, The Dixie Kid, Norm Erskine (Big Erko), Joe Taylor, George Wallace Snr, Jandy, Al Reynolds, and Honest John Gilbert. A very young and talented Warren Kermond was yet to arrive on the scene. There was only one other black face act around the traps. He was a banjo player too and called himself Piccaninny Pete. George Wallace was a mate of Maurie's and reckoned when Skit and Skat were on the same bill as Piccaninny Pete it looked more like 'The Minstrel Show'. Old George decided to gently explain to old

Pete that he was using the wrong kind of black make-up. 'What ya oughta do is cover ya face with paraffin oil then put a thick coating of lamp black all over it, then cover it with plenty of white talcum powder.' Well, he finished up looking up like a shiny black snooker ball. About that time Piccaninny Pete retired from showbusiness.

It's still traditional at Returned Soldiers venues (like RSL clubs) that before the fun commences, every night at 9.30 sharp everyone stands and respectfully bows their head in silence while the 'Ode' is read. All drinking, machine playing and conversation halts for the reading and the dedication to the fallen. The 'Ode' is like a solemn prayer. It only takes a few minutes, but for artists getting toey waiting to go on, it's not exactly a warm up. Maurie remembers the great comedian Slim De Grey. 'It was at Marrickville RSL. Slim had just finished his act and he had killed 'em. The idiot manager was waiting for him when he came off the stage. He was a smarty and said, "Hey Slim, when are ya gonna change ya bloody jokes?" Slim replied, "When are ya gonna change ya bloody Ode?"' Maurie continued, 'Some of those managers were amazing. I remember the one at Ashfield RSL. He was always pissed. The first time Kenny and I were engaged by him he was handing us over our pay envelope and he reckons "You're the best bloody act I've ever seen". Funny, cos' we hadn't even been

on. And we never did get on. He finished the show and didn't know the difference.'

A successful double act called The Dapper Boys mimed to records. Miming was still a novelty and not yet considered thieving. When Skit and Skat asked for more money at Five Dock RSL the stupid manager said, 'I don't even pay The Dapper Boys that much, and they sing better than you two.'

Skit and Skat were one of the acts that worked many venues all in one night, sometimes four or five a night, with the last one being a late show at Skelsey's. Maurie remembered Five Dock, Paddington, Bondi, Marylands, Liverpool, Bankstown, Leichhardt, Granville and many others. 'It kept us flat out and we had many transport problems. The flashy zoot suits and black make-up gave many an old sheila a fright, especially on a late night tram. Often times we were left standing on corners when cabs wouldn't stop for us.'

Bill Skelsey owned the famous 'Oyster Bills'. People came from everywhere to 'Oyster Bills' at Tom Ugly's point. When he opened Skelsey's at Lansdowne, it too became a very popular late night spot with good food, band, dance floor and variety acts. They stayed open until 5 a.m. Bill Brady was one of their favourite comperes. Skit and Skat played there so many times they became part of the furniture. They dared to do all kinds of double acts, breaking in gag

routines. Maurie was funnier but he always took the role of 'feed' for Ken. They say that a good straight man knows more about comedy than the comedian.

Chequers and The Celebrity night club were still presenting a great night out, with well-produced floor shows. Joe Taylor was resident comedian-compere at Chequers for several years. The spectacular all black female Norma Miller Dancers were imported to Australia for the first time. The Negro dance troupe were the talk of the town. They were to play the Tivoli circuit and were having a night out at Chequers, where Maurie and Ken were doing a season. The owner, Dennis Wong who was Chinese, successful, and inscrutable gave the troupe king tables around the edge of the dance floor for the midnight show. It wouldn't have occurred to him that a black face act like Skit and Skat could be offensive to black people. Joe Taylor however, who was on first, had time to check the house and knew that the boys' act could be in very bad taste. Instead of warning them

he decided to watch the fireworks.

Joe Taylor introduced Australia's favourite music and comedy act, and Skit and Skat bounced onto the dance floor with a big band intro and a blinding spotlight. In their check suits and black faces they sang and played 'I Got Rhythm' with scat vocals and funny strutting. Maurie gave his banjo a real workout and Kenny blasted away on trumpet. When the applause began and the lights came up, they were facing a sea of equally black faces. It looked like the main street of Harlem.

The Norma Miller dancers, although world famous, were nevertheless very gracious and after the show invited Maurie and Ken to join them at their table. Norma Miller said, 'Hey, I haven't seen an act like that for twenty years'. The boys relaxed and were pleased with the comment, until later when they gave it a little more thought!

In Melbourne 'Poverty Point' was outside the Tivoli theatre in Bourke Street. In Sydney it was outside the Criterion Hotel on the

❧ "I kept telling them I was innocent!"

corner of Pitt and Park Streets. Traditionally actors, agents, musicians and bookers would meet there at 9 am every Monday morning. Although the Criterion Hotel relied on its drinking trade, all sorts of business transactions took place there and 'Poverty Point' was aptly named. In the building next door the ABC employed the velvet tones of Skit and Skat, with no funny business. Burl Ives, Red Norvo and Helen Humes topped some of radios finest broadcasts. They considered their employment at the ABC a casual day job, an improvement on the Hasty Tasty and Silver's pancakes. Wormald's factory was another work experience for Maurie, where he mastered the untheatrical art of soldering. He soldered the outside badges onto the fire extinguishers. Sounds like the basis of a Benny Hill sketch.

Sydney's theatrical agents, although busy, weren't many. There was Ted James who was so busy he had a habit of double booking people. Ted drank only whisky— straight. It was understandable that he would sometimes get a bit muddled. Maurie remembered one Easter Sunday. 'Ted James sent Honest John Gilbert to a job at Chullora Train Work Shops, a "ten in the morning" gig. It was worth three "carries" (translation: guineas, from the song "Carry Me Back to Old Virginny"). When Honest John got there, there was this old bloke outside the gates sitting on a packing case and eating a hot cross bun. He wouldn't let him in. "No show here," he said. "Piss off". Well, it was all in the game.' Glorious showbusiness.

Another agent, Frank Strain, was also a stalwart of the then theatrical scene. He even wrote an act for a young Tivoli soubrette called Val Jellay, who at that time had never heard of Maurie Fields.

Two very young boys with a show-stopping dancing act were the Saddler Twins. Len and Hugh would later become theatrical agents, but in the meantime it was their father Bill Sadler, a Tivoli stage-door keeper with a gruff manner (matching his bulldog-like appearance), who coughed and spat his way through many negotiations. It mattered not who was within earshot when his big head burst out with a string of the worst four letter words. It was said that while on the stage door he was so strict he wouldn't even let the fresh air in.

At one time Bill booked a show into Melbourne's Princess Theatre. The lines of dancers were known as ballet girls. It was the last full dress rehearsal before opening day and Bill was irritable and oblivious to the invited audience of VIP's, backers and dignitaries. When the finale ended he strode down the aisle, leaned over the orchestra pit and bellowed, 'Righto all you ballet sheilas, you'll be goin' on tour with this show. It's 30 bob a week and ya keep yourselves, and if ya don't like it youse can all get to the shithouse.'

STATION·MASTER

The Tivoli circuit and Sydney's Palladium Theatre were doing great business with vaudeville, as were Brisbane's Theatre Royal and The Cremorne. Perth's Tivoli Theatre was thriving under Garnet Carroll's banner, and Tasmania also kept the vaudeville and variety performers busy. Many of the imported headliners however, were at the waning end of their careers. George Formby, Arthur Askey, Donald Peers, Winifred Atwell, and Gene Krupa were nevertheless still big drawcards in Australia. Maurie remembers when together with Joe Taylor they introduced Gene Krupa to 'Two-up'. They took him to Thommo's Two-Up School near Central Station. 'He seemed to be away with the birds most of the time. He smoked a lot, and I don't think it was tobacco.' But when Gene Krupa got behind a set of drums he was brilliant.

The Australian outback will always have its characters—people who are not necessarily

'Neighbours' – always happy with a fellow cast member.

162

among the highly educated, but are far wiser from experiencing life at the grass roots! Some appear slow because of level headedness, but usually they're a mile ahead of everyone. Experience has always been the greatest teacher. Sydney would surely have had more than its fair share of characters, with showbiz folk being top of the list. Maurie Fields too, would one day be taken into the hearts of Australians for the very reason that he never aspired to be anything other than an ordinary good bloke.

The Tivoli Theatre and the Palladium were also in the Central Station area of Sydney. There was one particular show at the Palladium which featured an array of acts and the usual line of ballet girls and sketch comedians. Norman Erskine was the compere. Life was never dull for Skit and Skat; they always had a spare bottle of grog stashed somewhere, and the dancing girls could always inspire the challenge for flirting and womanising in general. One night, after having done their act, they were waiting side stage for the finale run down when Norm Erskine whispered to them, 'The coppers are outside looking for you.' Norm had slipped out front to watch one of the acts and heard the police making inquiries about Ken and Maurie. In a flash they grabbed their instruments and flew out the stage door. It could have been a practical joke but 'Big Erko' didn't joke about things like that,

especially anything to do with police. Skit and Skat, complete with zoot suits and black face make-up, racing around the city's busy streets would have been a strange sight even for Sydney. Ken had a utility truck by then and he should have been arrested for dangerous driving. After reaching their car Ken drove like a maniac, going the wrong way up one way streets, along the footpath in Castlereagh Street and nearly crashing through a David Jones window. They never did find out why the police enquired about them.

Norman Erskine, a down to earth, boisterous sort of entertainer, was always fondly regarded. A typical rough diamond. He had been a pretty good heavyweight boxer. When an important boxing contest looked like being cancelled because of the fighter's withdrawal, big Erko obliged the promoter by filling in. Maurie picked up the story. 'It wasn't until he was getting in the ring that he saw his opponent. The bloke was an imported Negro boxer, eight foot tall and built like a brick shit house. He said to the manager, "What are you trying to do to me? I'm a singer!", and with that he ran to the centre of the ring where the announcer was in the middle of a big build up, grabbed the microphone and started singing. The crowd began to throw money. It was all around big Erko's feet and he looked at the big Negro boxer who didn't know what was happening, and said, "You'd better join in, you're half in this mate, cos I'm not gonna bloody fight ya.'"

Beryle Meekin was another theatrical legend, probably the female counterpart of Norman Erskine. A very talented singer and comedienne, big and buxom, she capitalised on her size with songs like 'Even a Fat Girl Has a Heart'. Offstage she had a mouth that would make a bullocky blush. She often worked with little Ronnie Shand which made for great comedy. Her father, Dave Meekin, was an important showgrounds promoter, along with Greenhalgh and Jackson, Jimmy Sharman, Des Wittingslow and Ma Short. Skit and Skat worked the showgrounds for Ma Short, who was considered the toughest. However, she loved the boys and paid them well, even though they would have sung 'Dinah' more than a thousand times for her sideshows.

Dave Meekin imported showground attractions from America such as the first Pygmies to be seen in Australia, headed by Ubangi Chillawinga. Dave took his daughter Beryle Meekin to America with him on one trip. They were at a very exclusive gathering of showbusiness dignitaries and Beryle was on her best behaviour. Her father had told her to act like a lady. Marlene Dietrich was at the society event and Beryle couldn't resist the opportunity. In her best affected English she asked, 'May I have your autograph please Miss Dietrich?' Marlene raised her head and over her shoulder said, 'I'm afraid not, I don't give autographs', and as she slinked away Beryle called out in her loudest Aussie voice, 'Think yourself lucky ya got f...ing asked!'

As the years roll by, people's tastes change. Sometimes they get recycled, like fashions and hairstyles, but for comedians it gets tougher. For the first half of the century audiences didn't probe and dissect what they saw as being funny. Racism was a word yet to raise its ugly head. There was no malice intended with jokes about Jews, blacks or the Irish—they were just jokes, not reality. Like homosexual jokes, the approach was light-hearted, as was a comedian portraying a simpleton, or lisping, and a stuttering joke was a laugh getter because of the way it was told. Not meaning you should laugh at handicapped people. All in all Mr and Mrs Everybody weren't openly malicious and the butt of the jokes laughed loudest. But in the nineties everyone got serious. No longer was it socially acceptable to laugh at homosexuality, black people, large families, Asians, ethnics, religion, or politicians. Even mothers-in-law were offended. The result? Penis jokes, toilet jokes, anatomy in general and the overdone four letter F word. Maurie Fields worried that the human race would eventually lose its sense of humour altogether.

The difficult art of comedy

There's a real art to joke telling. How many times have we heard someone say with great enthusiasm, 'I heard a funny joke the other day, wish I could remember it'. Then there are those who begin to relate a joke they've heard—only to falter halfway through, forgetting what it was all about but still laughing at the memory.

We are probably all familiar with the amateur joke teller who is determined to hold a listener's interest by making the joke longer and longer, believing that diversions in the telling will make the ending funnier. Usually all that is achieved is a loss of interest!

When silent movies burst open the entertainment scene, they relied heavily on visual humour—the jokes were conveyed to the audience through movement, not sound.

Subtitles were required for an occasional film frame or plot explanation, and the silent movie comedians usually wrote their own storylines, based on a good bit of comedy 'business'.

Hence, comedians who were also acrobats, dancers, jugglers, or even magicians were valuable, and novel ways of doing prat-falls were in high demand. Slapstick was the order of the day, some of it hair-raisingly dangerous, with the greatest comedy stars all doing their own stunts.

American vaudeville and its predecessor, burlesque, bred generations of versatile performers. English variety and revue also produced the popular all-round English entertainers.

This melting pot of talent influenced enthusiastic, but geographically isolated Australian humorists at the time, giving them a yardstick by which to create. Australians, however, have long since learned never to underestimate their homegrown talent, and to be proud of their individuality.

Many children learning musical instruments would probably never have predicted that their serious years of study and dedication could

eventually be presented as comedy, and even relied on by world-famous comedians.

When the world wasn't in such a hurry, before the electronic media played such a large part in our lives, people in general were more inclined to appreciate the advantages of entertaining by playing a musical instrument. Celebrated comedy stars used their serious musical abilities to great advantage. The famous Jack Benny, when doing a stage performance, relied heavily on his ability to play the violin. He used his own pre-recorded voice while he played the violin very seriously, and the laughs came thick and fast as the audience heard his private thoughts.

Another versatile American funny man, well known to Australians who remember the vaudeville era, was Wil Mahoney. His clever knockabout ability was used to the hilt in sketches like 'The Ice Man Cometh', in which he slid all over the stage on blocks of ice; and his boxing sketch, in which his small frame dodged and weaved around a huge opponent like an infuriating mosquito. The highlights of all his performances, however, involved the playing of a very large xylophone—but not in an ordinary way. Will danced with the musical hammers attached to the front of his shoes and made fantastic music by dancing on top of the instrument.

English comedians were often also talented musicians. George Formby, for example, was renowned for his banjo playing, Dudley Moore was a great piano player and Reg Varney featured music in his stage act, particularly the playing of the piano accordion. Victor Borge, from Denmark, remained an international favourite by centring almost all of his wonderful comedy routines around a legitimate activity that was no doubt his original goal in life: to be a great concert pianist. Of course, he was hailed as the world's funniest piano player!

Partnerships in joke telling have surely been around since the first joke was ever told. Today's audiences are familiar with the names of past double acts such as Abbott and Costello, George Burns and Gracie Allen and Martin and Lewis, whose fame reached Australia by way of the movies. Most of their successful movies were written around comedy routines that had been polished and perfected over many years of performing in front of live audiences in hundreds of venues, including the popular vaudeville and variety theatres.

Each partner in a successful double act is responsible for a joke and getting a laugh. If a joke isn't set up properly with the key words stressed in the right place, the comedian has nothing to bounce off. That's why the 'straight man' is called a 'feed'. He 'feeds' the straight lines to the comedian. Bud Abbott of Abbott and Costello was a renowned straight man. He pulled and pushed Lou Costello into physical as well as verbal situations, and most of the time no one noticed. That's the art of concealing the art.

With the exposure of joke tellers and comedy double acts in the world of television, one performance can reach millions in a matter of minutes. The constant turnover of comedy routines can become a nightmare. New ideas, new approaches and new jokes have to be constantly created. The likes of Morcombe and Wise, Peter Cook and Dudley Moore, Hale and Pace, the Two Ronnies, and so on, all successfully transferred their live theatre experience to television.

Traditionally, the main ingredient in a women's ability to be funny is the way she is able to exploit her unique characteristics and stereotypical views of how a woman is meant to behave. The zany Phyllis Diller, who garnered the majority of her laughs at the expense of her fictitious husband, Fang, had a wardrobe that was over-the-top girlie. The wonderful Lucille Ball could fall flat on her face in a pool of mud and still remain a lady. She played the unfortunate innocent to perfection, scoring off the fact that she was a girl. Carole Burnett and Betty Hutton had the same approach—win the audience over as a nice girl, then be a victim of circumstance.

Of course, in today's climate of political correctness this may seem by some people to be selling women short; however that ability to laugh at yourself, whether male or female, is one to which Australian audiences relate and comedians regularly employ in their routines. It helps the audience to relax and enjoy the show.

Every professional knows that the audience must first of all like them, otherwise resentment replaces Srespect and the audience will never laugh.

Being a likeable person can be cultivated like a façade, a veneer. But the comedian who is regarded as a mate, a friend, sharing fun happenings is, as they say, 'home and hosed'.

Laughing at others' misfortune seems to be a universal recipe for humour and can be purely visual. Long before film and television presented spoken comedy, Charlie Chaplin's humour was largely at the expense of some unfortunate so-called villain, and often very cruel. His clever acrobatics were incorporated into many a combat which produced hysterical laughter from his audiences. They would be lulled into accepting the downfall of his opponents because his clever plots usually began with him being kind to a blind flower girl, a crying baby or a poverty-stricken family, so that his subsequent exploits seemed heroic.

Buster Keaton, another very funny silent movie star, relied heavily on his exceptional talent for acrobatics—his fans and followers could always count on lots of prat-falls and falling about. This approach to getting laughs was so successful that many comedians over the years have incorporated it into their routines.

Knockabout comedians like Laural and Hardy formed double acts, then trios such as the Ritz Brothers and the Marx Brothers arrived, all exploiting the physical aspects of this kind of slapstick humour.

This zany, pre-television era of comedy involved a fair amount of physical danger. The Three Stooges' playful approach to mishaps verged on violence. At that time slapstick comedy evolved to such an extent that silent movie casts expanded to include the combined talents of non-star comedians, stunt men and knockabout clowns. The world-famous Keystone Cops were one product of this trend.

Slapstick is still universally entertaining—people tripping, falling, or on the receiving end of something physically hurtful in 'Funniest Home Videos' programs are extremely popular. When it comes to jokes, we have all become used to finding humour in others' misfortune—it can be positively hilarious!

Comedy is very difficult. But then — anything worthwhile usually is.

Surviving

The need to eat and drink and simply survive would see Maurie working in Perth. A successful season of *Pink Champagne* saw it come to the eastern states and Maurie with it. The show was owned by Maurie Rooklyn, who was also the star. The Amazing Mr. Rooklyn now had two magician's assistants, and the added attraction of Skit and Skat, along with George Wallace, Joey Porter, Helen Lorraine, Ray McGeary, Joy Clyde and Jandy. *Pink Champagne* also had a very successful season at Melbourne's Princess Theatre.

Most of the cast went to Sydney but the two now very experienced professionals were facing a busy time in Melbourne. George Wallace was doing radio for the ABC and Skit and Skat were first cab off the rank. Old George liked to have them in his shows and of course the feeling was mutual. Of all the big time star comedians, George Wallace was the only truly funny man off stage. That included Jim Gerald, Morry Barling, Will Mahony and of course Roy Rene, 'Mo'. Norman Shephard was in charge of light entertainment at the ABC. Maurie recalls the ever-reliable pianist Bernie Duggan being in the orchestra. The hallowed halls of the ABC were not attuned to vaudevillians. In the Melbourne studios of radio 3LO during one recording session, Maurie remembers moving a microphone closer to the piano. There was a sudden silence; the attention of every orchestra member honed in on Maurie and a voice like God from above came from the control room. 'It may be acceptable in the theatre, but at the ABC, never, *never* touch a microphone.'

This was typical of a situation that Maurie Fields could curl up and die over. He couldn't bear humiliation of any kind, whether it involved himself or anyone else.

Back in the fifties, after the season with *Pink Champagne*, Max Reddy was taking shows to Tasmania. Max and his wonderfully talented wife Stella Lamond, (mother of Toni Lamond and Helen Reddy), needed versatile performers who could sing, dance, work in sketches and do everything required in a vaudeville show. Maurie and Ken were ideal and to fill the time before departing for Tasmania, Max got them a six-week season at the Plaza Northcote, Melbourne.

Maurie never did any serious searching for employment but always went with the tide and had a marvellous time along the way. Now, it was winter in Melbourne and that meant the football season. Maurie and Ken worked for Ted Rippon, an ex-Essendon footballer who had the Auburn Hotel and loved to put on shows. All the football clubs had social functions. These family get-togethers were known as 'Pleasant Sunday Mornings' and went from about 10 am until 2 pm. Along

Maurie Fields, 1960.

with party pies, sausage rolls and the like, the beer would flow. Quite often those with hangovers were having a 'hair of the dog'. Amid the celebrations or commiserations, depending on the outcome of the previous day's play, there was entertainment. All kinds of acts worked the footy clubs. Jugglers, singers, magicians, mime acts, comedians—the brighter the better. Skit and Skat had plenty of different presentations and with Max Reddy's mad love of football, he couldn't wait to get the boys on the circuit. They played at Hawthorn, Fitzroy, South Melbourne and Richmond Football Clubs. Just as well these Sunday mornings were a party atmosphere as things did not always go to plan. Mime artists would have their backing tapes break down, tap dancers would have to dance on carpet, ceilings would be too low for jugglers. Microphones were often on the blink.

The six weeks at the Plaza Northcote prior to Tasmania were busy. With their policy of fortnightly programme changes, it meant rehearsals non-stop. Maurie and Ken met up with many old mates again like Beryl Meekin and Jandy, a wonderful musical clown who would spend three hours getting made up in a dark corner by candlelight. The Trio Fayes were on the bill there, also Joff Ellen, Eddie Edwards, The Brittons, Ruby Lacey, and David Sterle the tenor, whom everyone called Spangles.

Jenny Howard and old George Wallace also played The Plaza Northcote. Everyone who was booked to work there was very professional, as an early system of production had been long set in place. Just as well, because the management was taken over by a scenic artist whose real trade was as a butcher. His name was Alf Klimeck and he came from somewhere in Europe. He was torn between showbusiness and his butcher shop. One time there was a strike at the wharves and the boats couldn't unload. George Wallace overheard Alf Klimeck getting upset and saying, 'There's 600 pounds of my meat held up on that ship'. Old George leaned over and said, 'And that's not counting the fat.'

The Tasmanian tour went from all points north and south to all points east and west. Not many shows went to Tasmania. Max Reddy's standards were high, so he had Tassy all to himself and always 'did good biz'. 'Get Out Those Old Records' was a show stopping duet for Stella Lamond and Maurie Fields. Max's idol was comedian Jim Gerald and his work was adapted to that style. The character 'Bladebone Brady', that Maurie would later make famous, was inspired by George Wallace and his style of comedy.

❧ *'Always perfect timing.'*

171

How can I get into showbusiness?

1955. Back in Sydney the experienced reliables were still holding shows together. These were talented comperes who had a strong act like the under-rated Frankie Davidson, Bill Brady, Ray McGeary, Tim McNamara and many others.

Skit and Skat were again on the nightclub merry-go-round and were booked to play the RSL Club at Woollongong. The agent Ted James told Maurie that the prestigious touring show Sorlies Revue would also be playing Woollongong at that time, and he'd arranged for the boys to audition. When it was explained to Sorlies' boss, Bobby Le Brun, that a band rehearsal wasn't necessary because they were musically self-contained, he decided to slip them into the second half after their RSL gig and that way get an audience reaction. It was a curious situation for the regular cast when two men burst in back stage dressed in their outrageous check suits and black make-up. They did their act in the show then rushed away, back to the RSL, with no one knowing who they were or what they really looked like. The regular Sorlies cast were top professionals, drawn from the Tivoli Theatres and other vaudeville circuits. Versatility in all things was their strength. The producer, Bobby Le Brun, was the star comedian who only worked with strong character acts and experienced feeds. The choreographer had to incorporate the featured acts into the production, relying on everyone's varied talents. When the producer and the choreographer got together that night, on stage after the show, he asked for an opinion on Skit and Skat, the act that had auditioned. 'Their music is great, their jokes are lousy, but that can be fixed. I think they would be very useful in the show.' Bobby Le Brun agreed and booked the act, and they stayed with Sorlies for six years. The choreographer was Val Jellay.

Sorlies Revue toured the eastern coast of Australia for ten months of the year. From Albury-Wodonga in Victoria, through Sydney, Newcastle, Maitland, Scone, Muswellbrook, Armidale, Tenterfield, Inverell and across the border to Warwick, Moree, Ipswich, Dubbo, Gympie, Maryborough, Bundaberg, Gladstone, Apple Tree Creek, Homehill, Ayr, Townsville, Ingham, Gin Gin, Innsifail, Cairns, Coonabarabran, Mossman, Mareeba, Atherton, Stanthorpe and Goondiwindi, then back on the southern run to Bathurst, Hardin, Wellington, Orange, Parkes, Forbes, Cowra, Narrandera, Leeton, Griffith, Mildura, Broken Hill, Cootamundra, Junee, Temora, Wagga, and Mudgee. The river run came after Newcastle and Maitland and went to Kempsey, Grafton, Lismore,

With Daryl Somers on 'Hey Hey It's Saturday', in May 1992, being quizzed on longevity in marriage.

174

Murwillimbah, and so on, and so on.

Every town had their dedicated followers of Sorlies Revue. Families would cook and bake for days in preparation, making the cast welcome with stacks of food, and along with the big black teapot brewing on the fuel stoves, the ice cold beer would be flowing. Everyone mingled—business people and labourers alike. Even the local constabulary would join in the after-hours drinking in family-run pubs. Actors need to unwind after a show, and the country folk loved playing host. A piano was part of the furniture in those days, and whether it was a golf club, bowling club, (before poker machines in Queensland), a private home or a hotel, Maurie would eventually end up on the piano, surrounded by encouragement, just relaxing and singing blues.

The show had three short breaks a year and some of the cast would find time for their families back home, whilst others used the breaks to work in other situations. Television was in its infancy in Australia. Graham Kennedy compered *In Melbourne Tonight* and Keith Walsh compered *In Sydney Tonight*. Skit and Skat were ideal for the new medium, which literally chewed up talent. Instead of being seen by an audience of hundreds in a theatre, performers were being seen by an audience of millions at one time. This made material valuable, with everyone digging deep for ideas that were used in

an instant, and couldn't be re-used. When Skit and Skat appeared on *In Sydney Tonight* with Keith Walsh, the supposedly highly skilled television make-up artist became very indignant when they refused to let her apply their black-face make-up. Suddenly everyone was an expert. But not at everything.

Brisbane's Theatre Royal, starring George Wallace Junior, was a favourite with the public and performers. In fact Maurie worked there on three separate occasions. One break from Sorlies coincided with Brisbane's Agricultural Show, complete with side shows, rides, boxing tents and all the paraphernalia that went with showgrounds in the fifties. Theatre Royal's policy at that time was a programme change weekly, which meant working day and night at a frantic pace. The son of George Wallace Senior was also a very funny man. He could recycle and make topical any tried and true comedy situation over and over. He had a great brain for writing as well as being fun to work with. He was always in a hurry and wouldn't cream or wash off after the show; just a quick wipe with anything that was handy on his way out. Eddie Edwards, the great heavyweight straight man, was young George's rock, and with Clyde Collins in charge of music, combined with the ever-energetic Doris Whimp, the team worked like clockwork. Thursdays they didn't rehearse but instead did a radio show live from the theatre. It was aimed at housewives, with prizes and competitions. Give-aways were earned by owning up to personal questions like who had the most children, or who was the oldest lady in the audience! Maurie was entertaining on one Thursday, when Eddie Edwards issued an unusual command. 'Stand up the lady with the largest reticule.' He was relieved when a lady ran down the aisle waving an oversized handbag.

During the particular season that coincided with Brisbane's Agricultural Show, Maurie went along with Ken's scheme to earn extra money by doing a quick easy stint on the showgrounds. Didn't sound too difficult. Lloyd Nairn the juggler warned the boys that the life was tough and showground bosses tougher. He told them how he had to ask Arthur Greehalgh for his pay, and was told to ask Mr Jackson (his partner) for it—who in turn told Lloyd to ask Arthur Greenhalgh. The two partners were inclined to avoid parting with money. Maurie and Ken worked for Ma Short who paid them regularly, and even gave them somewhere to sleep. It was in a tent on two stretchers next to the Hall of Mirrors. The three-legged rooster slept next door chained to one of the mirrors.

The boys would do twenty shows a day, up on the board outside as well as inside. They always wore the thick wool check suits complete with full black make-up, and even their hands had to always be made-up. Gloves wouldn't have done because of their instruments. The weather was oppressively hot and after a hard day at the grounds they would work nightly at the Theatre Royal, then on to a nightclub with the great Len Bernard, who had his band there at the time. Len was a very good drummer but would often get on piano and have the place jumping with great solos like the life of Jelly Roll Morton set to music. The boys would finally get home to their stretchers. No sooner would their heads hit the pillow at 4.30 am, than the three-legged rooster would start crowing at full volume. Maurie handled everything in his usual amble-along style, whilst Kenny would be meeting himself coming back. Maurie smiles when he hears young actors complaining about the hours they put in. Perhaps he remembers having more fun as well.

Every December Sorlies Revue opened at Newcastle on Boxing Day, after rehearsals in Sydney at a first floor rehearsal room in Goulburn Street. A pantomime was presented twice daily with the revue at night. It was hard work. Three fully prepared productions were polished in Newcastle before the coming year on the road. If a season anywhere was for less than a week, the most practical features would be plucked from the repertoire whilst the

bigger elements involving special effects, cumbersome wardrobe, props and scenery would travel on to the next big date. Shows performed as one-nighters or two-nighters were called short packs. No less entertaining, just more practical for venues with smaller facilities. Usually it was a local town hall, sometimes known as The Mechanics Institute, or the local picture theatre-cum-dance hall. The Sorlies cast would be just as large, necessitating mixed dressing rooms, if any. Power was always a problem. The locals would presume that power was only required just prior to eight o'clock when the show started. This was before synthetic materials, and it took two ladies many hours ironing and hanging out costumes from the big travelling wardrobe baskets known as skips. Consideration for others was imperative. No setting up personal props in limited space, or hogging the best position for light, or commanding a solitary mirror. One way to

spot a performer who has had a touring theatre background is when they stand aside for someone else who wants to look in a mirror.

Every Saturday the pantomime was presented at 10.30 am, and at 2 pm. If it was school holiday time the pantomime appeared twice daily, every day. Each year it was a new production. The favourites with the youngsters back then were *Cinderella, Jack and The Beanstalk, Aladdin, Red Riding Hood, Mother Goose* and *Dick Whittington*.

The nightly revue had three productions. If playing a town for one week, the programme would be changed every second night. The majority of the audience attended each programme. It was the personal touch that made the years full of happy memories.

Apart from their acts, everyone was required to work throughout the show— running order permitting. Maurie was no exception. It was not only a great learning

Willy Lowman in 'Death of a Salesman'.

process, it meant being able to polish a performance. Television doesn't allow for getting it better the next time. If you haven't already learned the finer points of acting, TV directors don't have the time to teach them.

Maurie's natural aptitude was invaluable to Sorlies Revue. A good straight man is essential to sketch comedians, and observing some of the past greats like Len Rich, Les Ritchie, Buddy Morley, Mike Connors and Eddie Edwards had already left an impression on Maurie, but none more than Bobby Le Brun's team of Neil O'Brien and Stevie Doo. Maurie's shyness evaporated when he was on stage. He gave everything his best shot. He tap danced; played on a drum kit made of kitchen props that filled the stage, finally exploding; he sang tenor, baritone, soprano; he strutted with canes and straw deckers. He wore wigs, beards and an array of female drag; he soft-shoed and sand-danced; got doused with soda syphons and balloons of flour. He was the pantomime's Demon King, Baron Hardup, and King Bat. The young man who could have been hiding his shyness under black face make-up became a great comedy feed, and straight man. An all-round song and dance man and a master of timing. Off stage he remained quiet and unassuming as though everything he was asked to do was effortless. When he did talk, it was never meaningless and always jovial.

Maurie warmed to a memory. 'I had been with Sorlies for over a year, knew everyone pretty well, when I noticed this sheila staring at me while I played and sang at the get-togethers. Sometimes she'd just stare at my hands. If I caught her eye she'd look away. I knew her as well as anyone else in the show, but something began to seem different. It wasn't like I could go up to her and say, "What are you lookin' at?" Then I found myself doing the same thing. Each time she was on stage and I wasn't, I'd be side-stage watching her, just watching her do things that I'd seen her do dozens of times before. I started to think I was imagining things, but as the days and weeks went by I'd be playing someone's piano somewhere, with the usual mob of mates and drinkers egging me on, and I'd feel her eyes dragging me like a magnet. In the end I was singing just for her, and I knew she knew it. This was a girl I'd been working with for over a year, a friend. One day I got up enough courage to ask her to the movies. It was in Albury and the movie was the Hitchcock thriller, *The Man Who Knew Too Much*, starring James Stewart. It also starred Doris Day who sang 'Que Sera Sera, Whatever Will Be, Will Be'. Ever so slowly in the dark picture theatre our hands touched, and they were warm, even though I remember it was winter. From then on we began to realise we just liked to be together. She laughed a lot and brought out the big kid in me. Then later we also began to love a lot. It

was the slowest process. We had come from different backgrounds. Her entire life had been theatre, she could do everything, and I thought of her as "Ziegfeld". For three years we continued working together, while the courtship deepened. But in the end, Val Jellay became Mrs Maurie Fields.'

With the many weird and wonderful things happening throughout those years on the road, it's understandable that Maurie Fields was hard to surprise. He had known tough people, worked with the good, the bad and the temperamental, and was very hard to faze.

Ken Bowtell, AKA Al Kenny, married twice. He preferred the stationary life in Sydney. So during Sorlies' breaks, he teamed up with another good performer and called the act 'Big Red and Bojangles'. The lively act was a success on Sydney's club circuit where Ken worked until his untimely death. Alcohol combined with drugs were taking their toll,

but even so, his passing happened just as he would have (if he could have) planned it. He died of heart failure during intercourse with an unknown woman one Christmas Eve.

Travelling shows were beginning to disappear. No longer touring the country were Barton's Follies, Ashton's Circus, Coles' Varieties, The Great Levante, Max Reddy's Follies, or Wirth's Circus. Sorlies Revue was the last survivor.

At one time they were all playing side by side in the same cities and towns, doing capacity business on the showtime circuit, which had taken them all to every part of Australia. The new medium, television, would affect the Tivoli circuit and musical comedy houses. Even picture theatres folded, with only the input of millions of dollars saving some movie distributors. Cinemascope, Sensaround, and even movies in 3D all contributed to an eventual resurgence of bigger and better movies, but television would still remain the enemy.

❧ *'Make 'em laugh!'*

Surviving in television

Television, the new medium, caused much excitement. For many the change was too radical. Radio actors could no longer read from scripts. This was a visual form of entertainment—dialogue had to be learned and actors had to look the part. Drama therefore took a little longer adapting. Lots of radio personalities took to television like ducks to water. Graham Kennedy, Bert Newton and Bill Collins (the race caller), all became stars. It took courage and daring. Youth played a big part—it has no fear, and back then they were very young and of course, very talented. Roy Rene had created a successful radio character called Mo McCacky which didn't transfer. Neither did Jack Davey or the marvellous George Wallace. For some, TV came too late.

Comedy was heavily leaned on. Mistakes didn't matter, it made things funnier, therefore the variety shows were easier to present than drama. Jugglers, acrobats and magicians were good value, their acts having been polished and presented on stages for years. They also had band parts for the musicians, and only needed a camera rehearsal. Many circus acts were denied TV exposure. Studio lighting is ninety per cent from above and although some banks of lights and special effects come from floor level and surrounds, overhead lighting is massive. The performers who needed height, such as trapeze artists, high wire jugglers and the like, were very restricted. One big stage setting can be changed behind a set of tabs. Most television sets were permanent, with one host set, one music area and one comedy area, with cameras swinging from one to the other. Stage performers whose lives had been spent using a full stage had to condense, not only in area but in performance. What worked on stage didn't necessarily work in someone's lounge room.

Double acts, like Maurie and Val, along with many others, had a repertoire of material that had to be re-thought. Instead of acrobating from one side of a stage to the other while Maurie played a drum kit in the centre, the acrobating circled the drumming so that cameras could angle their shots. If an entrance had been made from either side of a stage, they now came on together from one side only. These were minor problems. Everyone had them—it was a pioneering time, a learning process in all departments. It surprised Maurie that the public was interested in his opinions and his private life. An often asked question was, 'Do you prefer film, theatre or television?' It's like asking do you prefer bread or milk. Each is very different. The craft and the techniques are not the same and the rewards are not the same. But for an extended life as an entertainer, the biggest plus is of course ... stagecraft.

In 1957 everyone was buying a TV set. Some resisted, but not for long. Variety shows were literally being churned out, with everyone's brains being picked. Channel Seven had *Hold Everything*,

◄ *Maurie with Honest John Gilbert, 'Sunnyside Up', 1957–1964.*

where three audience members stood on pedestals and were loaded up with anything from crockery to cabbages. They got to keep what they didn't drop. *Club Seven* was done in a nightclub setting, complete with commissionaire Roy Lyons on a prop footpath opening the big double doors for the camera. Frank Wilson was one of its comperes.

The youngsters were well catered for with *Brian and The Juniors*, hosted by Brian Naylor, (Pattie McGrath-Newton was one of its stars), and *The Happy Club,* hosted by Lovely Ann and Funnyface (Vic) Gordon.

Channel Nine's King Corky, Geoff Corke, was their children's presenter. Although Norman Swain attempted an inroad from his success in radio, he was foiled the first day when Uncle Norman made his entrance down a slide and promptly broke his leg.

The kids' favourite was the delectable Princess Panda, complete with diamante crown. She had a naturally effervescent personality that had been cultivated and encouraged by the uniquely wonderful Graham Kennedy. If barrel girl is still a respectable title, then she was it. She married the trumpet player Jimmy Allen and they left to live in Las Vegas.

In Melbourne Tonight was Channel Nine's flagship for many years. Channel Seven's *Sunnyside Up* held its 7.30 Friday night time slot for seven years with its permanent cast,

including Maurie and Val. Many things of personal importance happened during the long run of *Sunnyside Up*. There were deaths, marriages and a couple of births. Helen Lorraine added a baby to her family. And with his mother working through seven months of her pregnancy, young Martin Fields arrived at 7.30 am on Monday morning, December 18th, 1961. It was considerate of him to arrive at Christmas time when all television shows were in recess.

When *Sunnyside Up* returned to air in 1962, still on Fridays, so did Fields' parents. Baby Martin stayed with his maternal grandparents every Friday night until school age. From day one he saw his mum and dad on television. Throughout an education at Victoria's Brighton Grammar School, and twelve years piano study at the Conservatorium of Music, he too performed in TV dramas and live concerts. Young Martin's birth was an unexpected miracle. His mother had until then believed she was unable to have children. The youngster became the centre of their lives, their reason for achieving. In the nineties, his workload would become as busy and diversified as his mum and dad's.

Quiz shows were popular and inexpensive. Prizes were donated by sponsors, and by copying overseas successes, little was left to risk. There was *Coles Quiz*, *It's Academic*, and *Pick a Box*. Other forms of sit-down-in-one-

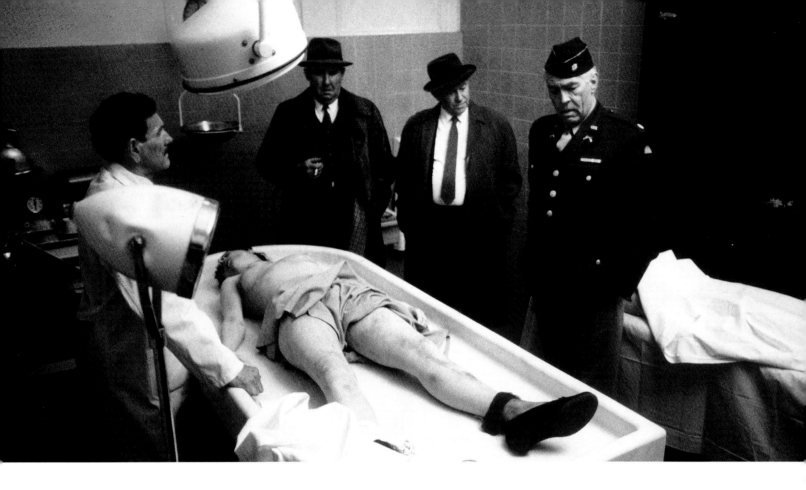

setters were *Beauty and the Beast*, *Celebrity Squares*, *Raising a Husband*, and *Name that Tune*.

Tommy Hanlon's *It Could Be You* and Larry Nixon compering *Lady For A Day* were huge daytime successes aimed at the local housewife.

Lots of shows came and went, but of all the live shows over the years, television's only survivor must be the eternal sporting panel. It could only happen in Australia.

In the beginning actors shunned working in commercials, believing it would affect their credibility. That attitude would eventually change when financially a commercial became irresistible. It was something that American actors had long revelled in. Many of the Americans were able to live in retired luxury from residuals received for promoting just one product. If that arrangement were paralleled in Australia, Maurie Fields for one could have retired many times over. The difference was the bigger population in America, and therefore bigger revenues.

While all the live-to-air shows were ironing out procedures, the big guns from radio's drama days were waiting in the wings. Crawford Productions were about to burst upon everyone's television screens with successes that had been planned and plotted to the 'enth degree. Glory days for actors were about to arrive. It wasn't a time for teenage stars and inexperience. Although some would grow up in the business, they didn't begin at the top. Not with the likes of Hector Crawford and his sister Dorothy at the helm.

Reg Grundy provided Australians with employment that was also prestigious. The Crawfords' stable was given a kick-start with the outstanding success of *Homicide*. Not only were the on-camera personnel being given opportunities, technicians with basic crash courses were being trained to a higher level, and none were more grateful than some of the sound recordists and cameramen who went on to be directors. In the nineties, some would bask in Hollywood fame.

❧ *The 1985 Leonski film 'Death of a Soldier' with James Coburn and Bill Hunter. Maurie received an AFI award for his role as Australian Police Chief.*

Homicide ran for many years, with the same actors returning many times as different characters. Maurie somehow managed to inevitably be cast as a heavy. He murdered so many people he lost count. He shot them, drowned, stabbed and strangled them. He remembers one time in someone's backyard when he was supposed to smash the top of a bottle and cut a bloke's throat. When the fake blood spurted out, the director said it looked too gruesome. So instead, he smashed the bloke's skull in with a house brick. Charming! At one time Crawfords' cast him as a plain clothes detective, and he was offered the part as a regular cast member, but he had already committed himself to a stage play. Don Barker, an Adelaide actor, stepped in and stayed with Homicide for years, and his portrayal was spot on.

It's probably the best compliment to have comedy make the strongest impression on the public, when every actor knows it is the most difficult. Granted *Sunnyside Up* left its mark as a great comedy vehicle for Maurie, but that came from experience in vaudeville and went to air in the fifties.

Maurie's contribution to the Australian Film and Television industry expanded from comic roles to straight characters—often with a nasty side. For ten years at the ABC he played the conniving John Quinney,

stock and station agent, in *Bellbird*, whilst being a tyrant in *The Box*. Around the same time he was a priest in *The Sullivans*, and in *Tandarra* he was a gun-happy ranch owner. In *Evil Angels* he sentenced Meryl Streep. There were leading character parts in *Taurus Rising*, *A Town Like Alice*, *Mr Doubleday*, and *The Banana Bender*. He was always the villain when guesting in *Cop Shop*, *Solo One* and *Division Four*. He played a sadistic warder for some time in *Prisoner*, breaking girls' fingers and committing rape. And still, not a day passed by without someone saying to him, 'Tell us a joke, Maurie'. He really should have burst into some Shakespeare that he did for the Melbourne Theatre Company. Surely they don't remember the great comedy work in *Last of the Australians*, or *Bobby Dazzler*, or the plays *Goodbye Ted*, *The Next Greatest Pleasure*, or *The Club* for the MTC, or the two year city run of *Dimboola*. Borderline comedy could be said of his portrayals in *Break of Day*, *Country Life* and *The Flying Doctors*. Even the sad old Syd in *Neighbours* was lovable.

Skyways could have been one of the most difficult series, especially from a director's viewpoint. The location scenes were filmed at Tullamarine Airport in Melbourne. The general public and their travel plans were not to be disrupted—very difficult for filming. Especially so as the cast, dressed as pilots, flight attendants or passengers, mingled perfectly with reality. Maurie's regular role in

Skyways was as the head porter named 'Chaz Potter', a lazy employee. His nickname was 'The Judge' because he was always sitting on a case.

All entertainment has its hiccups during the creative period, but none more than the making of a film. The expected hitches are those brought about by weather, availability of key people and a dozen other familiar hold ups. *The Leonski Story*, about the murder of young Melbourne women by an American serviceman during World War II, was written by Bill Nagle whose earlier screenplay, *The Odd Angry Shot* had received considerable acclaim. In America the files containing detailed facts on the murders were no longer secret, enabling Bill Nagle access and confirmation of details. His many trips to America involved the making and importing of authentic uniforms, flags, decorative medals and weapons. Everything was detailed, even to the uniform of General

MacArthur whose involvement in the case was considerable. The writing of that involvement was a delicate issue, as the Americans were still very sensitive about their heroes.

Maurie's AFI recognition for this sinister performance as Australian Police Chief was pleasing because of its dramatic content, even though lines like, 'get off your f...ing arses' left his family feeling a little uneasy.

Everyone involved with the making of 'Leonski', especially cast members, received an influx of mail and phone calls from every Joe Blow in the country, all giving their versions of the killings and what happened at the time. Everyone was an authority on the subject, and knew Leonski or one of his victims personally.

The city streets of Melbourne had never before been filmed on such a scale; a big screen movie with American stars. The print media was swamped with photo spreads, knowing that a large percentage of their readers had been touched by the subject.

Scene from the ABC 'Love Story' series titled 'Best of Mates'.

An actor's life requires stamina, and the mental strength to cultivate a facade when coping with the elements. When the end product is put together for TV and film viewing, nobody is interested in whether the actors are feeling hot or cold, if a family member died that morning, or if they are coping with earache, toothache or bites from sand flies or disturbed bees. During the eight years of filming *The Flying Doctors*, the regular cast learned to cope with many things. Grin and bear it. Whether it actually was summer or the depth of winter, the show had to have a 'hot' feel. The 'real' flying doctors tend to those requiring medical attention in the outback, and provide a service unique to Australia. The TV series achieved the outback feel but at times the cast and crew deserved a medal. Although the crew spent more time on the set than the actors, they could wear shorts and singlets in summer and layers of thermal clothes in

winter, with hoods and thick boots. Mud was always a problem, and you could bet that if scripts involved drownings, storms or boating accidents they would always be scheduled for a winter shoot. The directors would call out just before a take, 'Think hot! Think hot!' The chewed ice would be spat out, (ice prevents the breathing out of steam when talking), wardrobe people would run around grabbing coats and gloves at the last second, and make-up artists would spray cold water on faces to look like perspiration.

Is it any wonder actors are often mistakenly labelled, accused of being insincere or social frauds. The facade becomes ingrained. It's an actor's tool when beneath the surface is vulnerability, nervous anxiety, extreme sensitivity and an acute awareness of moods.

Brendan Maher directed a very funny movie about breaking into showbusiness and the humiliating experiences of bit players and extras. It starred Chris Haywood. Maurie played a professional 'extra'. It was entitled *The Bit Part*. The location, Maurie recalled,

❧ *Maurie with Val, Marty and the family pet Jade 1982.*

❧ *Fields Senior and Junior sharing their love of music and entertainment.*

'Was right in the Werribee sewage farm, and the stench was vile. After a couple of hours we sorta got used to the shocking smell, but when lunch was called the blowflies decided on a change of diet, us. Appetites were gone. The caterers tried their best, but their spread, which included fried sausages, had been set up alongside an open sewage drain. The "Richard the Thirds" were floating along on the surface. Amazing how they always float! *The Bit Part* company spent a lot of their lunch breaks heaving.'

Actors are not only forced to endure the elements, but often must confront the difficulties and complexities associated with working with animals. Maurie recalled, 'I can't remember how many times producers and directors have cast a dog to be with me. Even without talking to it or even patting it. They must reckon I look like a dog person. Most times it's been a blue heeler. I'm rapt in dogs and always make friends with 'em, it must be the old bushy in me. I reckon they went too far when I was cast with Googie Withers, Sam Neill and Greta Scachi in *Country Life*. I was the yardman in the story, a sort of boots who lived at the back of an old mansion, where the horses, chooks, and dogs were housed. When the character gets drunk on the squire's prized bottles of red, the director wanted to have me seen passed out and snoring in amongst the dog kennels, with all the dogs licking me face. It was a

night shoot, cold of course. The dogs looked scruffy because they had to be working dogs, not house pets. To get them to lick my face they smeared mutton fat all over me. Face, neck, arms—I was covered in the stuff. They wanted me to lay perfectly still, with me mouth open, snoring. The mongrel dogs were more than keen on what they had to do. But for me, it took about five takes. The crew loved it—bastards.

'The same location called for Googie Withers to throw a full bucket of water over me. It had to be done in a wide shot first. There were plenty of duplicate wardrobe changes for the many takes. For a stronger impact an assistant director threw the buckets of water over me in the close-ups. It too was a night shoot, in the middle of winter, and the hours of changing in and out of soaking clothes is something I'll never forget. That water was bloody freezing.'

❧ *Next page: Father and son with Wilbur and Red on 'Hey Hey It's Saturday'.*

Microphones

Being familiar with a sound system can give a performer a certain sense of security. For example, when doing a season as a cast member of a musical comedy in a purposely built theatre, the procedure is as follows.

After make-up, wardrobe and hair is in place, a sound engineer visits each artist with his tray of body-mikes and their attached battery packs, which are about the size of a pack of cards; after the cast hear the half hour call, there comes the fifteen minute call, and that's about the time the all important sound person arrives. Each cast member has their own microphone. Most are coloured black, like a tiny piece of licorice. If the wearer is blonde, a pink coloured mike is used. It is usually anchored into the wearer's hair with an appropriately coloured hairclip. Sometimes the mike is secreted in the costume or even a prop. (Did you see *Singing in the Rain*, where a vase of flowers was the focus! Hilarious.) However, the attached lead usually winds down through the back of the hair, down to its destination, and then the back pack gets tucked into either a pocket or a belt, preferably hidden. Mine was always pushed into the top and back of my panty hose. Some ladies tuck them into the back elastic of their bras. Males seem to have more secretive choices. Hmm! In any case it's always wise to visit the toilet prior to this last minute body invasion.

Everyone must go to the prompt corner for a mike check before the show begins. Nothing is left to chance. A million dollar production can be sabotaged by a sound failure. Audiences are now attuned to perfect sound reception and are rightly unforgiving if it's otherwise.

A second check involves speaking a few words, or singing a note or two, while standing beside a seated engineer who listens through headphones as he presses your microphone number on his console. He, or she, will nod or give the thumbs up that all is well. Then it's back to the dressing room, give the mirrors a good work out, let the nerves do what they will; it's adrenalin time. The overture begins, the murmur of the audience subsides, and the terror takes over. Chookas everybody—break a leg. It's time for all those other useless metaphors.

Once upon a time, one microphone on a stand was a luxury. At the famous Tivoli theatre, there was also one on either side of the stage—prompt side, and the o.p. side (opposite prompt). The stage manager in his prompt corner, controlled the mikes' up and down movement by manually handling the pullies. When the mikes went down, a little lid popped over them like a trap door and all was hidden. I loved those microphones; it gave one a sense of power to walk down stage and be greeted by a microphone coming up from its hiding place, almost like welcoming applause before you did anything.

The body mike became a popular choice, not only by artistic folk, but by anybody who needed to command attention, from politicians to real estate agents. Stand up comedians came to use them like a powerful weapon.

Heckle me all you like, I'm the one with the microphone, I will always win.

Is that your nose, or are you eating a banana!

It's not only the walls in here that are plastered!

If I need your help I'll rattle your cage!

It's wise, when using a stand mike or one that is attached to a lectern, to check its height before a performance, but never if there are any audience members present, in which case ask someone else to adjust the height on your behalf. Many a singer has unwittingly lost most of their individual personality by appearing to swallow a microphone. Ignore it, it doesn't need to cover your face. Chin high should be the maximum. My personal comfort zone is chest height, and leave the volume control to the sound man, the professional. If being incognito is the goal, wear sunglasses and keep the microphone covering the mouth. Many performers feel incomplete unless they are holding a microphone; others feel restricted and prefer to have their hands free for movement and expression. It was probably Madonna who initiated the wrap around mike—the one that appears to be holding the jaw in place like a surgical appliance.

No matter what choice is made, for whatever situation, a microphone is an undoubted necessity. The microphone, when thoroughly understood, is definitely among the artist's tools of trade.

Gimmee that old soft shoe

For those who began their showbusiness life as stage performers, the theatre will always remain a magnet. There is nothing like the feeling of knowing you are responsible for manipulating an audience. So many people at one time, applauding you, crying with you, laughing with you. And the times when the silence is deafening as you alone control their emotions.

Back in the late fifties during the years of television's *Sunnyside Up*, Maurie also had a night time cabaret act and played drums in a band.

Whilst playing the role of John Quinney in *Bellbird* for the ABC, those ten years were also loaded with parts in Crawford produced dramas, Grundy's panel shows, and the constant demands of cabaret, concerts, and various outdoor celebrations.

The successful two year run of the stage play *Dimboola* overlapped the daytime work on the sitcom *Last of the Australians*. Another tight schedule involved the role of Willie Loman in *Death of A Salesman*, whilst also working on the Johnny Farnham series *Bobby Dazzler*. Maurie was slow to acknowledge the fact that the sitcom parts were written exclusively for him by the late Terry Stapleton.

When the Steele Rudd yarns from *On Our Selection* were recorded as a four-sided cassette package with Maurie doing all the voices, it became, and remains a best seller—still available in ABC Shops. The voice of Wally Walpamur the chimpanzee in the paint commercials was then recorded. The movie *Eliza Frazer* starring Susannah York was also filmed at that time with Maurie playing a journalist. The interiors were filmed in the artistic Montsalvat buildings at Eltham.

Producer Frank Ward, with Joe Latona, found a huge audience with their presentations of favourite musical comedies. Under the ABC's banner, Val and Maurie recreated roles in *Kiss Me Kate*, *The Music Man*, *The Pyjama Game* and Maurie's favourite, *Guys and Dolls*. In amongst those productions were specials with Simon Gallagher, Debbie Byrne, Karen Knowles and a Christmas spectacular with Rolf Harris.

Three successful jazz albums were recorded.

'The Great Aussie Joke' segments on *Hey, Hey It's Saturday* were recorded during the eight years of filming *The Flying Doctors*. At least those two shows were done in the same building for Channel Nine, sometimes leaving on the same make-up.

It was in the seventies when Melbourne's first music hall theatre restaurant was augmented with the inclusion of Maurie Fields. The two stars of musical comedy, Tikki Taylor and John Newman had

Tikki and John's, 1979.

been taking Melbourne by storm with *Tikki and John's*. Over the years their original lavish productions have entertained millions.

Both Maurie and I would remember the Tikki and John years as the most enjoyable time of our professional lives. The working relationship lasted more than ten years; the friendship has lasted a lifetime. Some regular television roles were also fulfilled during this period, such as *Prisoner*, as well as doing

variety acts on Mike Walsh's midday show and later with Ray Martin at the helm. Day and night, year in year out the Fields' coasted along, working hard and loving it.

Maurie was not a small man. He was tall and very straight with a natural presence. It's not something that can be learned. It is probably best summed up by saying he didn't melt into a crowd. The old showbiz saying 'don't work with animals or babies', of

'Tribute to Vaudeville', Concert Hall at The Arts Centre, Melbourne.

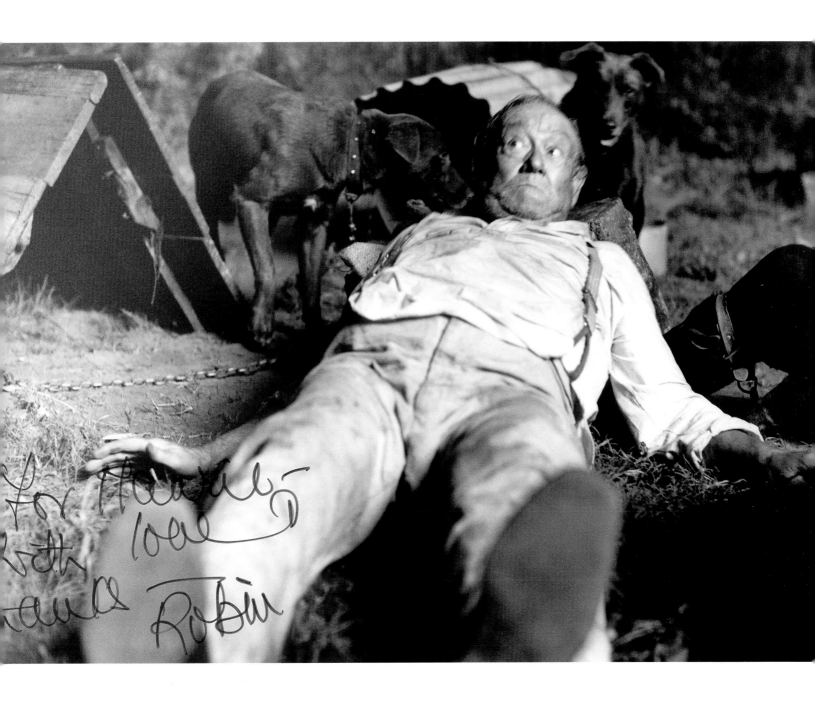

course means that they will naturally upstage you and command attention. After filming was completed on the successful mini series *The Dunnera Boys*, Bob Hoskins declared to the press—'Don't work with animals, babies or Maurie Fields.' It was a nice compliment.

During the many years working at Tikki and John's, Maurie and I were able to draw from our vaudeville backgrounds and put together many different double acts. The

harmony songs, comedy sketches, tap dancing, and smooth soft-shoe routines continue to be asked for. Perhaps an actor's life, as well as a show, does go full circle, and everything old is new again, and again, and again.

🌿 *Being woken by licking dogs in the movie 'Country Life'.*

🍂 *Next page: Aunt Aggie, the movie 'Dimboola'.*

Tips & dirty tricks

'Be on time, know your lines and don't bump into the furniture.' It's an old saying. It's what Maurie said when asked for some tips on acting. But what he would really have liked to have said was, 'Get twenty years of ongoing experience in dancing, singing, acting, music, enunciation, voice production and especially projection. Learn when and how to use props, how to listen, how to sit, eat, walk. And then say to yourself, "I know nothing". Only then will you be ready to receive advice. No matter how experienced, the learning never, ever ends.'

Being 'on time' is a courtesy; it's good manners and should apply to every walk of life. 'Know your lines' should apply to educators, to politicians, to boy scouts and elders of the church, not only to actors. Bumping into furniture is usually a cameraman's headache—they have trouble with mobile cameras colliding with anything that's near, because of tight squeezes in small sets.

Most actors don't play dirty tricks on others, but it does happen. Some unfortunates feel a necessity for one-up-manship, forgetting that the best result for everyone is a team effort. Maurie had seen others receive low blows and couldn't understand that kind of thinking. With an early education as a straight man to comedians, the instinct is to set up the next person's line or move, that's why they are called straight men. It's an unselfish approach and it makes things work.

Getting Maurie to talk about dirty tricks wasn't easy. He preferred to remember the good in people, but for the record he obliged. 'In TV I learned long ago not to give everything away at rehearsals. Save that little extra for the take. One actor I remember had a bad habit of copying little bits of business at rehearsals. Business like putting spoonful after spoonful in the teacup and not looking at it while doing dialogue at the same time. At the second rehearsal the said actor got in first with the same business, so I had to think of something else. Another unkind trick is to do something distracting behind the actor who has an important speech. Like straightening a picture frame, or even searching for a pen or hanky. The tricks of distracting are usually done only when the camera rolls, and a busy director may have to let it through.'

'Putting an unrehearsed look or move in on a take can throw the less experienced. I remember in *Division 4*, walking along a street doing two handed dialogue in a wide shot, and when it was my turn to talk I got a sudden elbow jolt just below my ribs. The move wasn't seen because of the camera's distance, but the sound recordist heard an unusual "ugh" at the start of my first word, and the rest of my line was weakened. A low blow.'

'Another two-handed scene comes to mind. I remember watching two ladies do a scene on *The Sullivans*, where the first one enters and announces the second lady's unexpected arrival. She had

❧ Multi-talented Maurie.

to say, "Guess who's just arrived", and in would come the second lady. But the first lady was eliminated from the scene totally when the second lady firmly suggested that the scene open with a close-up of her head coming through the door saying, "Guess who!" No further discussion was entered into.'

'Another time one actor had to pour a drink from a drink table by walking downstage. The pouring and drinking was therefore done facing away from the other person, seated upstage. The rehearsal was halted when the seated actor insisted that the dialogue be done facing upstage towards the one seated. This of course meant the non-seated actor's back would be facing the audience. That particular director said a definite "no" to that idea, but only after a time-consuming discussion. That was in a stage play.'

'Two people talking and walking through a doorway at the same time means one of them must speed up the move so that the other person is into the set in time for his or her dialogue. I remember the rehearsals working fine, but "on the day" the first person small-paced the walk and blocked the second actor's entrance whose dialogue was heard, but he wasn't seen on camera.'

'There are a million dirty tricks. The victim can be demoralised, especially in an environment that has no time for recourse. Every actor has experienced getting stuck on a particular passage of dialogue. It's everyone's worst nightmare. No matter how hard you try to get it right it becomes a psychological barrier, with the rest of the cast and crew trying to be patient, which reinforces the dreaded hurdle. The wrong thoughts start interfering, like wanting to swallow, or cough, or thinking of those in the green room waiting to do the next scene.'

'One poor bloke, a fine actor, was having a lot of trouble with one line. I remember it got up to "take fifteen" before he finally mastered the thing. Everyone knew he was feeling bad and made light of it, until one of the waiting cast from the green room walked onto the set and loudly inquired, "What kept you so long? Couldn't you get it right?" Trouble was, the soul-destroying inquiry was addressed to the wrong person, who quietly winked at the worn out actor. There was a knowing silence all round.'

Eight years in *The Flying Doctors* was a wonderful time for lasting friendships. Having an appreciation of others' difficulties may be something that is not learned but observed. Technicians, wardrobe and make-up artists, set dressers, props people, television and film crews, all work very closely with actors on a day to day basis. By the very nature of their work they share many things with the actors. But one glaring

exception to this bonding was a person who delighted in pronouncing, 'I'm going to complain', at the drop of a hat. On location the caravan phone ran hot with telling of tales. In the studio the poor producer was often seen trying to escape from the tirade of tiresome complaints. There was never confrontation with an offender, just continual reporting to the top brass. One young, hard-working driver was given the sack because of a complaint about loud rock music on the car radio. It would have been easier to ask the young man if he could find another station. But then there's no power play in that.

A dance hall full of extras were given an embarrassing dressing down by an actor who took the stage for ten minutes to shout at them regarding the importance of their attention while she was acting. A quiet word to one of the director's assistants was the way to go, if at all, but again, there's no power play in that.

Another time, a phone call to head office from the caravan was a failed effort to have an entire film crew fired. A bedroom setting had been dressed to resemble a honeymoon suite. For a finishing touch two little dolls were placed on the pillows dressed in bridal gear. 'There are two dolls fornicating on the bed', was the complaint, and, 'I can't work in that environment'. But eventually she did.

Props people are often in the firing line. A job was hanging by a thread when yet again the producer tried to sort out the indignity of a troublemaker who claimed 'her' shop window was inappropriately dressed. There was another uproar when an extra in a crowd scene was spotted wearing one of her hats.

Writers have been close to tearing their hair out, trying to appease an actor endeavouring to rearrange dialogue for personal gain. Compromising usually leaves the writer at the mercy of ongoing disruption. One actor's demands tested the management's desire to please. The imported actor whose accommodation had to have a heated pool available at any time of the day or night, also insisted that a car, for personal use only, be available at all times, with an unlimited supply of taxi dockets for working hours. This began a chain of non-work related demands. Keys to the flat, the pool, the car, all got lost at different times, with carpenters knocking down the front door of the flat and breaking into the car, as well as extra pool keys having to be cut. Mechanics were sent non-stop to repair or replace car tyres, fix the air conditioning or mend the windscreen wipers. This was all very peculiar because the actor, not knowing his way around Melbourne, didn't use the car at all.

Weird and wonderful things happen in showbusiness. One day an important actress caused a panic when she demanded to see the cancer specialist who was treating the boss of the company for throat cancer. She had discovered a lump on her breast and insisted that the renowned doctor drop everything and attend to her fatal condition. The lump was diagnosed as an insect bite.

Food can become an obsession, especially when hours are spent waiting on a film set. Tea breaks and lunch breaks are looked forward to like having batteries recharged. Greed has been known to take over, like one actress who must have thought every meal was going to be her last. Grabbing toasted egg and bacon sandwiches in both hands, she would be searching for a third hand for the pocketing of apples, oranges and an array of cookies. It was suggested that the home front was being supplied at the expense of the management. There were many problems in the company car when she was driven home. Often the grease from heavily buttered steak and onion sandwiches would be running everywhere, with a big load of fruit rolling on the floor. Driving is dangerous when fruit is rolling around under the pedals. When one driver pulled over to the side of the road and attempted to tidy up, he too joined the ranks of the unemployed.

Being difficult, selfish and mean takes time. It's easier to be pleasant—like the much respected and funny actor who was filming on location for *The Flying Doctors*. The previous day's shooting was part of the next day's scenes and everything had to match.

It was winter, everyone was freezing, and because his character wore overalls nobody realised he had left his personal jacket on throughout the entire morning's filming, so everything had to be re-shot. It involved extras, other cast members, unpacking of props and all sorts of re-setting, including lights. Nobody complained, they all smiled and got on with it because everyone liked him. He was upset and concerned about causing extra work. Naming him would only bring forth his dimples.

Maurie was reticent about giving advice and tips regarding performing—it was not his style to appear knowledgeable, preferring others to decide. With a sigh he reluctantly discussed his observations.

'For a camera, don't be afraid to underplay. Concentrate on letting the eyes do the work. And if you watch ordinary people in a conversation, they don't use hand gestures. Talking with the hands detracts from the words. Folded arms is a dead giveaway. It says that the mind is thinking, "What will I do with my hands?" Pretending you don't have arms can help when rehearsing alone. The words take on real meaning. Another private exercise is to keep the head perfectly still like a statue; suddenly you discover the eyes are doing the work.'

'If an emotional scene requires a total

⚘ *Happy jazz.*

collapse into sobbing, a couple of things can ruin an otherwise good performance. Stretching the sides of the mouth with tragedy in mind can photograph as smiling. A good set of teeth exposed can look pleasant instead of sad. There is plenty the mouth can do without opening it. All the crying and hysterical acting in the world won't be convincing unless accompanied by tears. Some actors are too proud to admit they can't produce tears on cue. It's easier for everyone if the make-up artist is standing by with the eye dropper, and very professional to ask for it.'

'Trying a line different ways, to get that elusive natural delivery, can sometimes fall into place by forgetting about the setting, the fictional situation and the fellow actors. Imagine you're talking to the checkout girl in your local supermarket, or chatting over the fence to a close friend, your postman, or even better your barman. It can suddenly sound like real conversation. Look 'em in the eye and tell 'em the truth.'

'Directors can be made unhappy by repetitive little tricks, like the sudden intake of a breath before speaking, licking the lips, or sighing when movements should be mute. Flicking hair back with a toss of the head is a contrived action, or worse, the continual placing of hair behind the ears. I remember a director asking for the hair of one actress to be put in one elaborate plait at the back of her head to prevent this, but because it was habit she still put her fingers around her ears without the hair being there. Hat touching announces that the wearer is a stranger to the hat.'

'Hitting your mark, (which is the exact spot to walk to for the benefit of lighting and a camera stop), can be made easier by lining up a mental spot that's not only a floor mark. Find one alongside a vase, the edge of a table or have a shoulder parallel to a clock or mirror. It's a personal thought, eliminating the otherwise necessary glance at the floor.'

There are bits of brief advice like:

'Don't act—react. Listen and believe the other actor. Wear rubber soled shoes. Make sure wardrobe is uncrushable before sitting in it. If it crushes show it to the make-up artist and change into it after being made-up. Go to wardrobe on arrival. Eating or drinking requires a make-up check. Always ask an assistant director and get permission to leave the set if it's urgent. Let the crew go first at catered meal breaks; they are called back to the set before the actors. Don't be afraid to ask a fellow actor to have a "read through"; they are usually grateful. If time permits, return wardrobe items to their hangers—the wardrobe personnel are also hard workers. Keep more than scheduled scripts on hand. Schedules change for many reasons. Be prepared. When drinking tea don't have a teaspoon in the saucer; it will be noisy. Have a reliable alarm clock. Some call times are outrageously early. Sleeping in is unforgivable. Marking scripts to denote wardrobe changes will avoid waiting time for others. Know every move as thoroughly as the lines; the editor will bless you. A technical fault is often the reason for having to "do it again", leaving an actor feeling responsible. A considerate assistant director will sometimes say, "our fault", or "once more for us". Overlapping dialogue is a no-no for film. The editor can't make clean cuts. It's acceptable with video-taping, but still a bad habit. When doing reverses (when only the other person is being filmed), try to give the same performance even though the feeding of lines is off camera. Being required doesn't necessarily mean being seen.'

'I remember the time an actor who didn't have dialogue was needed to stand there and listen. He thought he'd finished for the day and without being cleared, he went home. It was an over the shoulder shot, so they put the bloke's jacket on a coat hanger. The lone actor was talking to no one.'

How did Maurie learn lines? 'Well', he said, 'What works for some may not work for others. Everybody seems to have a different system. Even directors. Some keep the entire script in a protective folder, others remove the scene they're working on, even fold it and keep it in their back pocket. Same with actors. I remember the absolute

thoroughness of Bud Tingwell. Working on episodes of *Homicide*, Bud Tingwell would have the whole script close at hand at all times, and it was a beautiful sight to behold. His particular scenes had tabs attached to the pages, jutting out like an alphabetic diary, and all colour coded. In an instant he could flip to the required scene. I never saw how he marked the actual dialogue. Pity, there's probably some unique system to be learned there. Bud Tingwell—actor, producer, director, gentleman. Even as a presenter at the Logies or television appeals, he doesn't look at the porta-prompt, but carries his own small cards for safety, but of course he has learned the dialogue thoroughly.'

Maurie further explained, 'My system isn't one to be copied. First I read the breakdown of my character at the front of the script, mark the scenes against the shooting days, then pull my scenes out of the master script. I circle my character's name wherever, with a biro, and with a yellow marking pen mark the lines. Then I put the whole thing aside until the day before it's required. It's not a recommended system, it's just that I need to learn them as close to the day as possible. I must have a photographic mind. Young actors have seen me pick up a script for the first time and do it immediately. They ask how I do it. I say—terror.'

'I remember Lorraine Bayley and the big work load she had in *The Sullivans*. She'd have with her the pages she was doing at the time. Sometimes she sat on them, but they were handy.'

A stage performance is usually preceded by the luxury of weeks in rehearsal. It's an entirely different craft. Sitting down in a chair on stage can be done with a flourish. When being filmed it must be paced so that the camera stays with the actor, otherwise it's an empty frame with the camera trying to chase the actor. Timing a sit down or a get up can sometimes feel foreign to the dialogue, especially if the words are at a fast pace.

A prop on stage can be waved about for all to see, or held close to the chest. The camera needs an important prop to be still, alongside the body, not in front, and if it's shiny, tilted to avoid flaring. Even then it will probably have its own separate shot. For example, Don Bourke of *Bourke's Backyard* talked about our garden and gave special comments about some plants. Later his crew went around the garden without us and shot a series of close-ups while the sound man played back the dialogue to determine which plants were highlighted.

Sometimes an actor will be disappointed in their given wardrobe. Decisions depend on a number of factors. The colour must not be the same as the background, and others in the scene must be considered. Stripes and checks will flare. Red will drain everything else. Pastels film stronger. White is only

for uniforms when there is no alternative. Nurses photograph best in blue. Hats with wide brims hide the face. Bracelets jingle. Turtlenecks add to the number of chins. Purses need to be easily opened. (A purse is a good place to secrete a script). Pity the poor wardrobe people whose efforts are sometimes questioned, and as for make-up artists—ditto all of the above.

For Maurie Fields to discuss his methods and approach to his work was like pulling teeth. He would have much rather talked about football or how to paint a picket fence. He was not the kind of actor who liked to discuss techniques. There is the kind who hold up a whole day's work by dissecting a scene word by word, letting everyone know how they're getting ready. Maurie was the total opposite. He was the kind who just wanted to go in and get on with it, and do the best job possible in the least time. Besides, time is money.

Anything for a laugh

Fond memories surface when Maurie talked about the time *60 Minutes* took him all over Australia with Charles Woolley and a film crew, highlighting the actor and the man.

There were showbusiness roasts that he found amazing because they deemed him worthy. When a personal phenomenon was included in *The Extraordinary*, he was quietly complimented.

Being asked to host a major segment of the *Homicide Tribute* was an indication of how much his contributions were respected.

Return performances by popular demand brought a humble smile to his face, like the Melbourne Concert Hall's audience who have claimed him as their favourite. Fan mail from Europe gets answered by Vic Buckley, his character in *The Flying Doctors*. Even the sympathetic gardener, Old Syd, in *Neighbours*, has swelled the overseas fan mail.

Friends and family were shocked when he was hospitalised due to a heart attack. How could the jovial Maurie Fields have heart trouble? But it happened. A second heart attack happened on a return flight from Hawaii.

On arrival in Melbourne, there were enough medical teams, wheelchairs and stretchers to accommodate a small army. Custom checks were thrown to the wind. An ambulance with sirens blaring sped him to Epworth Hospital. The airline took a description of the luggage and forwarded it by taxi to his home.

Maurie was in hospital a little longer the second time, but still determined to fulfill commitments. He cajoled the hospital staff into letting him be chauffeured to 'The Great Aussie Joke' segment of *Hey, Hey, It's Saturday*. Host Daryl Somers went along with it, but all through the jokes he had his eye on Maurie's minder Val, who had his special tablets and was standing by. Afterwards it was back to hospital where he joined the skylarking of other patients who spent most of the time trying to bribe the poor nurses into giving them just one cigarette to share. Maurie's heart specialist put him on a crash diet. The weight fell off him dramatically, but he didn't look like Maurie Fields. Striking a happy medium, he became his old self in no time and never looked back, except for one health hiccup common to men. A suspected prostate problem was overcome, but not before humiliating treatment—that brought a tear to the eye.

For many years Maurie Fields' joke pages were a feature of *The Australasian Post*. Many joke books have been bestsellers, reaching wide and varied destinations, some without electricity and therefore without television.

When asked if there was secret to his success, he would say, 'You shouldn't be asking me that

As John Quinny, 'Bellbird', ABC television.

sort of question. I only know I must be doing something right 'cos I'm still working. And I also know that when people start yelling at each other on movie sets, or anywhere, it upsets everybody and there's no need for any of that garbage. Things work better if you care about other people's problems as well as your own. Mind you, if you're considered to be jovial, you're also considered to have a perfect life. It's a fallacy that high profile people can't get sad. Everybody goes through shutting down at times, everybody.'

'All the good things that happened to me throughout my life sort of happened by accident. The things that came my way interested me because they made me feel good. There's even a rhythm to heavy drama when you're really enjoying it. A certain something happens and you belong, like feeling at home. Knowing you can survive without all that fame stuff is the attitude that matters. Be yourself and be glad about who you are. If you can discover what you are best at, the pressure lifts. After all, just being alive

is a big job. It's best to make a lot less money and be a lot more satisfied.'

Maurie talked more on his down to earth views on acting. 'Sometimes to go on and on about acting as an art form can get a bit ridiculous. Some actors can't get into a character without taking a scene apart word by word, thereby holding everybody else up. You don't have to be a genius to say a line and hit a mark. Anyone can do it, with application. For me, the whole thing is an easy pleasure.'

Maurie Fields was a dedicated family man. Marty Fields his son had the unconditional love of both his father and mother. If the giving of love, joy and kindness guarantees a long life, then Maurie Fields will live forever.

'Vic' in 'The Flying Doctors'.

❧ *Roaring Twenties.*

Why —— must the show go on?

Close to his demise, Maurie was invited to do Bert Newton's morning TV show—an interview plus a song. He accepted the job, and although the Channel Ten wardrobe department did their best to conceal his predicament, it was noticeable but didn't affect the repartee between him and Bert. The song he sang with Alan Zavod's accompaniment was 'When Somebody Thinks You're Wonderful'. He even threw in a soft shoe dance chorus. All was well. The chat had been about the vaudeville years of the forties because suddenly it was 'Australia Remembers' time. All of Australia was celebrating 50 years of peace after six years of the Second World War. It was now mid August 1995.

It would have seemed unpatriotic to refuse the array of work that was expected of him, because he's a 'pro', and he was needed. The very next day after Bert's show, he fulfilled a promise to perform at the big opening of extensions to the Sunshine R.S.L. He was asked to also M.C. the occasion and introduce Bruce Ruxton—President of the R.S.L.

On the same day *Australasian Post* magazine wanted him to perform at their celebrity function, with both events happening as luncheons. For years 'Maurie's Funny Pages' had been a feature of *Australasian Post,* and he couldn't let them down.

When alone, Maurie and I discussed the cancelling of all work. Get the priorities in order. He said, 'Better not do that, don't know how I'm gonna feel yet, I might still be able to work.' Sometimes I wondered if he would rather die than not be able to entertain. It's a powerful feeling when everybody loves you; it's the biggest exhilaration. Could it be the best medicine, or the worst?

And so it continued.

'Meet my wife Agnes, you're her greatest fan.' 'How do you remember all those jokes?' 'Are you two really married?' 'Why don't they bring back vaudeville?' 'Meet our Eric, you should put him on TV. He's the funniest bloke alive.'

The large entertainment venue at the rear of the Wrest Point Casino had been built for Gala Concerts with a seating capacity of 1800. For Hobart's tribute to 'Australia Remembers, 50 years on', both the matinee and the evening performance on that August Sunday were filled to capacity.

Our double act based on 'Whatever Happened To Vaudeville' was lovingly received, as were the contributions made by the entire cast of 300, including Barry Crocker, Dorothy Barry and Bobby Limb. Peter Richman was congratulated on his production.

During those three weeks of daily radiology, the doctors description of a sore throat, difficulty swallowing, tiredness, some nausea, some weight loss and a sunburnt-like skin, all began to materialise. Determined not to divulge the problem, it was getting very difficult to knock back

"Who luv's ya baby!"

218

work from agents, because agents have to know when and where you're working, so the excuse of 'I'm working that day or that night, sorry,' wouldn't wash.

Many jobs shouldn't have been, but were fulfilled. The 'Sante' room at the Crown Casino got only conversation from us, seated on two stools, compered by Tony Barber and Patti Newton and it worked well, although Peter Beck also wanted us to sing and really found our reluctance uncharacteristic. I suggested that we save the vocals for another time, as the programme already had fine singers in Ronnie Burns and Matthew Newton. Another time, what other time? We even did a series of radio advertisements for a retirement village. Long scripts, and a stack of them. A personal appearance at the village was part of the deal. But we got it done. Even though Maurie's stamina was taxed during that period and his appetite was dulled due to

the soreness his throat was feeling, he didn't disappoint anyone.

In hospital there were deaths around him. Even his private room couldn't keep out the sounds of families crying in the passageway, the expressions of gratitude to the very special hospital staff who did everything they could. Such occurrences urged him to try harder, swallow nourishment no matter what, keep the kidneys working, and the bodily functions happening, take a determined interest in the daily steps onto the scales.

Being discharged from room 201 and the Freemasons Hospital had been eagerly awaited, but the day wasn't without another last minute blood test, and an enema with tubing that Maurie claimed was eight metres long. The male administer of same, Michael, by then had the job under control, with Maurie suggesting at least he should have given him a bunch of flowers.

❧ *Opposite page: Maurie with his famous instrument.*

The professional, doing it tough

I've found that a knowledge of comedy doesn't necessarily mean being a funny person. Humour can rely on many things, like the wardrobe. A situation can be killed by wearing the wrong hat, or trousers with pockets that are too small, or a shirt that takes too long to remove. A million little things become big things. Props must work. A property master must really be a master of prop making, always prepared for unusual requests, finding ways to make things work. The lone stand-up comedian usually has no need of these production assets, unless he's doing a complete one-man show. Then he needs all the help he can get.

Learning the art of 'feeding' a comedian was a very serious part of my theatrical education. Comedy is a very serious business, and for this youngster, at the time, almost frightening. Distraction of any kind while the comic is speaking or moving, is a no-no. To blink in the wrong place might kill a laugh, apart from taking your life in your own hands!

Knowing how to set up a gag for the funnyman is an art that can't be learned overnight—it takes experience. The reason being, every audience is different. A good audience can throw the timing out, just the same as a quiet audience can. Imagine a huge wave in the ocean's surf; it's about to reach its peak then it subsides before the next wave. That's how it is in comedy. When feeding an important line after a laugh, it's like waiting for the crest of a wave and catching it halfway down before the laughter completely subsides, then in you go and plant the next feed line for the comedian to catch his wave.

Perhaps getting through one's life is exactly the same. A strange analogy? Not for me.

I was happy to attend the varied and many fundraising events to which I was invited.

The very knowledgeable Frank Van Stratten invited me to an evening at an arts complex in Caulfield. It wasn't so much a fundraiser as a tribute to Roy Rene ('Mo'). As a part of the speaking panel, I called to mind suitable anecdotes from my Tivoli Theatre years.

Addressing a large group of St Michael's Church congregation in Collins Street wasn't exactly easy. The subject was Living Successfully. At Berwick I was guest speaker at a gathering of successful fundraisers for the Arthritis Foundation. Kew Town Hall was the venue for an after luncheon speech.

Because I had worked for Hoyts movie circuit as a teenager in the 1940s as part of their stage-combined-with-movie-presentations, an invitation to visit an actual restoring process received another 'Yes I'd be delighted'. After the manager of the incredible restoration staff showed me around the magic that was taking place, I found myself facing a film crew and interviewer as I ad-libbed on the magnificent re-birth of the Regent Theatre Melbourne. The charming Elaine

❧ Enjoying the hospitality of a Queensland VIP appearance.

and David Marriner thanked me, for what resulted in an ongoing TV promotion. It was encouraging to know I could still wing it.

Brighton's Bay Street reception rooms were the location for the Diabetes fundraising luncheon. The public still felt that Maurie & Val belonged to them—with affection.

The Players and Playgoers association were considerate. As was a literary luncheon in a formal reception room at Frankston had them calling for more. It was very encouraging, as my predecessors had been Ita Buttrose and Hazel Hawke.

I spoke at Daffodil Day, the annual highlight of a week which promotes Cancer research. It was a big week. The Novotel on Collins Street had a cocktail bash in Michelle's Brasserie, featuring music and the comic talents of Jack Levy, better known as Elliot Goblet.

The Anti-Cancer Awareness Week also held a big promotion day at Melbourne Central. Among my fellow performers donating their talents were a delightful children's choir featuring my friends Pattie Newton and Tottie Goldsmith, with prominent sports identities and VIP's all contributing. The busy personal appearances kept me on a merry-go-round of diversion.

The Melbourne Town Hall played host to the Australian Film Industry awards, where I was invited to be a presenter. Entering the long wide passageway at the rear of the stage, a tall lean man strode toward me, his arm outstretched. With a friendly smile he shook my hand and said enthusiastically, 'Hello Val Jellay. I'm Geoffrey Rush'. Just as I was placing the name he was pleasantly on his way. This was the star of the much-awarded film *Shine*. What a nice man. He couldn't possibly know what he had done. His greeting was the first of dozens that night, when I was still wondering what I was doing there.

Just when all the after-dinner speaking and the charity appearances began to get bigger and more frequent, Bert Newton's producer invited me to be a semi-regular on his high rating television program *Good Morning Australia*. My job was to review and give a criticism of the latest videos. It was one of the sweetest gigs I'd ever done on television. A limo collected me from my home and returned me. A courier would arrive prior to the day and deliver the video for me to watch. I was always taken to a screening room on arrival at Channel Ten in Como Melbourne, where the 'grab' or 'clip' from the video would be shown for me to comment on. With old friend Bert Newton compering the show, it was always fun to do.

An audition for *Showboat* got me a wonderful role in the Melbourne season of *Crazy For You*. It had been two years since both Maurie and I had auditioned in Sydney. The role in *Showboat* went to Nancye Hayes.

❧ *Opposite page: The Daffodil Day Cancer Appeal.*

223

1. *At the dressing room door, Melbourne State Theatre,* 2. *Costumes belonging to Maurie and Val displayed in Melbourne's Performing Arts Museum.* 3. *Travelling in style in the Royal Melbourne Show Parade.* 4. *Crowning the winner of the Toddlers' Show at the Royal Melbourne Show.*

A publicity shot for 'Once Upon a Pantomime: a Topsy Turvy Exhibition', at the Performing Arts Museum, Melbourne.

The agent

Finding the appropriate agent for one's particular talents does not happen overnight. Being on the books of an established and respected agent is comparable to reaching an inner sanctum of recognition. The best agents are relied upon by their clients to know in advance when the appropriate job will be coming available. Managements contact agents, not the artist direct, although many artists have been known to lobby their own cause by making direct contact with managements, which quite often can backfire, even with high profile entertainers. The agent arranges auditions and interviews and acquires every detail including audition scripts. He or she is in constant need of updated professional photographs. The flow on then involves publicity, rehearsal times, locations, etc. In fact every detail becomes the realm of a good agent.

How to achieve this status, this acceptance into the hallowed realm of being on an agent's books, is the hard part. When it happens, that's when all the years of dedication and determination bear fruit. No agent in their right mind can promote an unknown, just on their say so. But how does one go about it? Every artist will give you a personal account of their experience, and each story will have a new approach, but all of them will reveal the same attitude.

It's a serious business, showbusiness. It's natural for the unsuspecting general public to see only what's on the surface, and therefore believe that an artist's life is one of glamour and excitement, of never-ending fun and games. It's only fair that we don't disillusion our necessary audiences. We shouldn't remind them of the percentage of mental breakdowns that occur, often at the height of a career.

Do you still want to be in showbusiness! Alright, let's get to it.

First, grab everything with both hands, the earlier in life the better. Put your hand up in every classroom for parts in school plays, musicals, debates, anything that requires getting in front of an audience—any audience—parents, grandparents, other schools, do it all.

Giving up the childhood pleasures may seem hard at the time, like Saturdays at the movies and the like. It's dedication, it's groundwork. Lessons and classes can be costly, but most parents forsake their own pleasures for the many hours required for dance lessons, piano lessons and the encouragement needed for years of never-ending practise.

Many agents make the rounds of amateur presentations, looking for new and promising talent. Never underestimate who is in the audience. It may be a school concert, a talent quest or an amateur or semi-professional musical comedy. They attend incognito, that's their job. So, one never, ever, knows exactly who is looking for what in audiences. Always do your very best. Accept with gratitude every performing job, no matter how menial. That way, when the big one comes along you will be ready.

Another approach if an agent is out of reach is to make a video for their visual files. This can be expensive. Finding a technician who understands what is needed can once again require determination. Compile, for instance, a three minute montage of all your attributes. It can be an investment. Remember to ask for many copies. Place it on the internet.

Some agents rely on a theatrical bible called 'SHOWCAST'. Once again it's an investment, like a business being in the Yellow Pages. There are also agents who specialise in children, which is a hard area to crack, but persistence can pay off.

An agent can see good work and inquire about representation, but it doesn't often happen. It's a mysterious business, acquiring an agent. There are no rules, except, no agent wants to handle a no talent. This may be why, when we go through the early years in search of a career in showbusiness, that the constant cry is Good Luck!

There'll be some changes made

It has been well documented by successful authors, no matter the subject, that the process of creative writing requires isolation and uninterrupted silence, so the thought processes are without distraction.

It's an often-asked question: 'How do you go about writing a book?' Another familiar query: 'Have you always been a writer?' Or the truly confounding question: 'How long does it take to write your books?' That's the one question I don't understand. It has always made me feel that my acceptance as an author depended on how long I took to write a book. Do I make a better impression by saying something about it only taking a very short time, or would that lessen its difficulty, or should my answer convey an agonising, lengthy period of time like some blockbuster movie—'Quo Vadis, five years in the making?' I have often felt that my efforts were judged on how long the project took to accomplish. Would I be more worthy if sleep were to be forfeited altogether, and I wrote with the speed of an Olympian athlete? Or perhaps true appreciation comes with years of plodding and persistent re-writes. That idealism could be likened to those who spend their lives digging for ancient fossils. It's not possible for any one person to constantly write day and night; inspiration is quite spasmodic. We all have different ways of doing things. My system, however, is probably the most unorthodox.

During the long run of *Crazy For You* I managed to break a bone in my foot and also had gall-bladder surgery to remove 13 stones, which were presented to me in recovery, in a small glass jar, by a smiling surgeon who looked as though he was presenting me with a Logie.

Wasn't it enough to have to cope with the changing times and the additions to the English language? We senior citizens were here long before VCR's, frozen food, credit cards, automatic teller machines and ball point pens. We surfed on the waves, not on the Internet. A chip meant a piece of wood and time-sharing meant togetherness. Hardware meant nails and screws etc, and there was no such word as software. We were before electric blankets, washing and drying machines, drip dry clothes, and we shopped at the nearby grocers and had no supermarkets.

In our youth cigarettes were fashionable, grass was for cows, and pot was what you cooked in. A gay person was the life of the party (probably still is) and AIDS were the means of beautifying oneself, or helping someone in trouble. We were before Batman, vitamin pills, disposable nappies, instant coffee, McDonalds and takeaways.

We got married first and then lived together. Girls thought cleavage was something the butcher did. Think of how the world has changed and how hardy we must be to come through all the

❧ *Val marvels at Cinderella (Helen McFarlane).*

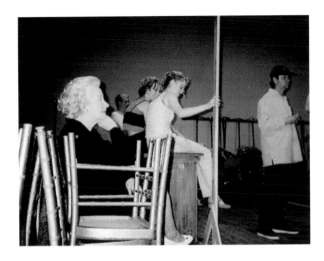

constant changes we had to make, all the necessary adjustments, and still survive. Is it any wonder that along the way something gives under the strain. We feel confident knowing that problems like illness or accidents only happen to someone else, not us. But we are *all* that someone else.

The critics all loved *Crazy For You*. Each newspaper headline was fulsome in its praise. Perhaps the one I really enjoyed was the national *Australian:* 'And, for sheer stage presence, there's Val Jellay in the role of the rich imperious Mother.' (Obviously unaware of the crawling on hands and knees bit.)

Life goes by so quickly, on reflection. Each day is such a bonus. My career began when I was four years old; at seven I was a seasoned professional. At seventeen I was loving my success with the Tivoli circuit. At twenty-seven I had toured the world performing in the great theatres of Europe, England and Ireland. By thirty-seven I had become a wife, a mother and a television personality. By forty-seven, fifty-seven and sixty-seven I had achieved what life was meant to be about—love, contentment, respect and good health. Everything that is worthwhile attaining.

When work takes Marty and Jenny to America, their non-committed evenings are spent attending as many Broadway shows as possible. They see plays, depending on the cast, but mostly the latest Broadway Musicals are given priority. With Marty's high profile in that area, it's good business to know and see what may be coming to our country. Let me tell you about one such journey in the year 2002.

Back home I was in Marty's car, and as he was driving me to a luncheon with Jenny, he said, 'Listen to this song Mum, it sounds like you, it's your kind of song, its range is your range, it could even be *about* you. It's sung by an old actress Kathleen Freeman believed to be in her eighties. She received a Tony Award for her performance in a show called *The Full Monty,* a smash hit on Broadway, and London's Westend.'

At the opening function, the owner of Her Majesty's theatre Mike Walsh said, 'Val, I've got to tell you about a show that's coming to Australia, it's called *The Full Monty* and there is a part in it that you've got to play.' I remember feeling surprised and saying something like, 'It's been so long I'm amazed you remember me'. He replied with something polite about Maurie Fields and Val Jellay but was urgently trying to tell me about the part of Jeanette.

The nice things said to me by Mike Walsh were surely stimulating, but through experience, I'd learned not to count on anything. But the conversation did at least

A pensive moment watching Marty during rehearsal for the Melbourne season of 'Crazy for You'.

231

confirm that the Broadway production of *The Full Monty* was definitely coming to Australia.

The next morning I mailed a courteous note of thanks to Mike for giving me a 'bunk up'. To my surprise he answered my note, and confirmed our conversation re: the show in question.

Christmas came and went and various big shows fulfilled their commitments: *Cabaret*, *The Witches of Eastwick*, *Singing in the Rain*, *The Lion, The Witch and The Wardrobe* and *Oliver*. So now there was a flood of available performers. My agent informed me that should she hear of anything about *Monty* she would let me know, and that was that.

Marty had made it possible for me to have access to all the dialogue and music from this big show that was beginning to feel like some kind of challenge. Doing auditions can be heartbreaking, but should I get the opportunity to audition for *The Full Monty*, at least I tried, at least I gave it a good shot.

Almost every day I played the music on the cassette that I had copied from Marty's CD.

As for the many scenes with dialogue, I wandered around the house daily for months, talking to myself out loud, trying the dialogue different ways, as one does when learning a part. Actually getting this coveted role was just another 'maybe', a 'what if?' There were so many fine actresses

in Australia who were more than capable of doing this part, and all with a high profile.

The character needed to be at least in her seventies, an old vaudevillian, a comedienne, used to working all her life with comedians and musicians. Sound good? It sounded to me like the only truly great role ever to be have been written for someone with my background. Not a Shakespearian actress, but an old vaudevillian who had spent her life working with comedians and musicians, and everything else that came under the heading of 'entertainment'.

Television welcomed me again as Connie, with Bud Tingwell. We were grandparents in the legendary series *Neighbours*, and all of it kept me in touch with the only thing I really knew how to do—perform. Which is not a way of life to be recommended. Nevertheless it was nice working with friends in the cast and crew of *Neighbours*.

Whispers around the industry confirmed that auditions for *The Full Monty* were back in Sydney.

I began to hear news that many of our musical comedy people were finding it difficult to get an initial appointment in Sydney and call-backs were few.

Not only did I know all the scenes involving Jeanette, her song was imprinted on my brain from months of listening and singing with the original actress. But this wasn't enough for me, the research wasn't complete

🌿 *"Bobby, in the ten years since you left Harvard, you have accomplished nothing". A dramatic moment in 'Crazy For You' as Mother.*

unless I made an effort to look like the character.

Once again Marty's library of Broadway shows contained photos of Kathleen Freeman, as Jeanette, wearing a type of hip length denim jacket, kind of country, with out of place sequins on it. Here was another challenge, something else to add to the effort.

It was at the South Melbourne market that I saw a jacket that just might do the trick, pale blue, patch pockets, with a collar, and it was denim. The little Chinese owner of the store wanted to sell me the three-piece outfit. Explaining that the jacket was all I needed, the conversation became very involved with the result being that I paid for the three pieces but only bought the jacket. No matter.

It was a 40-degree heat that day, a heat wave, and the search was tiring. From the market I walked several blocks in the sun to a warehouse that I hoped would sell loose pale blue sequins, and fabric glue with which to stick them on, one by one. Success! All was found. The chore of sticking sequins on denim at home in my kitchen was frustrating, they only wanted to stick to my fingers. Why was I bothering! After all, this spangly jacket would never ever get worn again. But I couldn't stop preparing.

Auditions for musicals always require one song to be sung; this is to be a personal choice, not one from the show. Sheet music must be brought along, in the correct key, with no transposing to be expected from the supplied pianist. An audition pianist has the unpleasant job of having to sight read all sorts of melodies and tempos. Strict instructions are also given—no movement, and a second song may be asked for. If dialogue is needed it will be handed out on the day. Too late for this old pro, I knew every scene.

Relying on the supplied piano player was too risky for me, I needed all the help I could get. So I phoned an old mate who first played for me years earlier during my ten years, with Maurie, at the famous Tikki and John's music hall. Will Conyers was only too pleased to help, in fact he had students who were going for different roles in the same show so he was on tippy toes with anxious interest.

The song I wanted him to accompany me with was one he'd recently played for me with a big band at the Palais Theatre. The song was 'Broadway Baby'. Another mate, Kirk Skinner, originally handed me the great song to do in Sondheim's *Follies*. Still leaving nothing to chance, another good musician friend John Foreman wrote out the music for me, with lyrics inserted, in case amongst us all we didn't have the music. So, I'm a worrier, but at my age it's too late to change.

Meanwhile the phone call came for me to attend an audition at the rehearsal rooms of the Melbourne Theatre Co. in Port Melbourne. It was to be on a Friday. Will Conyers, 'my' personal pianist came to my house for a rehearsal and together we joined a room full of aspiring cast members in the Port Melbourne rooms on that first day.

The air was electric, most of us knew each other, and swapped relevant small talk. Auditions are part of an actor's life. It should be taught as a subject, and so should 'how to handle rejection'.

Walking in and singing a song to a bunch of strangers was just not going to satisfy me this time, not after all the anticipation. Some of the actual dialogue in *The Full Monty* is about auditions, and how these out of work mill workers try to put together a Chippendale's type of show, but nobody has an ounce of talent. In the story they hold their own auditions, which are less than successful.

Jeanette the old vaudevillian-come-pianist tells them not to worry. So I decided to brazenly start with the actual dialogue from the show. This was against all auditioning formats. Would they bring me to a halt, throw me out for disobeying the conditions outlined, or perhaps call out 'that's enough thank you—next please'. Who could tell! But I was going to make the most of this opportunity. Even Will Conyers joined my unusual approach by throwing a feed line to me, a line from the show. We were kind of in daredevil cahoots!

'Val Jellay, they're ready to see you now'. So, this was it. Get through this, be courageous, don't just stand there and sing a song, these auditioners must be so tired of the usual format. Good or bad to my mind wasn't the question, surely they were looking for

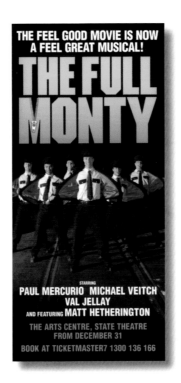

something different, at least something interesting.

I was introduced to the panel, the I.M.G. people, English representatives, and our own David Atkins. I nodded and smiled acknowledgement, whilst exchanging a quick hug with David. All these niceties go out the window in such business-like situations. Will Conyers had gone to the piano, which was to the left of the panel. Without waiting one second and privately thinking, 'Here goes nothing', I launched into the actual dialogue from the show, complete with American accent.

'Don't worry, when the right guy walks through that door you'll know it, he'll glimmer, he'll light up the room. I've seen it happen a thousand times. You audition for days, they're all dogs, you're ready to slit your wrists, when in walks "Jeanette". (Laughter from the panel). *Besides you're not just offering these guys a job, you're offering them hope. And I'll tell you this—my heart beat a little faster when I heard*

about this gig.
Do you know heartbreak hotel? (From Will at the piano)
'Honey, I wrote it. Do me a favour, try to keep up.'
(Intro music 'Broadway Baby' <u>with movement</u>.)

Sure the appointment instructions said 'NO MOVEMENT', but once again I defiantly ignored that. For me that would be like not breathing. (Even working with a hand held microphone I find inhibiting and distracting.)

The panel applauded wildly, were they being polite! How could I possibly tell! I left that rehearsal room with David Atkins in pursuit. He explained that the Americans would be in Melbourne the following Monday, Tuesday and Wednesday, they would need to see me, choose which day, and do exactly the same thing for them. Because the next Monday and Tuesday I had work commitments at functions, I chose the Wednesday at noon.

❧ *'The Full Monty' poster.*

🌿 *Scenes from 'The Full Monty'.*

Once more I donned the denim jacket with the glued on sequins. Once more Will Conyers was with me as we trod the same path at the Port Melbourne rehearsal rooms complex. This time others already waiting were few, the obligatory smiles were exchanged in an atmosphere of those who are about to receive major surgery.

David explained that he wanted me to do exactly what I'd done at the first audition, including the few lines of dialogue. Was I feeling alright, he asked. 'Fine', I replied. When, by now, I felt like I was standing outside myself watching somebody else go through the motions.

'Broadway Baby' came to an end. Applause! So, now, what next? The panel of experts nodded and smiled to each other. My mind was trying to anticipate, remembering the struggle going on outside in the 'green room' with actors pacing up and down, urgently trying to learn unfamiliar scripts in the minutes available.

Before anyone could suggest I do likewise, a cheeky request came from my mouth. 'Would I be able to try a scene for you?' There was general agreement. 'Perhaps the scene with Horse, the black man', I suggested. I knew it was a particularly naughty scene. Played sadly.

The actor who had been hired to read with all the characters quickly found the script for the scene. He placed a chair in the centre of the room and took up his insignificant position. A script was instantly offered to me, I waved it aside with a smile.

> *'SO, ARE YOU TRYING TO TELL ME YOU'VE GOT A SMALL DICK HORSE!'*
> *'I'm telling you no such thing—I'm average.'*
> *'MOST MEN <u>ARE</u>, THAT'S WHY IT'S CALLED AVERAGE. LET ME LOOK. I'LL TELL YOU IF YOU'RE AVERAGE OR NOT.'*
> *'Are you crazy woman?'*
> *'NO—BUT I HAVE BEEN MARRIED EIGHT TIMES, SO I GUESS I'D KNOW WHAT AVERAGE IS.'*

I played out the rest of the scene 'word perfect'. It was naughty, funny, with plenty of light and shade. Because of my determination to learn everything about the show and its script, I'd had time to study where the laughs were, and my lifetime of working in comedy fell perfectly into place.

The panel of decision makers were laughing as though they were hearing it for the first time. Was this only American courtesy, how could I know?

This call-back audition was taking a long time. Surely now I would be dismissed. But no. The American director suddenly said— 'The character of Jeanette has a big song in the show.' I nodded with interest. The show's musical director picked up the score and went to the piano.

237

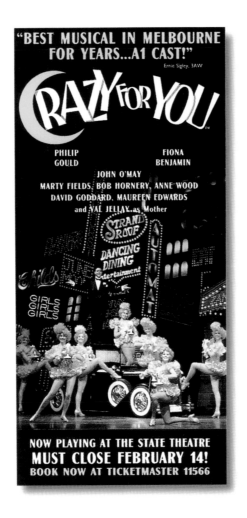

Still standing on the opposite side of the piano, I looked at the new piano player as he started playing the intro to the all important song. This is what I'd hoped for, after the many months of polishing the dialogue and the big song. I had finally been given the final big opportunity to do the only thing I really knew how to do—perform.

Being under a microscope, with the air electric, whilst trying to convey that the moment is the happiest, most carefree time of your life, is a very stressful experience. Auditions are a cold ordeal, usually taking place in a bare, unfriendly space, devoid of embellishment. It's a part of the business that all of us are aware of and have to face.

'Thank you Val.' The powerful people applauded my efforts. 'Jeanette's Song' apparently pleased them. I apologised for augmenting the vocal with my own movement. A pleasant lady said, 'Don't be sorry, we will probably use most of what you did.' Knowing that the lady, Kathleen Freeman, who played the role in America was in her eighties, I asked—'Did David (Atkins) tell you how old I am?' David chipped in and laughingly said 'Yes—fifty.' I said 'Sure—and some months. I am seventy-five. It's no secret, all Australia knows it.' The nice lady then said, 'Maybe all of America will soon know it.'

They all thanked me and I left the room. I

❧ *'Crazy For You' poster.*

could do no more.

By now it was Easter time. Offices close for the holidays. I started to get a strange pain in the bridge of my nose, and then it worsened to behind my right eye. A day later the side of my head pounded with a pain like nothing I'd ever experienced. I would have to put up with it over the weekend until after Easter Monday. A rash came out on my temple and the side of my forehead. Tuesday I went to my GP in an awful state. He took one look and said, 'You've got Shingles'.

It was as a very small child that I last heard of the condition known as Shingles. At that time it was spoken of in hushed tones, as though it belonged to the dark ages, much like the plague. Definitely not contagious was the best news. It was so painful and so itchy, and swollen.

When my doctor was explaining the pitfalls of Shingles he asked, 'Have you been feeling stressful of late?' How could I explain to a medico the urgency of wanting to be in a musical? It wasn't life threatening—or was it? 'No more than usual', was my reply.

While trying to lay low and cope with the agony of Shingles and my less than attractive swollen itchy face, my agent Claudia phoned me to say that she'd heard from *The Full Monty* company and they would like me to play the role of Jeanette.

Such news is usually greeted with squeals of delight, much jumping about, and excited celebration. Alone, sick and feeling miserable, my verbal reaction was a very flat and seemingly disinterested ... 'Oh really.'

The most important and influential impact on my determination to be fit was walking—yes walking. It was once again Marty who encouraged and got me walking every evening, for months and months.

Some don't have the dedication required for a career that isn't steady. The ups and downs are not for everyone. Not only physical stress takes its toll, severe mental stress is commonplace. Given the chance, I will work until I drop—which *has* happened. Retire—never! Actors never retire. We sometimes 'rest' and quite often have been known to 'rust'.

This was a special project for us all. Before rehearsals had begun we knew we had to be one hundred per cent fit, and we privately worked hard to that end.

We were all going to be pushed to sustain these strong characters. My character of Jeanette would be like nothing I'd played before.

In film and television, the less you do the better. More work is done with the eyes than

🍂 *As grandparents on the 'Neighbours' set, with Bud Tingwell.*

anything else. The director puts it together with the shots, angles and editing.

With theatre you get a story from beginning to end. You can create more from your own special feel for a character.

For me, it's called stage craft, and I love it.

Rodney Dobson, David Harris, Bert Labonte, Matt Hetherington, Paul Mecurio and Michael Veitch were cast as the male leads in the show. Matt Heatherington received a Green Room award for his performance. Each one of them was great.

Life should become more passive as one continues to climb the ladder of life, but not so for this very senior soubrette! It was a case of action stations in every way possible. The stamina required for rehearsal every day for five weeks, then eight shows a week for three months, was going to take a big effort on my part.

The role of Jeanette is a very energetic character. She has to take over totally in every scene, a bit of a dynamo, full of wisecracks and wisdom. Now that I'd succeeded in getting the part, I had to throw myself into solid 'get fit' exercises, lose more weight, cancel all other commitments, personal and professional and be ready. Rehearsal clothes were retrieved from dark depths of my closets. Old theatrical make-up was tossed out. The old false eyelashes had seen better days, needless to say the accompanying eyelash glue had totally sealed itself up like glazed toffee—out it all went. I was like a child playing with new toys as it was all replaced.

For my own peace of mind I had a complete medical check-up for almost every condition known to man. The hair got tinted before it needed to be. A pedicure was a necessity, even my house got an unnecessary spring clean, and most important of all, I had swatted over my script of *The Full Monty* so that I'd arrive on the first day of rehearsal—word perfect.

With all this excitement and activity going on in my private little world, an even bigger cause for celebration was about to absolutely floor me beyond belief. Martin and Jenny informed me that they were expecting a baby. I was going to be a grandmother. A different mindset was needed for that wonderful news. Being a grandmother was something I had given up on. Perhaps I thought I was too old to have grandchildren. But then, it doesn't happen that way does it! It requires no input from the grandparents. Accepting the new title is all I had to do whilst the pregnancy proceeded.

When my agent told me we would be rehearsing in an area of a large building in St Kilda Rd called 'The School of Dance', I

❧ *On the set of 'Neighbours'.*

was delighted. We would be having all the latest in rehearsal requirements needed for the many weeks of concentrated hard work. Wrong. Oh yes, I certainly got that wrong. One should always remember, never presume.

For a start, there wasn't any air-conditioning. Our usual January heat wave decided to arrive in November and December. It was cooler on the ground floor, but the ground floor was all office-staff allocated. The building was impressively tall and we were to rehearse on the top floor. Heat rises as we know, so windows were opened to let in 'fresh' air, (hot north wind), which did little to ease the plight of those who had to give their all for the choreographer. Buildings with three, four or more levels usually have elevators, but not this one. Even the entrance to the front courtyard had two flights of stairs going down before one could approach the actual glass-doored entrance. Perhaps The School

of Dance meant no pampering. After all, students of dance are all young, fit and energetic. Not this old pro! I got to dread those stairs.

Everyone playing a major role in musicals has an understudy, someone who is already in the cast. My understudy was the high profile Rowena Wallace. When the show was to move to the Theatre Royal in Sydney for a twenty weeks season, Toni Lamond was going to take the baton and play my role of Jeanette. Rowena was also understudy for Toni. During the Melbourne initial rehearsals for the show, I had both of them watching me intently, listening, and marking their scripts accordingly. It was very strange but only at first. I soon forgot they were there. These ladies were very respected in our industry, and were friends. Particularly Toni, (who by the way is five years my junior). We are truly close friends. We all wished each other well.

As it happened, *Monty* didn't play Sydney

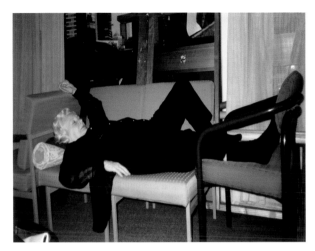

A much needed break in rehearsals for 'The Full Monty'.

or anywhere else.

During each lunch break at rehearsals I dared to adjourn to an area which was down two flights of stairs. Unlike the landing on the rehearsal room floor, there were a few stray chairs. By moving these chairs around I was able to stretch out these old bones and endeavour to lay flat for a precious half hour (see photo). Tea, yoghurt and an apple would have me up and going again.

'The success that is enjoyed by our big achievers isn't just because of good luck. The thing about Australian actors and actresses is, despite having this reputation for being laid-back, we're bloody hard workers. We don't put on airs and graces, we're very well trained and we are desperate to work.'

Hugh Jackman
(Sunday Herald-Sun April 30)

On my first entrance in the show, when I turned around from the piano, stood up and said 'Are you talking to me?' I inevitably received applause from the theatre-going public. It was always extremely heart-warming and joyous, particularly because of the way I looked. Barely recognisable. I really did appreciate that audience loyalty.

One day some of us were comparing Equity membership cards. Union cards are probably the same as one's driver's licence, permanently amongst the everyday identification we carry on us. Someone noticed that my Equity union card year of joining said 1944. Knowing that I was the most senior in the cast was no surprise to me, but my current cast members were amazed, wanting to know all about theatre and what it was like all of those years ago. Vaudeville is foreign to our current wonderful young performers, and the two shows a day every day, with rehearsals in the morning is always met with disbelief. As for the stage stars of the time, names like George Wallace, Jim Gerald, and Roy Rene 'Mo' are met with blank stares. It's understandable; I probably did the same thing in 1944.

Coincidentally or not, the very next day after the equity discussion I received a formal notice that I was to be honoured with lifetime membership in our union. No longer would fees be involved. 'I had done enough for the industry.' It was a very nice acknowledgement of having spent a lifetime in showbusiness. But of course I had to privately admit that some awards are based on longevity. Nevertheless it was nice.

With the aid of blue-tack, I was able to

The growing Fields family.

❧ *A regular on Bert Newton's 'Good Morning Australia'.*

⚜ *College of the Arts, rehearsing 'The Full Monty' with Paul Mercurio.*

make my already splendid dressing room full of happy, encouraging vibes. The various cards and messages that accompanied gorgeous flowers were attached to the mirror and walls. I appreciated them all so very much.

Thoroughly dressed up in the character of Jeanette with my make-up perfectly in place, there was nothing to do but wait, anticipate the overture and the inevitable – 'YOUR CALL TO THE STAGE MISS JELLAY—MISS JELLAY THIS IS YOUR CALL TO THE STAGE.'

Staring at myself in the mirror, the reflection also included my dressing room and its delightful surrounds. How many dressing rooms had I sat in and stared at myself in the mirror. Reflections! So many. It's true about getting older, that long ago memories become clearer, and you can't remember yesterday.

From some of the world's biggest and finest theatres to some of the world's smallest in size and stature, it had taken seventy years to come full circle. From sumptuous dressing rooms to those with bare minimum. Here I am still staring at the same face in a mirror surrounded by traditional light globes. As the years have taken their toll a little less sparkle is in the eyes, but the opening night nerves behind those eyes has never changed. It has always been unbelievably urgent.

The audience applauded the overture as soon as it began. The three thousand seats were filled with the A list of guests. Politicians, high profile celebrities, sponsors, stars of sports, our families, and the all-important media.

Was this going to be my last hurrah! Probably. At my age it would be nice to go out with personal success. Opening night of *The Full Monty*.

It had been quite a ride.

You don't know what lies ahead. When you find happiness grab it with both hands, because all there really is, is now.

❧ *With Matt Hetherington in 'The Full Monty'.*

❧ *At the dressing room door, Melbourne State Theatre, Arts Centre Complex in one of Mother's costumes for 'Crazy For You'.*

Dear Val,

It's an honour to share a stage with you. You are so classy! Your talent is an inspiration.

Much love. Matt Heatherington

Val, what a treat it is to be sharing this crazy journey with you. Enjoy!

Rodney Dobson (Dobbo)

Dear Val,

Lovely getting to know you. Chookas for tonight and the rest of the season.

Love Donal Forde

Dear Val — You're a gem!! Have a wonderful, wonderful night with "your boys".

Love Rowena xxx (Wallace)

Dearest Val,

Have a wonderful season — can't wait to see you up there! We'll be down in February to start rehearsals for "The Producers" so see you then. Lots of love,

Tony Sheldon

Dear Val, Have a wonderful opening night and a great season here in Melbourne. It is a joy working with you, and look forward to many good memories. Chookas!

David (Harris)

Beautiful Val, I feel so honoured to share this stage with you, you truly do have 'a lot of glimmer'. Shine tonight as you always do! Chookas. All my love,

Deone (Zanotto)

The Full Monty Opening Night.

Dear Val,

Have a wonderful opening — It is such a privilege to work with you, a true first lady of the theatre, and a lovely person as well. We are honoured to be working with you. I hope you enjoy it all.

With love, Queenie (Van De Zandt)

Val, great work! Knock 'em dead!

Love and Chookas. David Atkins x (Producer)

Val, fantastic! Congratulations and best wishes from all at O.M.G. Enjoy the moment. Love Wayne Jelly (Producer)

Dear Val, Chookas!

We know you will kill them you talented old broad.

Love Pat and David Argue xx

Dear Val, This is for you Babe.

You climbed this one on your own. You deserve it all. So enjoy it and give us that old Pizzaz.

Rita and Gus Mecurio

Dearest Val.

Opening Night darling. All the best.
Milton Neely (American Import)

Dear Val,

Just know you will be a knockout. Have fun. Cheering you on to a great success. Love David Goddard.

Dearest Val.

You'll be swell — you'll be great. Have a wonderful opening night and a fantastic season.

Lots of love. Maryanne McCormack

Dear Val, the big moment has arrived. Thinking of you today. Wishing you an exhilarating and exciting opening night. I'm sure your "Jeanette" will have them shouting "Encore".

Chookas and lots love, Claudia xxx (Agent)

Dearest Val,

Best wishes for tonight and for a great season. I really hope you enjoy Jeanette because she's sure giving us all some laughs at rehearsals! Have fun tonight — it's great to have you on board.

Natalie Gilhome x x (Resident Choreographer)

Dear Val,

You are such a gem. I'm so happy to be witnessing your talent on stage each night. Truly inspiring. Have a lovely opening night and here's to a wonderful Melbourne season.

Love from Emma xxx (Langridge)

Dear Valerie. Make it look easy

But we know . . . .

Shine as always. Your Family. Marty, Jenny, Hayley (your unborn grandchild) & Steven the dog

Dear Val,

Just think. Some old pros would kill for this role. Have a great time and stay well. Love and kisses

Toni (Lamond)

To Dear Val,

To a true professional that never ceases to amaze us! Have a wonderful night — we will!

The Coppings xxxx

To Val,

Good to have you back at the State Theatre. Chookas. xx. Walter (Dressing crew)

Very simple rules

Always clean, even where it can't be seen.

Care about the problems of animals.

Floss.

Never do anything for the sole purpose of hurting someone.

Listen to all kinds of music. As long as it's good.

Don't hold your knife like a pencil.

Remember money can be your best friend.

Don't be a slave to fashion.

Always get someone else to do the dusting.

Speak with respect, it will earn the same.

Most problems are not life threatening.

Don't make complicated things simple, or simple things complicated.

Bad language denotes a lack of vocabulary.

Punctuality is the hallmark of good manners.

Prelude to an opening

Nervousness is only caring. Some of us care more than others, some of us care to the extreme, some of us care so much we make ourselves ill. But then if you don't care, you're no good.

It's all so worth it. That adrenaline rush, the roller coaster ride that takes your stomach to your heart and back again. I've known and felt it all my life, always a new thrill, a new love.

It's a wonderful feeling to be praised for hard work. Some may say they are not personally affected by critics who write adversely. I don't think they are being quite honest. It's magnificent when you receive a flattering review, and devastating when you don't. After all, who is more sensitive than an actor?

The accolades continued. The print media continued to use every opportunity to compliment the show and its individual cast. Radio talkback and serious critics gave *The Full Monty* ongoing praise. Television chat programs itemised the show's many highlights and fine performances.

And so I achieved what I had tried so hard to do. Prove to myself that I could still 'hack it'.

Reach high, for stars lie hidden in your soul. Dream deep, for every dream precedes the goal. May you live in interesting times.

We had experienced something that only we knew about. During the season personal accolades were many, from sources great and small; all were heartfelt and welcome. None was more meaningful to me than a formal letter from Actors Equity, our showbusiness union.

Life is wondrous, but so fleeting. It's all over in the blink of an eye, and I wouldn't have missed it for the world.

VAL JELLAY

Itemising the performing credentials of Val Jellay would amount to a dictionary of show business; it's been a non-stop seventy year career.

Being a dancer, acrobat and comedienne in vaudeville at the age of four was to launch this versatile Australian on a world wide journey, constantly entertaining.

Her school days were combined with performing nights. Teen years were committed to the demanding high quality productions of the Tivoli Circuit. Always a choreographer, she became involved with Garnett Carrol Presentations who became a springboard to the variety theatres of England and Ireland. Contracted to the Moss and Stoll theatres meant adapting her talents to the demands of diversified audiences. Max Miller enjoyed her creative input in his tours of Great Britain. Joyce Grenfell's management was quick to sign her for tours of Europe.

Upon her return to Austalia, she spent six years choreographing and directing for Sorlie's Revue Company. But the new medium in Australia in the 1950s was television. She made an instant impression in locally produced variety programs. The top rating *Sunny Side Up* with its comedy team enjoyed a seven year run. Drama followed, as part of the Crawford's stable of actors, and her involvement in all their dramas culminated in an eight year run in the hit series *The Flying Doctors*.

Always keeping in touch with her theatrical background, Val's lifetime journey of commitment has taken her full circle. The recent past has seen her featured in the huge musicals *Crazy For You*, Sondheim's *Follies*, *Anything Goes* and now playing Jeanette in *The Full Monty*. The role could have been inspired by her own life. Now considered an Australian show business icon, she was a subject of TV's *This Is Your Life*. Val Jellay is one of our most endearing and enduring talents.

```
VAL JELLAY                          JAN 2004
FULL MONTY CAST         MEMBERSHIP NO 1500
VICTORIAN ARTS CENTRE      JOINED 17-11-1944


DEAR VAL,

THIS LETTER IS TO NOTIFY YOU, THAT
DUE TO YOUR LONG STANDING IN THE
EQUITY COMMUNITY, WE WOULD LIKE TO
RECOMMEND YOU FOR HONORARY MEMBERSHIP
OF THE MEDIA AND ARTS ALLIANCE. YOU
WILL BE NOTIFIED FURTHER.


THANKS ONCE AGAIN FOR YOUR MANY YEARS
OF COMMITMENT. WE LOOK FORWARD TO
KEEPING YOU INVOLVED IN THE EQUITY
COMMUNITY.


KIND REGARDS,

ELEISHA MULLANE
INDUSTRIAL ORGANISER
LIVE THEATRE
```

Foibles fail to foil Follies

The Crown entertainment people assure me that tonight and tomorrow night's concert performances of *Follies* will go ahead, despite backstage rumblings and personnel disappearances.

I was surprised by how many hits Stephen Sondheim has crammed into this one. *Those Beautiful Girls, I'm Still Here, Would I Leave You?* and more.

But the showstopper is from the grand old lady of the Melbourne stage, **Val Jellay**.

She proves she still has what it takes and more and brings the house down with her rendition of *Broadway Baby*.

Sunday Herald Sun, April 16, 2000

This is your life

When Mike Munro with his grin of boyish devilment sneaks up on his unsuspecting victims, armed with his hallowed big red book, and pronounces—'*This Is Your Life*', an emotional fuse is lit. Some recipients have replied 'No It's not', and have plain walked away. Others have cried, some have giggled uncontrollably, some have come close to passing out.

The experience can be likened to a policeman knocking on your front door. Although innocent of all dastardly deeds, it is human nature to react with thoughts of 'what have I done'!

With *This Is Your Life*; it's similar to feelings of 'what are they going to tell about me'. Because that's exactly what the experience is—a detailed emotional exposé.

Please allow this one such honoured subject to humbly take you into the receiving side of what really goes on during the making of an episode of *This Is Your Life*.

I was made aware of the extreme research done by a team of dedicated and determined staff. They who pull all the strings together, the detailed dates, the relevant anecdotes, the on-screen guests, family and faces familiar to the public.

That research team at Channel Nine in Sydney spends many months on each subject. They are television's detectives, the ultimate goal being emotion, joy, sadness, and surprise, all adding up to entertainment, and therefore ratings for the network.

There were many things I learned about the process, long after my memorable episode. Firstly the unbelievable revelation that my son Marty Fields had been helping the research team in Sydney for six months. Very difficult when he lives in Melbourne. But he had grown up a showbusiness kid. Things he had been used to as part of his everyday life! Actors, theatres, TV shows, friends' names, phone numbers, photos, all sorts of information suddenly became important, as he passed on all the required memories to the researchers.

Marty is not one inclined to keep a thing to himself, but this time he did. He and my 'so called friends', were all in on the secret, like an underground network of informants.

When the subject of *This Is Your Life* is inundated with old friends appearing as surprise reminders of important moments, it barely touches the surface of one person's life. Research results in the showing of old film clips, where applicable, plus recorded messages from remote parts of the world. When Bud Tingwell was the honoured subject of one episode, I was very pleased to be invited to join the parade of friends who surprised him. In fact they made me the final friend in a

❧ Bud Tingwell and Val Jellay on the set of 'This is your Life'.

distinguished parade. From that experience I learned what goes on from the side of being an included friend.

As each guest surprised me, I was reminded of their involvement in my life, and the incredible workload I had crammed into a career in showbusiness.

With Bud Tingwell it was drama in *Homicide*, *Cop Shop*, *Solo One*, *Division Four*, *The Sullivans*, *Carsons Law*, *Prisoner*, and later *Blue Heelers* and *Neighbours*. *The Flying Doctors* kept me busy for eight years. Maurie and I were the publicans, Vic and Nancy Buckley. A lot of subtle comedy was written into those roles. Seven years in *Sunnyside Up* for Channel Seven, coincidentally, had given both Maurie and me a thorough knowledge of comedy. The birth and basis of it all had begun in vaudeville, decades before television. Most of us learn something every day, oblivious to the fact that one day it will be useful.

When Maurie died, Bud's Tingwell's quote to the press was:

'Over many years I have been privileged to work with some great people, but none better than Maurie Fields.'

After Mike Munro surprises his featured guest, which is referred to as the 'Sting', he goes back to Channel Nine and rehearses with the 'surprise friends'. Standing in for the star guest is the floor manager. He doesn't attempt dialogue, he wears his usual headphones and microphone set, carries his trusty clipboard and is responsible for everything that happens while listening to the director in the control room.

The guest of honour is firstly secreted into the studio by chauffeur driven limousine, then protected from sight and earshot by various production assistants who will not open a door unless cleared by an accomplice. Black curtains are draped like corridors, preventing anybody accidentally being seen by the star, thereby spoiling any surprise. The importance of this security is the basis of what makes the show a success.

It was five years after being on Bud Tingwell's tribute that I was again invited to be part of the accolade given to Helen Reddy. Helen's parents had been our close friends Max Reddy and Stella Lamond, vaudevillians from the days when Maurie and I trod the boards. So I should have been beyond surprising.

Nobody could have been more shocked, surprised and alarmed when Mike Munro, complete with devilish grin, approached me with his big red book and said, 'Val Jellay, This Is Your Life.'

Here is how it happened.

'We're here to pay tribute to one of Australia's

Taken aback by Mike Munroe.

most enduring and endearing entertainers. She thinks she is coming here to dine at the home of her son. So—let's go and surprise her.' This is how Mike Munro introduced the audience to the episode of 'my' *This Is Your Life*.

Mike's smiling countenance was surrounded by other sneaky conspirators. The script assistants, continuity people and other essential crew had obviously contracted the contagious moment of happy surprise.

'This is such an honour,' I managed to blurt out. Mike showed me the famous red book. 'But me, why me?' was my sincere question. Still holding my hand Mike replied—'Because we love you'.

Everybody was smiling. The cameras stopped filming; it was time for Mike and the crew to get back to the Channel Nine Melbourne studios.

Somebody quietly explained that I would have about three hours to spare before being required at the studio for the recording of the episode. 'Thank goodness for that,' I sighed, 'I need time away, home on my own to calm down and hold myself together'.

'No you can't be left alone now', I was firmly informed. 'We will take you by limousine anywhere you want to go, with one of us by your side every minute. Everything must be monitored by our staff. You must not answer your phone; you must not go to your front

door or speak to friends. Should you get any idea of the show's content, it will all be cancelled.'

I kept pestering my lady 'carer' for clues to the names of contributors to my life, but she kept assuring me that I would be very happy. Everything was going to be marvellous. Mine was a particularly beautiful story.

It was her job to keep telling me that. As it turned out, she was telling me the truth. I had been through many things in my lifetime, all of us have. Even so, I was about to go through one of the most emotional experiences of my long life. But then, it could be said that I am very emotional. A perfect subject for a show that relies on tugging at the heart strings.

Television cameras don't scare me—we had been co-workers for fifty years. The house lights or rather the studio lights were on as together we stepped through the sliding doors. Between the cameras and their capable handlers, I saw a mass of familiar faces greeting me with big smiles and lots of

applause.

The producers cleverly stack the audience with people who are part of one's day to day living. My wonderful next door neighbours were enjoying the deceiving situation. Liz Copping is my best friend, we tell each other everything, like sisters both of us never had. How did she look me in the eye every day and manage to keep this secret? Her husband Tom and family Asher and Adam, were all there, dressed to the nines. Maurie's gardening mate Lloyd Williams and his wife Betty seemed to be as proud as punch to be there. Lloyd was looking particularly

unfamiliar in a smart business suit—over the decades I have never seen him in anything other than overalls and gardener's gear. Some of these old friends had never been inside a TV studio, especially the postman.

Maybe the biggest smile that I could see was on the face of Maryanne Worth, my local hairdresser. This is a lady who literally sparkles in her demanding job as hairdresser and mother. A hairdressing salon is a breeding ground for chatter and swapping of what's what. It must have been so difficult for her and my other dear friend, her husband Terry Worth, to keep all this to themselves.

I would have said impossible. But they all managed to obey their apparent instructions. So many friends were in that audience.

When Kevin Swain, my childhood dancing partner was introduced, I was reminded of the depression years and us pre-schoolers, earning precious shillings. The acrobatic troupe famous as the 'Melbourne Marvels' always had my gratitude for knowing how to fall without being hurt. Jumping over fences, falling downstairs, being shot in a dozen different ways. It was all in the drama years.

The years were certainly crowded with showbusiness memories. None more significant than my years at the Tivoli in Bourke street, as I was reminded of when Mike Munro surprised me when he introduced two elderly ladies who had been beautiful Tivoli showgirls in the 1940s. It was time to laugh a lot as actual film of the time showed us all looking rather gorgeous. The Channel Nine researchers had film clips of everything relevant.

Maggie Fitzgibbon also reminded me of our years with her late brother Smacka Fitzgibbon.

Maggie:

'I did my first show at the Tivoli and you were there. This is a very wonderful tribute to all the joy, the fun and the laughter you've provided for so many people for so many years, particularly with your darling Maurie. And now you have Martin to carry on the tradition. That's so special. My fondest wishes to you, to Martin, and any of the old gang who may be walking down memory lane with you tonight.'

When Maggie was saying all the nice things about me on that show of tribute, sad thoughts were hard to suppress.

Once the Tivoli had been mentioned, the era of vaudeville and its effect on my life became paramount. These were my teenage years. It was the early 1940s. We were all in the thick of World War Two, the public desperately needed escapism, and vaudeville at its best provided it.

While Mike spoke of my having to do anything and everything at the Tivoli, the studio television screen continued to flash

Alma Jellay in her Sorlies Revue days.

on various photos of me during those years. So long ago. It made me feel so old, and yet grateful for having been given such a great theatrical background.

Alma, my proud mother adored the theatre. Being a wife and young mum had cancelled out her career, with her ambitions being transferred to her little daughter. I was proud of her too. She taught me that showbusiness was not only enjoyable, but it was a serious business, with ethics, morals and discipline.

It did take dedication and discipline to handle the workload at the Tivoli. We did twelve shows a week. A matinee every day at 2 pm, with an 8 pm show every night. We rehearsed in the mornings for the following programmes which changed every five weeks. Some of the show's titles were, *Paris Le Soir*, *Make It A Party*, *Clambake*, *The Naughty Nineties*, *It's Foolish But It's Fun*, *Get a Load Of This*, *Greet The Fleet*, *Americana*, *Forbidden City*, *Follies Bergere*, *Artists and Models*, *Stars and Garters*, *Ballyhoo*, *Forever Glamour*, *Starry Nights*, *Cavalcade of Varieties*, *The Gay Nineties*, *Beauty on Parade*, *Laughter Invasion*, *The Sky's The Limit*, *Atomic Blondes*, *Let Er Go*, *Design For Glamour*, *Laughing Room Only*.

Some of the headliners were Jim Gerald, Will Mahoney, Roy Rene (Mo), George Wallace and Jenny Howard. Of the second string comedians there were Morry Barling, Syd Beck, Joe Lawman, Buster Fiddes, and

so many others but the big name comics, except for George Wallace, were very serious people.

Because of my solo work as a child performer, it took no time before the management had me working in the comedy sketches.

Working in the sketches with great comedians was probably the best education I ever had. The discipline was truly severe. To breathe in the wrong place, or a slight move of distraction would earn a serious reprimand. To not deliver a feed line with the correct timing would mean getting jumped on and lectured severely. Those great comics weren't only wordsmith perfectionists. They could tap-dance, sing, acrobat, and extract pathos as well as laughs from an audience, this was their life, before writers and television cameras and laugh tracks changed the world of entertainment forever.

The same could be said about the acts of the time. Gone are the days when a strong sight act would have them working the same act forever in the many variety theatres around the country. A television performance can only be done once because it's seen by millions, all at the same time, and can't be repeated. It's easier to be a singer. One song can bring fame and success. Besides singers have all the best writers, where repetition is expected.

The dancers during my era were beautiful

261

❧ *With Marty Fields, Liz Burch and Andrew McFarlain.*

girls in every way. Classy, elegant, dedicated. I was indeed proud to be one of them.

Of all the performing arts, ballet is probably the most valuable. If not pursued as a career many things remain with the student. How to stand, sit, walk. Like learning piano, ballet is the basis of dance, as piano is the basis of music.

Then there were the productions of Harry Wren, a very smart scallywag. Garnett Carrol and his Australia-wide circuit with management represented by his brother Bruce, and later son John. There was Max Reddy's Follies. Variety shows from The Great Levante and Rooklyn. Barton's Follies toured Australia, as did other smaller companies. The big and constant touring company was surely 'Sorlies'. A revue company that brought together the pairing of the double act of Maurie and Val. That double act enjoyed a forty-five year run.

Being only sixteen when I began at the Tiv', it felt as though everyone was older than me, maybe they were. The beautiful showgirls would have had a short career in showbusiness. They weren't required to sing, dance or acrobat, therefore their immediate future was usually a marriage that took them to the four corners of the globe.

When Toni Lamond made her entrance for my episode of *This Is Your Life*, it felt like old times.

Toni:

'Long ago when I heard that Val Jellay was joining the show that I was in, I was worried. Val was from the big time, the Tivoli, and I was somewhat intimidated, but I needn't have worried, Val was a true pro'. She taught me the right way to make an entrance and an exit.' (Toni demonstrates the remembered moves.)

Toni:

'My Mother Stella later worked with Maurie in *Bellbird*, and at my Mother's funeral Maurie gave a most moving eulogy. Years later I found out that it was actually composed by Val. That was the first hint for me that she would become an accomplished author of several best-seller biographies.'

Later another moving eulogy for Max Reddy's funeral, also presented by Maurie Fields was a Val Jellay tribute.

Toni was in her element, enjoying her memories of a past we shared. We hugged as she walked to the guest's seating area. I remember feeling grateful for her kind input.

Mike:

'When you unexpectedly fall pregnant, you and Maurie are over the moon. And on December 18th the light of your life Martin Fields is born. Here he is now with your grandson Steven.'

A sudden murmur and flurry of gasps immediately erupted from the audience. 'She doesn't have grandchildren! What grandchildren!' The blue sliding doors opened and there was Martin, looking resplendent in an Armani suit and tie. Standing beside him was his Blue-Heeler dog Steven—also wearing an Armani tie. I swear they were both grinning with delight. Marty then said to Steven, 'There's grandma'. With that, Steven ran to me, immediately jumping up on the little settee beside me. He even turned around, sat and faced the cameras

before leaning over and giving his grandma lots of loving doggie licks.

I have to admit that Steven's appearance gave me the biggest surprise, and joy, of the entire evening. Later that night Toni Lamond told me that my reaction to Martin's dog coming on was definitely my greatest, in order of importance. It's a known fact that I'm an animal freak. It's true that during my lonely, only childhood, a dog was always my best friend.

I learned later, that when the producer/director of *This Is Your Life* asked Martin whether or not the dog 'would go to her', his reply was—'You're kidding!'

Martin:

'I don't have any children yet, so my dog is like a surrogate grandson to Mum. She spoils him rotten, and babysits him when I'm away. As a kid it was never unusual for me to come home and find Mum and Dad rehearsing dance steps or comedy routines. They bought a piano for me before I was born, wanting me to have the value of musical knowledge. Mum always drove me to piano lessons at the conservatorium. She was in such a state once when the car broke down in the middle of a city intersection and the police towed us away. We've had some great times together and I love her very much.'

The media

Photographers, radio and television news readers, the press, the paparazzi. Collectively are known as the media. Their work is a necessary part of our lives, whether we like it or not, the media is crucial. It's part of what makes the world go round. There are some who declare the media intrudes on their lives, whose fault is that! It cannot be blamed solely on the paparazzi; they are just doing their job, obeying the rules of mercenary editors who by necessity must beat their opposition to the big story or the important photo.

It's not only show folk who, and can, become famous. Show folk have the media to thank for their high profile, for being on the A list for invitees. They are highlighted at opening nights, at other people's weddings, at the Melbourne Cup and so on. And then there are those who become famous for just being on somebody else's arm. While this situation interests the public, and while magazines highlight what they consider to be news, nothing will change, and the world of showbusiness is undoubtedly among the grateful. When the very big stars, usually from overseas, complain about the media intruding on their lives, perhaps it is realistic for them to understand it is of their own making. There would have been a time in their youth when they would have begged for a published photo in the press, or just to see their name in print. It seems that it's when they get their name in lights that the trouble starts.

For performers, publicity can be the making or the breaking of success. Those who say 'the critics are not important', may be being totally truthful. A good 'write-up' is a wonderful form of approval, and is always spoken about, where as a bad write-up is often referred to as 'really, I didn't see it', or 'it's only one person's opinion'. This latter attitude is simply covering the hurt.

Fact: there aren't any other people more sensitive than show people, believe me.

And as for the media, there is an old, but very true saying: Be nice to them on the way up, because you never know when you might meet them on the way down.

Exposed

The very nature of a program such as *This Is Your Life*, is to trigger the minds of those involved.

The magnificent English variety theatres that were under the banner of the prestigious Moss and Stoll management, took me to the length and breadth of England, followed by Belfast and Dublin.

It wasn't possible for reminders of those years to be announced by Mike Munro and have English stars step through the sliding doors. They were times of pride in 1952-3 & 4 when working on the same bill with Max Miller, Diana Dors, Donald Peers, Morcambe and Wise, Syd and Max Harrison, an aging Laurel and Hardy and so many others excited me. All of those stars had long ago passed on.

The years away from home became even more exciting when I was invited to join a concert party headed by the much loved English comedy actress Joyce Grenfell. The publicity machine billed me as 'The Shape from Downunder'. I was twenty-four years old. Malta, Tripoli, Benghazi and Fayid were fascinating. We entertained forces and their officers who were still stationed in far off places immediately after World War Two and into the 1950s.

Germany, Austria, Oldenberg, Nuremburg, Italy and Trieste were also part of the same itinerary, which included BBC stars Louise Traill and Harry Andrews.

Back in Australia, Sorlies Revue played an exceptionally important part in my life. It was 1955 and it's where I met Maurie Fields. It was a love that erupted like a volcano. It never diminished. For well over forty years it continued to bubble away with extraordinary effervescence.

Work took Maurie and myself to wonderful destinations to entertain corporate seminars. They were a case of B.Y.O Aussie entertainers. Vanuatu was a favourite. More than four work trips to Hawaii meant that it became a familiar destination. Strange how these organised soirees of Australian business folk preferred their familiar performers instead of the locals.

Mike:

'In 1966 *Sunnyside Up* is coming to an end, and your career starts heading in another direction.' (The screen then showed a sketch with Syd Heylen and me, from the many such sketches we did over seven years for Channel Seven in the much loved and fondly remembered *Sunnyside Up*.)

My life's lessons were learned at the Tivoli from the greats.

Encouraged by the Producer of *Sunnyside Up,* Alf Spargo, I would write out comedy scripts word for word as my youthful memory capitalised on the past. Detailed outlines of sets were drawn, wardrobe lists itemised, even explaining how certain bits of 'business' were executed. I didn't mind, I was proud to be part of the new medium, we all were, and especially proud of being in a successful show.

⤺ With good friend Toni Lamond.

*When vaudeville died, television
was the box they put it in.*
— Bob Hope

Variety shows were destined to have a shorter life on television than drama, although we didn't realise it then. The great visual acts, known as 'sight acts' because they didn't have a language barrier, were most severely affected. Jugglers, acrobats, wire walkers, magicians, teeter-board acts, risley acts, trick cyclists and the like, would have trained from childhood to reach the necessary standard for success. Once precision perfect, which was the ultimate goal, they could then perform in the many theatres with a thousand or so audience capacity. The act could keep going for a lifetime.

Not so with television. The ability for TV to reach so many audiences in one sitting destroyed many specialty acts, who were never replaced. It all became too hard. Much easier to learn four chords on a guitar and become a rock singer. Reading music was not a requirement. Singers had it even easier. An overnight star could be made by one successful song, no stage craft necessary, and access to all the best unpaid writers, Gershwin, Porter, Bacharach. Personal managers and record companies made millions.

I remember once talking to Bill Collins, the great race caller. He was reflecting on the halcyon days of *Sunnyside Up* and the great comedy team we had. He was an integral part of that team, when people in their houses would sit on the loungeroom floor every Friday night at 7.30, eating fish and chips while watching our fearless exploits.

It was probably about 1996 when Bill Collins, himself battling bone cancer, began reminiscing about our successful comedy team. 'You know love, it's sad that Maurie has gone, Syd Heylen's gone, Honest John Gilbert's gone, there's only you and me left and my money's on you.' Two weeks later Bill Collins died. A lovely man, missed by many, including the racing fraternity. His widow Robyn still dances with the Tivoli Lovelies. She is forever lovely, and a good friend.

Many performers survived the transition to television, combining their theatre skills with camera skills, ten times as many fell by the wayside.

Professional actors are trained to study scripts and learn dialogue. This 'homework' is essential, enabling the actor to arrive for work, word perfect and thoroughly rehearsed. One feels in control. It's quite frightening just having to sit on that little settee and wonder who and what will happen next. Mike Monroe kept the surprises coming. My long time friend Bert Newton reminded me of past experiences shared. Cast members of *The Flying Doctors*, Andrew McFarlane and Liz Burch, had us all laughing. I silently thought about Maurie and the great

2005 TV WEEK LOGIE AWARDS
PRESENTED BY GARNIER

Pat Ingram, Publisher, TV WEEK,
takes pleasure in inviting

Val Jellay
& Marty Fields

to attend

THE 47TH ANNUAL
TV WEEK LOGIE AWARDS

Palladium at Crown
8 Whiteman Street, Southbank
Melbourne
Sunday May 1, 2005
4.30pm sharp
Cocktails and Canapés
Main Course
Live Telecast
TV WEEK Logies After Party
Black Tie

Please RSVP by April 4, 2005 to 2005TVWEEKLogieAwards@acp.com.au
Enquiries to Liz McKenzie: Phone 61 (03) 9846 7100, Mobile 0411 614 523
email: liz@eventtoremember.com.au
Strictly non-transferable

TV WEEK GARNIER 9 CROWN

eight years we had on that show.

It was at the 2003 Logies, when Peter O'Brian introduced me to his beautiful new bride Miranda Otto, that we talked about the earlier years we spent together in *The Flying Doctors*. They were tough times but wonderful memories.

Peter and I talked about a conversation that took place in the pub set when he was playing the role of a pilot. Rebecca Gibney was an overalled young mechanic and Maurie and I were behind the bar as publicans.

The scene involved our four characters with Maurie having the bulk of the dialogue. Some actors have a system of line learning that works for them. Others slog away non-stop, never managing to completely get on top of the stress. Doing one's homework is really where the toil takes place. At home, I don't remember seeing or hearing Maurie swat over his lines, other than marking his scripts with a yellow marker, and an occasional mumble to himself in front of the bathroom mirror while shaving. He was a genuinely calm bloke, who never got rattled.

As we rehearsed this particular scene the day before shooting, Peter, Rebecca and myself, with scripts down, of course, worried our way through it. Not Maurie. As usual he was holding his script in one hand, the other hand was holding the last mouthful of a

Every year a Logie invitation.

This is Your Life

15 May 2000

Ms Val Jellay
57 Page Street
ALBERT PARK VIC 3206

Dear Val,

Producing "This Is Your Life – Val Jellay" has been exciting and inspiring. The show wouldn't have been the great success it was if it weren't for the constant support of your wonderful family and friends.

At this stage the show will be going to air on Thursday 19th October, 2000. I will let you know if this changes.

Enclosed is a copy of the show and your album filled with photo's of the night.

Thank you for your good grace and relaxed approach to the show.

All our best wishes.

Kind regards.

Julia Holdstock
PRODUCER

NINE NETWORK AUSTRALIA PTY LTD
ACN 008 685 407
24 ARTARMON ROAD (PO BOX 27) WILLOUGHBY NSW 2068 AUSTRALIA
TELEPHONE: (02) 9965 2955. FACSIMILE: (02) 9965 2893
WEB SITE: ninemsn.com.au

hastily, discreetly eaten meat-pie.

'Do you wanna go for one mate!' Maurie said to the director. 'Standing by'—'rolling'—'mark it'—'action', came from different crew members. They all knew him well. No one else would get away with this casual approach.

After working on *The Flying Doctors* for a long time, Peter O'Brian had watched Maurie's attitude to the responsibility. We filmed the scene, and as usual, the director declared 'that's a print'. The crew immediately began their moving on routine for the next scene.

Peter said, 'Maurie, how do you do that! We watch you and wonder. You don't appear to study your lines, you don't seem concerned about thoroughly rehearsing, and yet it comes out word perfect, performance perfect, how do you do it?' I listened as Maurie thoughtfully replied with one word—

'Terror'.

Peter O'Brian told me that he had carried Maurie's one word of advice with him throughout his busy career here and overseas. 'Terror.'

He said it's fine to be scared, to feel afraid, to be daunted by the situation—every actor is stressed. Face it, admit to yourself that you have the right to feel terror. It's when you push the anxiety aside, bottle it up, pretending everything is easy, that trouble can take over. I've always admired Peter O'Brian (he's a down to earth country boy at heart) and a fine actor. His understanding and admiration of Maurie once again reinforced my own respect for Maurie's uniqueness.

When Mike referred to Maurie's heart condition whilst film clips of us singing,

Previous page: Passing parade of Tivoli dancers.

dancing, laughing, and acting were on the screen I began to fall apart.

Mike:

'On his son Marty's birthday, Maurie suffers his third and final heart attack. He passes away in your arms, and you've lost your best friend and soul mate.'

'All of Australia mourns the man who for decades had entertained them. It was like a national disaster as we all lost the man who always acted and joked his way into our hearts, bringing smiles to everyone's faces. Tributes flood in, and in 1996 Maurie is honoured when he's inducted into the Logies Hall of Fame. Naturally the other half of the act is there to accept on his behalf.'

Mike:

'Val you've certainly come a long way from a four year old child performer. The years

on the Tivoli Circuit. Those hectic, frantic, chaotic years in vaudeville. A television pioneer in comedy and drama. You've now spent seventy years in showbusiness, now starring in musical theatre. You've never tired of it, never dreaming you'd achieve what you have, and you've done it with enormous style and grace. And of course there's only one way to end a show like yours, and that's what you do best. So would you please join your son Marty by singing one of your favourites, 'Mandy'?'

This surprise request really took me aback. Mike had requested a song from a repertoire of duets I had performed only ever with Maurie. After putting me through the wringer, my emotions were truly stretched and the tears and laughter brought on by the whole experience wasn't the best warm up for singing. It must have been obvious that I was floored by the request.

Val to Mike:

'I don't think I could do it without Maurie, I haven't sung any of our songs since his passing, please don't ask me to do it without him.' I started trembling.

Marty, who had been sitting beside me on the little blue settee, then said 'I'll do it with you Mum—trust me.' 'But you've never sung it, you don't know 'Mandy', we've never sung it together'. Panic was mounting. With that, Marty took my hand, dismissed my objections, and quickly escorted me to a grand piano, which was discreetly set to one side of the central shooting area. A microphone stand with its microphone set at the exact height I preferred was also waiting for me.

I discovered later that Marty had been very explicit about the microphone situation. Things I didn't realise he'd taken on board from the past. Holding a mike I find unacceptable. It limits my feel and selling of the song. I prefer to be hands free. If a body mike isn't available, (in this case surprise being foremost) the stand-mike must be neck high, not masking the face. Singers who hold the mike up to their mouth are losing expression. The sound department is there to take care of the volume. Don't hide the assets. However, Marty was familiar with my idiosyncrasies and had this situation well and truly covered.

The song Mike asked for seemed simple, but having a counter melody was its charm. It was tricky. I was suddenly very nervous about it. But my fears had to be pushed aside. Like the rest of the research that had gone on, Marty had risen above being a son who had grown up surrounded by old songs and gag routines that he'd not truly taken much notice of, and actually listened to the recorded words sung by his father.

Getting the song started was really difficult. Maurie wasn't beside me with his trusty ukulele playing the introduction. Marty could see hesitation on my face, he played a four bar intro in the correct key and said 'sing Mum'. It was an order, and just as well—I needed to be jolted into action. Faith in Marty's input was never in doubt; he is a superb piano player and a natural perfect pitch vocalist.

The three video cameras swung around to face the new performing area. Between the cameras I caught glimpses of all my friends in the studio audience. They were all wearing smiles of encouragement; they knew this wasn't going to be easy. My thoughts were mixed. The producers of a show like *This is Your Life*, rely on exposing one's innermost feelings, they too knew this was going to be a tough call. The network knew me well, they had been close to Maurie and myself since the early days of television, why not turn those emotional screws one more time. Channel Nine had always done their job well.

❧ With son Marty at Maurie's posthumous induction into the Logies 'Hall of Fame', 1996.

Like going into battle I gathered up my performing instincts and gave our dear old 'Mandy' a full on attack. It was hard, very hard. Maurie's strength wasn't beside me, but I couldn't let down the side. Behind me at the grand piano, my trusty son was singing the busy counter melody, with its complicated words. Maurie would have approved, his kind smile would have surfaced, with a customary wink.

It was near the end of the song, was I going to get all the way through it without breaking down! The big finish was coming up… 'For my Mandy and m…'. The last note stuck in my throat, and stayed there. Loud sobs took over, and I broke down completely. The on-stage guests all flocked around me as the theme music began playing. Mike Munro walked onto the set.

'VAL JELLAY, THIS IS YOUR LIFE.'

The big red book was presented to me. I weepingly accepted it with pride as the music swelled and the credits rolled.

The red book was retrieved by the floor manager, it contained only Mike's notes. Two weeks later I received a shiny red and gold duplicate. It contained everybody's dialogue along with photographs taken from the episode. Attached was a delightful letter of thanks.

Audiences continued to make me welcome.

Fortunately, the lifetime of performing in live theatre made working solo once more not so much a challenge, but an invitation to be appreciated. And appreciated I was. It was a very different time for me, the work was more like being a special guest. Compering functions, presenting at awards nights, fundraisers, with interviews in every media. The television morning programs kept me really busy, which was very satisfying. Self doubt quickly disappeared as the power, and it is a kind of power, enabling me to enjoy the audiences who had come to know me. The cabaret audiences were always receptive, as though they knew me personally, and I began to realise how much I needed them, more than ever. They kept me going, it was and is, a dependence. And yes I was, as ever, addicted to the love from audiences.

"Mandy", a long established Maurie and Val duet. Marty filling the emotional breach on 'This is Your Life'.

Bare facts

Shopping for baby furniture became urgent, with only the best for baby Fields.

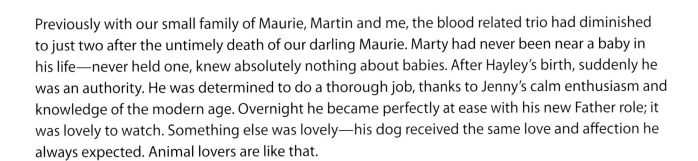

Previously with our small family of Maurie, Martin and me, the blood related trio had diminished to just two after the untimely death of our darling Maurie. Marty had never been near a baby in his life—never held one, knew absolutely nothing about babies. After Hayley's birth, suddenly he was an authority. He was determined to do a thorough job, thanks to Jenny's calm enthusiasm and knowledge of the modern age. Overnight he became perfectly at ease with his new Father role; it was lovely to watch. Something else was lovely—his dog received the same love and affection he always expected. Animal lovers are like that.

The workload seemed to get heavier for Martin.

Then, my busy son was asked to join the cast of television's cop show *Blue Heelers*, as a Sergeant of Police.

Fortunately Maurie had taught his son by example to be versatile. Don't rely on one skill alone. That way you can turn to other work. The 'fifty-two weeker' workers are all-rounders, that is, unless you're lucky enough to be in an ongoing series. But even these disappear by their use-by date.

It's rather gratifying to be able to spread the 'in demand' skills over a variety of areas. Life is therefore never dull, although meeting the many challenges can sometimes be very unnerving.

The dramatic acting required in *Blue Heelers* was probably one of Martin's most happy experiences. The workload was heavy. The regular cast accepted him into the fold and he truly became close to them all. I enjoyed listening to his views on various scenes, especially the scenes where he had to run around in the country completely nude—a situation that was a late surprise. He wouldn't explain to me how the storyline got him into that predicament, I had to wait to see it when it went to air.

He was the only actor involved that day in the unusual filming. The director made the most of it, he even had him going deep into a lake—and it was in winter—of course. The crew, which by

Maurie's 60th birthday at the Roxy Hotel.

necessity are many, and rugged up for the winter, were amazed at Marty's professional attitude. They tried to keep him warm and dry, but with the shooting of takes happening over and over, it was impossible.

Although he was actually completely nude, his 'tilbury' had to be covered by sticky tape, which also held up his 'orchestra stalls'. When I asked about who did the strapping up, his reply was; 'Everybody, although Alby in wardrobe was most helpful'.

All was going well until he had to run, and the pubic hairs which were glued to the sticky tape held fast. Apparently the pain was beyond description. By the way, he didn't have to audition for those scenes. Actors become accustomed to doing the unusual. As Maurie used to say—'You're workin' aren't ya!'

Every theatre and TV production is anxious for complimentary media coverage, especially from those who are known as critics. When total strangers are enthusiastic in their flattery it is truly a delight. It takes time, and some effort to put pen to paper for expressions of appreciation.

Although not having the same thought in mind, I too have not been shy in sending similar messages to those I have thought to be truly worthy of more than just receiving their monetary reward. One such occasion had me reaching for pen and paper in my urgent need to acknowledge a job well done.

It was just a quick note to a Melbourne radio station.

The 5.30 until 8.30 am slot is not the most convenient time to entertain and inform. Two of Victoria's most successful are the team of Ross Stevenson and John Burns. I would say that they are slick. What their background is—I have no idea.

It surprised me no end, to receive a reply from my fan letter to Ross Stevenson. He apparently appreciated my note, and I was ecstatic to receive his reply.

I was delighted when Channel Nine invited me to join the ten year celebration of *This Is Your Life,* to take place in Sydney.

I pondered the persistent loyalty to Australian showbusiness by the likes of Mike Walsh, David Atkins, Kevin Jacobson, John Frost, Simon Gallagher and Jeanne Pratt. The financial ups and downs are always a risk-taking heartache. God bless them all.

The Wentworth Hotel Sydney had been a particular favourite of ours when Maurie and I enjoyed the hospitality of various sponsors. But the recent billion-dollar makeover made the new Wentworth Hotel almost unrecognisable to this stranger in paradise.

I arrived at the specified venue for the *This Is Your Life* celebration to find the party in full swing. It was fun to see so many familiar faces. Around the room

were many TV monitors, without audio (sound), endlessly rolling through the many honoured recipients during 'the sting', when the host surprises the unsuspecting with the profound statement 'This Is Your Life'. The actual dates were displayed under each 'sting'.

Everyone was enjoying the mood. Ten years is quite a run for any format. Drinks were enjoyed, finger food was eaten. Photos were taken. Many honoured ones could not be present due to commitments, including my friend Bud Tingwell who had asked me to convey his regrets. I couldn't help thinking of those who didn't need an excuse for their non-attendance, like Tommy Hanlon and Slim Dusty. How does that song go 'I'm Still Here'.

I reminisced with Normie Rowe, Glenn Shorrock, Peter Phelps' delightful sister Dr Kerryn Phelps, Cornelia Frances, Judy Nunn, Toni Lamond and Debra Byrne, who was the first to be honoured in Australia.

Tony Bonner and Ian Turpie reminded me of the days long past. The irrepressible

'Carlotta' was still hilariously defying nature, as were we all, and the gorgeous Mike Munro was quick to plant a meaningful kiss on my cheek. Dear Mike, who had just arrived that day from a *Sixty Minutes* assignment in the States, looked handsome and proud; he had always been kind to us all. Without the hardworking Paula Duncan whose charity work is renowned, the ten-year birthday celebration would not have been the same. All of a sudden it was over and I was on my way back to Melbourne, for next morning, to take on a different mindset for a different television network, Channel Seven's *Blue Heelers*.

This time the make-up department did their work to make me not look like Val Jellay. I was playing the part of an old lady who thinks she is dying of a brain tumour. Familiar faces in the crew gave me greeting hugs while reminding me of past creative times we shared. Steve Mann, the director, always a

As Maurie used to say, 'You're working aren't ya!'

delight. Christian Robinson, the first assistant director, was holding down his usual important job on *Blue Heelers*. I honestly proclaimed his forever handsomeness, and still being slim. It was truly a comfort zone. Even in the make-up room, the star of the show, John Wood, came over to the make-up chair, and without a word leaned over me and planted a big kiss on my cheek, and I never saw him again. We didn't have any scenes together.

My role in that episode could have been done by any experienced actress, it wasn't difficult, it was enjoyable like old times when all of us were cast in most unlikely parts. Most of the crew that day had worked with Maurie and I on *The Flying Doctors* during its eight year run. They had always treated me royally.

In my third and last scene that day I didn't have any dialogue, 'lovely', I thought. Julie Nhill (publican) and Samantha Tolj (policewomen) had to unlock the door on my room at the hotel to find me collapsed on the floor unconscious. It was like a comfort zone, being part of a successful television drama again.

Here is a unique display that should only be performed by professional stunt people, who are experts in spectacular falls down stairs.

Managing to purchase a single ticket to the Saturday matinee performance of *Carousel* at the State Theatre Melbourne, the elegance of the surrounds were totally inappropriate for my yet again disturbing behaviour. Oh, the shame of it! My fellow audience members had all returned to their seats after interval, as I too had intended. The dress circle seating fans out at the sides, going down, which was my destination, but for a friend who needed to chat at the top of the stairs, which was where she was sitting. By the time we said our farewells, the auditorium was in darkness, ready for the second half of *Carousel*. The orchestra was playing the entr'acte prior to the curtain rising.

At this capacity performance, by now, everyone was back in their seats, except for me, who was still at the top of the side dress-circle aisle, needing to get down to the second front row. My usual sense of urgency, and the darkness caused me to miscalculate the stairs, which are uneven. So away I went, as Maurie would say, like a big heap of mullick, whatever that is. Clutching my handbag as if my life depended on it—why we do that I wonder—I rolled and bumped uncontrollably, whilst the orchestra was playing the *Carousal* theme most appropriately. Several ladies screamed amongst the general disturbance. I couldn't stop the momentum, the speed gathered, and I swear I would have gone straight off the edge into the stalls below, if it hadn't been for the design of the fanned seating.

Two ladies sitting at the end of an aisle were shocked when the full force of my rapidly descending body came to an end by impacting at the back of their seats. My head was the last part of me to stop. It landed directly between the heads of those two astonished ladies who stared at my sudden arrival. Could I move? Not a hope in Hades. Apologising profusely, I tried to get up from the carpeted stairs that had probably prevented something from being broken. Or was it my early acrobatic training in knowing how to fall! I flatter myself. Strange though, with a capacity audience, not a soul attempted to come to my assistance, or to verbally venture the useless question, 'Are you alright?'

The complete darkness, which caused my judgment to go haywire, was now the means of hiding my embarrassment. Eventually clambering back into my own seat I remember feeling disorientated and in pain, and I also remember silently crying. Had I known that the next day would begin the most colourful bruising ever to be seen down one side of a human body, I probably would have excused my lapse into that indulgent weeping. The bruising evidence remained unseen, although it covered the torso, and remained for the best part of a month. My backside and hips looked like the result of something far more sinister. Perhaps I shouldn't be allowed out alone. Amen to that.

Well I certainly wasn't alone when I walked behind a set of tabs, again in total darkness, at the Lido Theatre Restaurant during an annual concert presented by The Limelighters. My shin clipped the sharp edge of a ground row of lighting. It didn't hurt all that much. I just thought of it as a collision in the dark, until I emerged into the light, where the Tivoli Lovelies were dressing. These tap dancing old friends of mine were also preparing for the show, when one of them said, 'Val you're bleeding', and another said, 'You're gushing blood', and another, 'Quick, put her leg up, elevate it'. And with that, many change bags were thrust under my leg as I was seated on a chair. They fussed like a flock of mother hens. From out of nowhere came the Lido's owner, the marvellous Rene-Ann Martini, complete with first aid kit.

The first thing Rene-Ann did was to get me to remove my black pantyhose. As the hose lifted from the wounded skin, the skin of the gash also lifted in two sections like small flaps. I remember the other 'lovelies' trying to clean up the blood with tissues but the bleeding was uncontrollable. Rene-Ann tried to disinfect the area while applying a thick pressure bandage. I will always be grateful for her calm expedience. She even took off her own black socks which she was wearing under black pants, then quickly cut the tops off them with scissors and put them

'Blue Heelers.'

on my feet saying, 'You can't have bare feet!' She knew a sock wouldn't go over a thick bandage. I don't remember much about the performance that night, only that I brushed aside all suggestions of hospital or not doing the show. The next day the fun started in the treatment room of my local GP.

Leaving Rene-Ann's bandage on all night had been the right thing to do, because as soon as the doctor and two nurses removed it the bleeding became uncontrollable. This, they assured me was good, because it not only self cleansed the area but enabled them to shift the 'flaps' back to where they belonged. This they did together from both sides of my leg, with green surgical tweezers, explaining that stitching in that area wasn't an option. I looked away during this procedure but it sure was painful. After surgical dressings and a pressure bandage, a tetanus shot was administered. Every second day I went back for a dressing change and each time the bleeding would continue. That situation lasted two weeks during which time an allergic reaction to the tetanus injection caused my arm to swell, become red, and itch like crazy. That problem was treated with Cortisone cream. It was four weeks before I was free of the fat bandage. The dressings

began unsticking themselves from the wound and showering became less awkward.

Like everything in life it all came to pass. I have a permanent scar on my right shin, which is better than life's scars that can't be seen. My relating this kaleidoscope of mishaps is to illustrate my one deep desire in life—managing to stay upright! It's very important.

Time takes its toll on the advanced years of once-upon-a-time dancers and acrobats like me. The knees are a big give-away. I have a right knee that pops in and out with regular monotony. It's called a dislocated patella.

An unpleasant pelvic ultrasound revealed nothing. A pap smear revealed plenty. Shingles in my right eye has left me with headaches that are like a smithy's anvil pounding in my head. An irregular heartbeat is a permanent condition. At least I haven't got dandruff.

There are wonderful compensations for this advancing years situation. Respect is everywhere I go. And it's very, very, nice. I enjoy the invitations to opening nights in the theatre, also the annual invitations to the Logies are a privilege, especially as a presenter. Being assigned the prestigious position of the Victorian Seniors Festival's face of the year (2006), made the passing of time more acceptable.

The group at the Channel Seven celebration of fifty years of *Made in Melbourne,* made my decades of input feel worthwhile. The *Neighbours* twenty years celebration at Channel Ten was a privileged and fun party. Being a special guest at functions, being on various selection boards, a compere at others, and the many interviews about vaudeville, the theatres in Europe and variety in England, all keep me busy and gratified.

family.

Through the years it has been hard not to notice how some young performers find it tiresome to do unpaid promotions, to sign autographs and take a moment to acknowledge a devoted fan. Without our audiences and their interest we would be out of a job. It's a good idea to remember that one day your autograph may not mean a thing. Coping with fans is after all, part of the job. I have never found it tiresome.

Talent helps. Being prepared to strive helps more.

My mother's death was difficult to accept; my father's passing meant memories could no longer be shared. Life with Maurie Fields filled both our lives with everything we needed.

When our son arrived unexpectedly we had everything anyone could want. Never rich, always just managing. Martin, or Marty as he is known as professionally, is a compassionate man, kind, funny, loving and thoughtful. Always anxious to get everything right, happiest when he is doing too many projects at once. Now he is also a devoted father, a role he had no idea about, but being a quick student and very determined, their love is mutual—his little daughter adores him. Beautiful Jenny is a wise and happy mother. They make a loving family—my

Managements know the value of audience acceptance. If an audience knows cast members by past reputation, by standards set, they know their faith won't disappoint.

I have now shared with you the intimate feelings of just one member of a crazy business who has tried desperately to do a good job. Not seek fame or fortune, which can be short lived. To cope with setbacks, enjoy the good times. Applause is a great adrenalin rush, it's precious, like the loyalty of love. Be enthusiastic. Stay healthy. Happy endings are possible.

Fallacies

Doing one good show, and receiving all the accolades and publicity that goes with it, does not automatically provide financial stability. Many a well-known actor has faced lean times because the high profile has created a star-like presence. When starring roles aren't available, and the lesser parts are demeaning, the decision not to work at all is often made so as to preserve the high status. The solution to all this is to aim at being a fifty-two weeker: keep working; do everything; forget about stardom. If you have star quality you will be one anyway.

There are many well-known sayings that are meant to be helpful, but they don't really help. Here is one of them: 'There are no small roles only small actors.' In other words, 'it's what you do with what you've got'.

After a long run in a play, musical or performance of any kind, friendships are made for life—wrong! Most players never see each other again. Some do form ongoing friendships due to situations that keep them in touch.

The public, bless them, often believe in the characters that actors portray. They are disbelieving when told of lives having gone in different directions.

Actors are the life and soul of every party. Not so. Most are reserved and often shy. This is prevalent with comedians. 'It must be a laugh a minute in your house'. Wrong again. Where the next job is coming from usually takes priority, followed by health issues, closely followed by the ever constant letters with windows (the bills). We all have them. Would I change my life on that roller coaster, when the lows have been lower and the highs have been higher? Not for one minute!

Other fallacies:

Being in a show means access to free seats.

Being in a show means keeping the wardrobe.

Being in a show means stage-door fans bearing gifts.

Being in a show means you can ad-lib your lines once you've learned them.

Being in a show means you can see your friends in the audience.

Being in a show means you will hit the notes you did at the audition.

Being in a show means priority service in restaurants.

Being in a show means a hectic private life.

Being in a show means you will always be in a show.

Surprise! Surprise!

The following, although not meant to make for entertaining reading, will no doubt be of interest to those who like me, believed that to become unhealthy, you must have an unhealthy lifestyle. Bad things happen to other people, not me—never me. Now hear this. We *are* the other people. Fate has no favourites. 'Me' is all of us. To tell about what happened does necessitate some explicit describing of events. I can only hope that this does not offend. It's a matter of honesty.

Take for instance—spotting. It had been a long time since menopause. So this must mean to be some kind of node, such as singers get in their throat. Or perhaps a one off strain of some kind. The showing disappeared. Only to come back for one day, a couple of months later.

I made an appointment to see my GP of many years, who I shall call Doctor John. The St Vincent Place Medical Centre has a group of doctors who all have access to computer information on each patient. Doctor John unfortunately was on holiday leave, so a doctor who I shall call Fred was able to see me. He listened to my queries and sent me to the Chelmer Imaging Group in St Kilda Rd for a pelvic ultrasound.

You may have seen the movies with an animal theme, where the busy veterinarian examines the insides of a cow by forcing his entire arm, right up to his shoulder, inside the poor unfortunate cow, who can do no more than stand there and let out a bellowing moo-like roar. Well, I could think of nothing else, as a very efficient, but tiny female, endeavoured to force from me the equivalent of a moo-like roar. She did say, 'We can do this another time if you like'. But I didn't like. I wanted to get it over with and get out of there. I was informed that the results would be sent to the referring doctor. So with my son Marty by my side, we headed home and waited for the outcome.

A week went by, so I phoned the GP's clinic, and asked to speak to Doctor 'Fred'. The receptionist informed that Doctor 'Fred' was away on holidays; they had even received a post-card from him at the Taj Mahal. My results from the pelvic ultrasound were there for me to collect.

Not having succumbed to the lure of the Taj Mahal, or similar exotic locations, my personal GP Doctor John was back from his holidays. So there I was in his office, sitting across from where he was reading aloud from a computer, the results from the invading 'veterinarian'.

'Kidneys, ah yes, nothing sinister there.'

'Bladder, hmm, nothing sinister there.'

Followed by further um's and hmms, until he ventured … 'Did you have a Pap smear?' I said 'No'. It had not been discussed. 'How long since you've had a Pap smear?' 'Gosh,' I replied, 'About thirty years. I had them regularly until menopause, then gradually stopped.'

Hayley and a proud grandmother.

Doctor John went into action immediately—in no time I was on the table having a Pap smear. It took about five minutes. Back at the desk, he told me I had a polyp, which was causing the blood spotting. He could remove it then and there in his surgery, but just in case of bleeding he would send me to a gynaecologist.

The specialist's gynaecology examination revealed that the polyp wasn't small and a general anaesthetic the following week would ensure the correct procedure. Fasting all night and into lunch time the next day wasn't pleasant, and even more unpleasant whilst waiting a further three hours dressed in cap and gown and wondering. Marty was there when I regained consciousness. It was over, and once again I was feeling glad that it was done. A follow up check-up would be arranged for a few days hence. I was feeling pretty pleased with myself.

Then, the phone rang days later and a male voice said, 'This is 'Doctor Peter' here'.

'Nice of you to phone Doctor', was my polite reply. Then he said, 'I have the results of your surgery. The polyp was benign, but you have cancer cells which must be removed. You will need a radical hysterectomy and removal of lymph nodes to determine how far the cancer has spread. When can you come in for further arrangements?'

I became totally frozen to the spot, alone in the house, glaring at the walls, willing them to crash down around me and wake me up from this nightmare. My mouth was dry, I couldn't speak. Was that really how doctors deliver bad news, suddenly, over the phone? But it was real, the frightening news wasn't a nightmare, the doctor was just stating the facts. Clutching the phone and staring into space, I was paralysed with fear. A man of authority in the medical profession had just told me that I had cancer. It was unbelievable. There wasn't any pain, I was healthy, or so I thought. Still in a state of shock I managed to suggest that he phone my son.

Poor Marty. Five minutes passed before he phoned his mother. 'The doctor has filled me in on the situation. I'll be there as quick as I can. Try not to worry, we will get through this together.' Two days later we were back in the doctor's office, facing him across a desk. After outlining the situation he showed us a large sheet containing six colour enlargements of my insides. Apparently a camera had been doing undercover security work during the polectomy. I couldn't help feeling invaded, but thank heaven for modern technology.

The first photo was of the polyp before removal. The next photo showed what was behind the polyp after its removal. And there they were, a mass of cancer cells looking like sticky honeycomb. It was quite startling. Absolute evidence, no guess work here. The cells were up against the endometrial wall.

The rest of the photos showed the retreating camera back through the birth canal. As Marty was watching all of this with me, his usual defense mechanism kicked in with, 'I remember coming down there, and don't need to see it again'. The doctor explained that the polyp was unrelated to the cancer cells, and without the Pap smear it would have gone undetected.

An appointment had already been made for me to see a surgeon at the Freemasons Hospital in Melbourne. This gentleman, in his sixties, was an oncologist gynaecologist, which Marty remarked was too many vowels for one title. So there we were in another doctor's office, looking at him across another desk, willing him to relate some good news, but it wasn't forthcoming. This was the last stop before major surgery.

Perhaps it was best that I had no idea what I was in for, and for how long. Initially the hospital stay was going to be for five to seven days—it became closer to two weeks. Nobody told me that going home from hospital was when the real pain began. It's like a big secret. Regaining consciousness after surgery is very vague. I remember the oxygen mask and Martin stroking my forehead saying, 'It's all over now, it's all over', and the face of my friend Liz on the other side of the bed, comforting me.

Prior to the operation, the discussions with the surgeon were hard for me to absorb. Over the years we hear words like uterus, fallopian tubes, womb, ovaries, but not many of us know what their functions are. I for one took little interest in how it all works, even when having my one and only baby all those years ago. But I soon took a more than curious interest, when the surgeon told me that all of the aforementioned had been removed, plus lymph nodes from the cancerous area to determine if the disease had spread. There are many reasons why women need hysterectomies, but not always because of invading cancer. The radical surgery was indeed major.

It was days later that the surgeon informed me that the cancer cells had not gone through 'the wall', and the lymph nodes had proven to be negative. I remember showing signs of relief on hearing that fortunate news. Perhaps it was then that I could have been told of the long and painful road ahead. But then, it wouldn't have really helped or lessened the ordeal.

Wearing those white elasticised pressure stockings wouldn't be so bad if the holes at the ends didn't cut into one's toes. The nightly injections in the upper legs to prevent blood clotting had that very area bruised and punctured. Initially the morphine helped the pain but that was replaced by eight a day Panadol. To consider coughing or at worst sneezing was to rip everything apart, or at least that's how it felt. Nevertheless

an,

I was encouraged to cough—apparently it's a must—to prevent lung congestion. But by golly it hurt. Five or six pillows were responsible for the permanent half sitting, half laying position that was bearable. The nurses explained the reason for the bruising which apparently was quite colourful.

For the first days after surgery the meals—meals, ha! Dishwater is a description that comes to mind. But they knew what they were doing. The bland and tasteless liquid was to help internal healing.

The nursing staff were dedicated to the constant need for pain relief; their patients were in desperate and constant need for their professional help. This was a cancer-gynaecology ward. Each private room with its door always open was not a happy place. I tried hard to master the drawing up of my knees then rolling on my side in endeavoring to get out of bed, for getting to the adjacent toilet and shower, which was always done in a stooped position, as was standing up to eat. It seemed as though every little movement involved stomach muscles. Internal healing was going to be a long haul. Not one movement was possible without help from those wonderful nurses.

Marty and Jenny by now had a beautiful one-year-old baby girl, Hayley. Marty's workload is enormous, taking him interstate several times a week, for all kinds of corporate functions. Jenny works from home, with accountancy being one of her specialities. Marty's work has always overlapped, like the many months when he played a crooked sergeant of police in the television series *Blue Heelers*, he was also hosting, playing piano and singing at the *Howl At The Moon* chain of venues. Playing lead roles in musical comedy seems to keep him constantly learning new songs and reams of dialogue.

My cancer situation happened during a very busy time for him, not the least being cast as a gangster opposite Marina Prior in *Kiss Me Kate.*

Although he was mid-rehearsals, he managed to visit me in hospital both morning and night. Marty, Jenny and baby Hayley were there for me every day, so supportive and full of encouragement.

My little family of three were worth more to me than anything else in the world. Many of my own professional commitments had to be put on hold, and some cancelled altogether. I didn't want to make a fuss and tell everyone I had a cancer problem. Some of the cancellations did cause upset but it was definitely out of my control. A good friend Robin Collins stepped into the breach at short notice, for which I was truly grateful.

Just when Marty was in the thick of *Kiss Me Kate,* which played to packed houses during its run, he was asked to take over a role in *My Fair Lady*. Jon English was to play

Doolittle but had collapsed unexpectedly with blood poisoning. It meant Marty would finish one show that Saturday night, start rehearsals for *My Fair Lady* on the Monday, and open Friday night. The dialects went from broad New York to raucous London cockney. Apart from the pages of dialogue, there were important songs to learn. 'With a little bit of luck' and 'Get me to the church on time' were but a couple. With his perfect musical 'ear', the melodies and the accents weren't the problem. There were moves and choreography to learn. Marty told Bert Newton on *Good Morning Australia* that he was probably the only bloke in Australia who hadn't seen *My Fair Lady*, and the role of Doolittle sounded like he didn't have to do much—wrong!

The nursing staff at the hospital were relentless in their endeavours to relieve pain. In my room alone, there was a constant parade of those who had their various duties. There was the blood pressure machine—you know the one that only ceases to crush one's arm when it reaches the point of amputation. Then there's the one that measures the depth of breathing, (I was a shallow breather). There are constant blood thinning injections; the little cup of pain killing tablets. It seemed forever before I was back at home in my own house, which was more frightening than the hospital. There wasn't anyone at home to help, and I truly needed help. One

293

🌿 *Marty as Police Sergeant Roy Holland in 'Blue Heelers'.*

of my constant visitors whilst in hospital was the doctor in charge of the five weeks of radiology that I had yet to undertake.

He patiently explained to me the importance of radiology. It was a necessary precaution to prevent the cancer appearing somewhere else in the body in the future. He likened it to mopping up any seeds or cells overlooked. Statistics had proved that of those who didn't opt for the radiology treatment had a thirty per cent chance of the cancer recurring, whereas patients who had the radiology treatment had only five per cent chance of recurrence. The course would take five intensive weeks, every day, except weekends, beginning as soon as I was at home from hospital after the surgery.

Everything was unpleasant. My lack of appetite was accompanied by nausea. My bladder was weak and was about to get weaker. There wasn't much I could do for myself; I needed help. Phoning for my GP, Doctor John, made a big difference. He

arranged for assistance that I didn't know existed. Everything became manageable through council carers. The housework was done thoroughly, showering was supervised, a hot meal was delivered daily—all done by strangers whose days are spent helping others. Food was a big problem because of what I wasn't supposed to eat. The list of what to avoid was endless. Anything bland was OK, without skin, seeds or bulk. Even porridge had to be strained.

My good neighbour friends, Liz and Tom Copping, had been interstate for weeks and had come home in the middle of my attempted recuperation. Most treatment patients in the radiology area of Freemasons have a relative or friend to take them there, daily. Marty, Tom and Liz worked out a system between them to ensure that I was driven each day by one of them. They also made sure that my food problems didn't allow me to starve to death. Kindness came to me in many forms. The ritual of attending opening nights, especially if one's son is in the show was not an option for me. I was still feeling too much discomfort. But due to the efforts of Marty, his Jenny, and Rachel Taylor from The Production Company, wheelchair access was made for me in the State theatre. I was so grateful to Rachel for making it possible for me to see the last matinee performance of *Kiss Me Kate*. My confidence in attending the theatre was zero, but it was worth everybody's effort. Jenny and Liz made sure all would be well. I was so nervous that day, weak and fearful for myself. Sitting for so long in one position was what scared me, because of all the stitches internally and externally. It was very painful. I managed to get myself into a half stretched position most of the time, which meant I couldn't see the stage from our high dress-circle area, but I forced myself to sit up straight whenever I heard Marty's voice on stage. And the big highlight for me was the duet 'Brush up your Shakespeare', performed by Marty Fields and Gary Down.

Those who are familiar with *Kiss Me Kate* will understand my pride. The song incorporates many visual changes, from straw-decker hats to bowler-hats, to slick Fred Astaire type hat and canes. All the time singing complicated lyrics with tricky choreography. I don't know how Marty learned it all, when he had spent most of his time with his ailing mother. It did my heart good that day. I was so proud, knowing what was really going through his mind. I'm sure Jenny and his baby daughter gave him strength. With the help of Tom and Liz Copping I even managed to stagger into a matinee of Marty's other overlapping commitment *My Fair Lady*. There is no way of adequately thanking people who really make you feel as though nothing is a trouble, when it obviously is.

I remember the first day attending radiology. It's called planning, which means mapping and pinpointing the exact location for the radiation treatment. Liz came with me that day, thank goodness—I was so afraid of the unknown I was trembling with fear. The planning room had one of those big tunnel machines that allows the patient to be moved in and out, the sight of which sent my claustrophobic fears into overdrive. Wearing only my underwear, I was measured by two young men with a variety of appropriate instruments. Each measurement meant the tunnel went on its claustrophobic journey. The young men asked me if I objected to being tattooed. They explained that the tattoos were black and the size of the head of a pin. They would be placed at the upper outer thigh, and be permanent. I agreed to the tattooing, it was necessary for the planning, which was being overseen by other young men behind glass, rather like a control room in a television studio. Texta

markings were also drawn over various parts of my body. It was explained to me that all this measuring was being transferred to a computerised image of my body which would be used in the forthcoming radiology treatment. Many others just like me must have felt apprehension at these unfamiliar proceedings. All of it painless, but it was necessary to have trust in these people who were there to help. Nevertheless I was glad when it was over, and couldn't wait to get out of there, and back to my loyal friend Liz who was waiting with my clothes.

Why am I detailing all that happened? I am hoping that by talking about it, others may realise the importance of the medical messages. Wear that sun hat. Have that Pap smear, it only takes a few painless minutes and those minutes could save your life.

When I was first given the news of having cancer, apart from feeling paralysed with fear, there was an urgency for secrecy. At the time there seemed to be so many people selling their stories to magazines and television stations for large amounts of money. This approach to my problem horrified me. I didn't want money or sensationalism. I wanted others to maybe one day hear about my problem and learn that it can happen to anyone. Sensationalism wouldn't help, it would seem like publicity hunting. Not until I was nearing the end of the radiology treatment, and cancer awareness through Daffodil Day was looming, that I decided the

❧ *'Kiss Me Kate' with Gary Down.*

296

time was right to speak out and hopefully help others. Through Sunday Herald Sun journalist Fiona Byrne, my story went public, with the strong message of prevention. The sudden flood of get well messages, cards and beautiful flowers was very heart-warming but definitely not why I went public. The news certainly explained to a lot of people the reason for my appearing anti-social.

The initial surgery and the weeks that followed left me in so much pain I could hardly think. The doctors give no warning in their 'matter of fact' pre-hospital admission discussion, which is probably just as well. The only clue to the forthcoming ordeal is the absolute over the top smiles and pleasant consideration given by the surgeon's reception staff. All absolutely charming and considerate, as though you're checking into a five star hotel. They knew their stuff. After the surgery and subsequent discharge from the hospital, the pain lingered for weeks. I became irritable and short tempered, rejecting any interest in others who tried to occupy my mind. My previous dedication to reading the daily newspaper and watching television could not hold my attention; the pain and discomfort was all consuming. The nurses had told me to persist in trying to walk to strengthen the stomach muscles. Marty tried walking me around my grassy backyard, but it hurt so much. I moaned out loud with every tentative step. Perhaps my

recollections are too graphic, and may upset those who perhaps are about to experience the same surgery. My hope is that I somehow reach those who think having that Pap smear is not important.

I clearly remember my first actual radiology treatment. It was exactly ten years since I had accompanied Maurie into the very same building at the ground floor of the Freemasons Hospital. The sliding glass doors were the same, the large waiting room was exactly the same, the pictures on the wall of underwater fish were still hanging in the same place. The reception desk was exactly the same. The memories flooded back, and now it was my turn. Maurie's problem had been throat cancer after two heart attacks. No pre-surgery. His radiology treatment was getting on top of the throat cancer, but in the end his heart couldn't take it. I didn't believe the world could go on without Maurie Fields, he was indestructible. And therefore I still felt guilty at my apparent lack of compassion. But that man must have been scared out of his mind and didn't want me to know. Well now I certainly knew about it in all its unpleasant detail. That first day, whilst laying on the intricate equipment, I started shaking uncontrollably. It took a few minutes for the specialists to calm me down. They said it was normal, that many patients are apprehensive and suffer anxiety because of the daunting machinery and fear of the unknown.

The sight of the big bare room with the enormous machine that weaves its way over one's body certainly was unsettling. After five weeks of having treatment every day, I got to know the powerful radiology machine, and I dreaded every minute of it. Trying to consider the thousands of other poor souls who had gone through far more than I would ever know, did little to make me feel grateful. At least my surgery was successful and the follow up radiology was meant to be preventative.

Nevertheless, I will never, ever forget that scary huge machine that wound its way over and around the exposed area of my body. Only after a team of radiology staff pinpointed my exact position on the solid

glass table did proceedings commence. Measuring tools of all kinds were placed on my chest and my 'tattooed' thighs, with texta markings drawn in various other areas. My shoulders would be slightly moved, as would anywhere else that made my position perfect for 'zapping'. That's when I was left alone in the larger vault-like treatment room. It's probably the noise of the machines that I will remember most. As well as the bright red laser-like beams there was loud clicking sounds then sudden noises that reminded me of door locks opening and shutting. But it was when the huge machine began its four-part rotation, that a huge roar like no other became unforgettable. During each treatment I tried to imagine what the noise

❧ *Hayley Kate Fields.*

was like. The roar was deep and guttural, like a cacophony of ferocious pre-historic monsters preparing for conflict. Add to this a pride of lions all roaring at once in their best bass baritone voices and then there is some semblance of that distinctive and unpleasant sound. With all that went on, there was absolutely no pain involved, only some discomfort, but then again, I do consider myself to be one of the more fortunate patients. No doubt others have unhappier tales to tell.

It wasn't difficult to feel sympathy for the many unfortunate folk who spent many hours in that building's waiting room. Young people, old people, many with varied standards of living as was obvious by their

apparel, especially ladies with scarves, tied with the tell-tale style of also having chemotherapy. To me they all seemed so brave. Many arrived and left alone, which made me appreciate even more my close network of friends, which included Liz, Tom, Maryanne Worth and of course my rock solid son Marty. Many friends had offered their help in ways that were extremely caring and generous, for which I will always be grateful. Many a true friendship is tested in times of trouble.

An appointment was made to see my surgeon two months after the completion of the course of radiotherapy, which left me quite tired and weak. I had severe bouts of bowel trouble, which see-sawed between

Marty as Sgt. Roy Holland with Danny Raco in 'Blue Heelers'.

299

diarrhea and constipation, and my bladder was still weakened severely. A strict diet of very bland food still had to be adhered to. I was warned of these side affects, that were due to my internal healing taking a severe pounding from the radiology—the equivalent of extreme sunburn. It was months before the various discomforts eased. Stamina and strength eluded me for a long time. Having an appetite again became a goal.

Fighting all these problems would not have been so difficult had I been twenty years younger. Perhaps health is to be somehow likened to money, in that we don't worry about it until we haven't got it.

My cancer will always feel like I was waking up in the middle of somebody's nightmare. As it stands now, there will be periodic check ups for the rest of my life. The sun will still come up every day. No matter how carefully we tread through life, we are mortal, we are fallible, in the hands of the unknown, and every day is a gamble. It's never too late to heed those persistent warnings we get. Take off five when driving, quit smoking, wear a hat in the sun, don't drink and drive, be a man have the prostate check up, and ladies please have that Pap smear. I consider myself very lucky indeed that my local GP, in passing said, 'How long is it since you had a Pap smear?' Don't wait for your doctor to ask you that question.

I consider myself extremely fortunate to have survived this medical setback. Being a non-drinker and a non-smoker, I had to ask my surgeon what would have caused the problem. Did I drink too much milk! Did I squeeze too much orange juice, use too much lipstick!? He looked me in the eye and said, 'We don't know'. So what's the answer? Grab life with both hands, follow your dreams with enthusiasm. No matter what life dishes up—you will be ready for it.

We are all important to each other, even if unknowingly.

To me, you are part of the much needed audience who have been there for me all of my wonderful life.

My beautiful little granddaughter has filled a huge void in my life. I stare at her in disbelief, she is such a perfect miracle. Born May 23rd 2004, Hayley Fields smiles a lot and laughs easily, especially at pratfalls. She loves music, moves to all rhythm, and melts my heart when she says… 'P'ease Gammah.' She has wonderful parents to guide her.

My days and nights are now pleasantly peaceful. Medical check-ups will be constant. I will always be grateful to the decades of audiences who encouraged my theatrical journey, they will forever remain, my million lovers.

Perhaps it's a form of role reversal, when due to advancing years, I have become the face of 'Seniors Festivals', and invited to meet council dignitaries at Melbourne Town Hall and Government House. It was fun with long time friend Bert Newton on Channel Nine's *Family Feud*. Being captain of fellow vintage actors in Stuart Wagstaff, Bud Tingwell, Val Lehmann, Toni Lamond, Alan Hopgood, Barry Crocker and Noeline Brown was true vintage fest. Like 'everything old is new again'.

Invitations to opening nights and festive occasions give me great satisfaction. Guest speaking and being on selection committees keep me in touch, none more so than being asked by TV Week and Channel Nine to present the prestigious Gold Logie at a recent TV awards evening. The ABC welcomed me back to record a recent episode of their popular *Spicks & Specks* program. It's gratifying that my accumulated experience is acknowledged. But every day I still yearn for the love of my beloved Maurie. He would have said, with a knowing smile—'Hang in there Kid'.

Fan mail is always answered and requests for personal appearances continue. I am always ready for the unexpected. Due to changing times many things come under the heading of entertainment—but I will continue to be thrilled by attending the theatre. I will be seated earlier than necessary, to watch the house coming in and assess the respect the audience has for the performers by the clothes they wear. I will continue to stare at the front curtain (the act-drop) and anticipate the magical secrets it conceals. I will enjoy wondering about the moods of the actors. Are they nervous? Are they pacing? Are they making last minute make-up and wardrobe checks? Will the stage manager be reaching his final call over the P.A. system: *'Overture and beginners please?'* My interest will have me looking for the sound console, counting the spotlights on the lighting rigs, checking the angles of their throw. As the orchestra enters the pit from their private world beneath the stage I will stretch forward and endeavour to count the sections and how many musicians are in the band. As the act-drop rises I will, for an instant, recall the beautiful odour of paint, size and sweat that swept over the Tivoli audiences. The impressionable times of my sweet youth!

Still stage-struck? You bet!

❧ *Rehearsals for 'The Full Monty', empty State Theatre.*

Stealing that extra bow

What a bumpy ride it has been. Who could know, at the age of four, that over 76 years later I'd still be at it—performing that is!

I had a stage mother and a relentless multi-talented dancing teacher, but it's the fellow showbiz folk that always inspired my enthusiasm. There have been hundreds of them, and each and every one of them has my gratitude. The highs have been magnificent, the lows unforgettable. Life is a lottery; I was a big winner with an amazing husband and an extraordinary son.

Why do we show folk persist with the exciting tortures of such a lifestyle? Perhaps it's for the ongoing love affair with audiences. Perhaps it's the earned respect. Nobody really knows. This book may solve the mystery.

And the show goes on . . .

🌿 1. With the cast of the ABC play 'Inheritance'. Val as 'Girlie'. 2. With Damien Leith, Winner 'Australian Idol' 2006. 3. With comedians Denise Roberts and Dave O'Neil. 'Spicks 'n'Specks Xmas special'. 4. With Adam Hills.

Very Dear Val,

Thank you *so* much for your loving note. It was a great honour to meet you at that crazy TV show, and I very much enjoyed your witty contribution.

I'd love to invite you to my show. If you'd like to come,

Meanwhile a Happy & HEALTHY new year to you.

With all warm wishes

Truly Yours.

Barry x

🔸 *Christmas special with Dame Edna Everage.*

Catwalk modelling for Myer—the little black dress promotion. Lindy Rama, Denise Drysdale, Val Jellay, Dawn Fraser, Patti Newton, Lady Sonia McMahon, Belinda Green, Nicky Buckley and Kate Ceberano.